RAMONA MEMORIES

Published in cooperation with the Center for American Places
Santa Fe, New Mexico • Harrisonburg, Virginia

RAMONA MEMORIES

TOURISM AND THE SHAPING OF SOUTHERN CALIFORNIA

DYDIA DeLYSER

UNIVERSITY OF MINNESOTA PRESS
MINNEAPOLIS • LONDON

Letter from Reginaldo Francisco del Valle to Ysabel (Varela) del Valle, 1 October 1888, reprinted with permission of The Huntington Library, San Marino, California.

All illustrations from the collection of the author unless otherwise noted.

Published by the University of Minnesota Press
111 Third Avenue South, Suite 290
Minneapolis, MN 55401-2520
http://www.upress.umn.edu

Library of Congress Cataloging-in-Publication Data

DeLyser, Dydia.
    Ramona memories : tourism and the shaping of Southern California / Dydia DeLyser.
      p.   cm.
    Includes bibliographical references and index.
    ISBN 0-8166-4571-X (hc : alk. paper) — ISBN 0-8166-4572-8 (pb : alk. paper)
    1. Jackson, Helen Hunt, 1830–1885—Homes and haunts—California, Southern. 2. Jackson, Helen Hunt, 1830–1885—Appreciation—California, Southern. 3. Jackson, Helen Hunt, 1830–1885—Knowledge—California, Southern. 4. Authors, American—Homes and haunts—California, Southern. 5. Literature and history—California, Southern. 6. California, Southern—Description and travel. 7. Historic sites—California, Southern. 8. California, Southern—In literature. 9. Tourism—California, Southern. I. Title.
    PS2108.D455 2005
    813'.4—dc22

                                            2004023150

For Paul, and for all the girls named Ramona
—it has not been for nought

CONTENTS

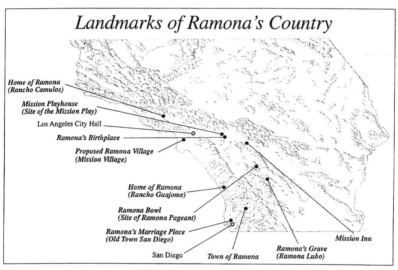

Landmarks of Ramona's Country

Home of Ramona
(Rancho Camulos)

Mission Playhouse
(Site of the Mission Play)

Los Angeles City Hall

Ramona's Birthplace

Proposed Ramona Village
(Mission Village)

Home of Ramona
(Rancho Guajome)

Ramona Bowl
(Site of Ramona Pageant)

Ramona's Marriage Place
(Old Town San Diego)

San Diego

Town of Ramona

Ramona's Grave
(Ramona Lubo)

Mission Inn

Within a few years of the publication of Helen Hunt Jackson's novel, places associated with Ramona drew tourists all over southern California. Map by the author (locations are approximate); reprinted courtesy of the Association of American Geographers.

INTRODUCTION

The shepherds, the herdsmen, the maids, the babies,
the dogs, the poultry, all loved the sight of Ramona.
—*Ramona*, 23

T he most important woman in the history of southern California never
lived. Nor has she yet died. She is Ramona, the fictional heroine of Helen
Hunt Jackson's 1884 novel of the same name. This book explores her impact on the region—a region that, for several decades around the turn of
the twentieth century, came to be known as "Ramona's Country"[1]—and
examines the impact of a person who never existed, the powerful significance of fictional places, and the commemoration of a past that, though
partly made up, was and is deeply felt in southern California. Exploring a
phenomenon now widely known as the "Ramona myth," this book looks
at how Jackson's work of fiction changed how people remember southern
California's past, how a new past was inscribed on the landscape and
marked on tourists' itineraries as thousands flocked to the sites the novel
described, and how this new past was enacted in the lives of both tourists
and locals.

Author Helen Hunt Jackson was already a successful travel writer, novelist, and poet when, in 1879, she resolved to help Native Americans by documenting their oppression at the hands of American settlers and the U.S. government. With a commission to write historical sketches on the missions,
she traveled southern California extensively. Compelled by her cause and
captivated by what she perceived as the region's romantic Spanish/Mexican
past, Jackson later resolved to use southern California as the setting for an
Indian novel—an *Uncle Tom's Cabin* for Native Americans that would dramatize the plight of the California Mission Indians. But in disguising her
message of Indian mistreatment in lavish descriptions of life on the aristocratic Mexican-owned rancho where the half-Indian heroine Ramona

At a time when California citrus growers were embroiled in fierce competition, elaborate labels on their fruit crates were intended to attract attention to the product inside. Ramona-themed labels included this Ramona Memories lemon label (circa 1930).

is raised, readers could readily focus not on Jackson's message but rather on those rich descriptions of a rapturous landscape and a romantic-but-vanishing ranchero lifestyle. Jackson, considering her novel a failure, died of cancer in 1885, just one year after *Ramona* was published. But her novel's fame would far outlast her lifetime and far outreach her expectations, though not in the manner she had hoped. Even before her death, devoted fans had named a California lake for Jackson's heroine,[2] and within a year readers of the novel would begin scouring the southern California countryside for the places Jackson appeared to have described.[3]

Published in 1884, *Ramona* is still in print today and was once said to have been read by nearly every visitor to California. Between 1885 and roughly 1955 so many places sought affiliation with the novel—either by naming themselves for the novel's characters or by claiming they were described in the text and were therefore authentic Ramona locales—that one booster wrote, "I doubt if there is any town in Southern California that does not boast of a street, hotel, garden, park or public place named 'Ramona'" and tourists flocked to see them. So great was the fame of the story, that same commentator wrote in 1928, "no matter on which highway you travel in California, signs, booklets and people inform you of Ramona landmarks."[4]

Significantly, *Ramona* was published at a time of immense popularity for regional fiction. Novels like *Ramona*, as well as similar shorter works published in popular magazines, portrayed remote corners of the country where the quaint customs and colorful preindustrial livelihoods perceived as living representations of the past still survived.[5] With first rail and, later, automobile travel becoming available and then affordable to the upper and eventually the middle classes, the picturesque places described in regional fiction became accessible. And, with the simultaneous emergence of popular tourism, and its focus on domestic travel in particular, the fictional landmarks were incorporated, along with sites like Yosemite and Plymouth Rock, into the canon of tourist sites as tourists explored, experienced, and narrated the nation for themselves.[6]

In southern California these changes were intensely felt: a region formerly isolated and rural, it was, in the 1880s, newly reached by fiercely competing railroads. Amid a flurry of regional promotion, and in a responding rush of incoming upper- and middle-class white tourists and homeseekers, the region was transformed into a seat of Anglo population and power, cementing the displacement of one hundred years of Hispanic rule.[7] By 1886 the romanticized version of that Hispanic past as portrayed in *Ramona* became a focus of tourist interest, as readers of the novel sought out its scenes, recognizing landscapes familiar from fiction. At a time of immense social change, *Ramona*'s romanticized images of what came to be seen as southern California's "Spanish-mission" past were blended into the region's culture, inscribed onto its landscape, and manipulated by California boosters with results far removed from the novelist's reformist intents. What emerged most prominently was not a call to aid the Indians, but rather a vast series of books, brochures, and magazine and newspaper articles serving as guides, and fueling the proliferation of Ramona-identified sites across the region. By the 1890s, for example, two adobes were known and advertised as the "Home of Ramona," and a third emerged as "Ramona's Marriage Place." Ramona sleuthing took on aspects of the personal as several women were identified as the "Real Ramona." One, hired to use her title to advertise other places and events in the region, now lies buried beneath a headstone labeled simply "Ramona," and that site too became a tourist attraction, marked "Ramona's Grave" on tourist maps.

But even as fictional places became popular tourist destinations, other locations sought to identify themselves with the novel and its characters as well. Towns, subdivisions, and roadways of various size were named for the novel's heroine and her martyred spouse, Alessandro. Likewise, businesses of all kinds appropriated the names of Jackson's characters. With lifestyle advertising newly on the rise, a host of products such as Ramona Face Cream appeared on the market. The novel even inspired a theme park, Ramona Village in Culver City. And, through continually emerging new media like postcards, snapshots, records, and films, Ramona and Ramona attractions reached a public far beyond the boundaries of the state of California.

More than tourist hype, however, Ramona-identified locales became meaningful places of memory and reflection for visitors to southern California. Nearly all were visited by tourists *before* being developed as tourist attractions; it was in large part the tourists themselves who demanded that Ramona-related places become visitable parts of southern California's landscape. Though some scholars have implied that Ramona tourists were simple-minded dupes who readily confused the fictional Ramona-inspired past with the real one, and who were easily lured to phony Ramona sites where they could be relieved of their moneys by an array of superficial Ramona souvenirs,[8] the reality is far more complex, for through the landscape these fictional places in fact became real. Countless thousands of tourists made a point of visiting Ramona-related sites, documenting their visits, and commemorating them for the future by purchasing teaspoons, rosary cases, or pottery, by posing for photographs and then carefully pasting those images into photo albums and scrapbooks, by inscribing their copies of the novel with details of their travels, by mailing Ramona postcards home, and even by naming their daughters Ramona. Between 1885 and roughly 1955, Ramona-related landmarks became important, even canonical parts of a visit to southern California, as tourists sought to appreciate the region's landscape partly through a novel they had read, to enjoy the novel again upon recognizing its landmarks,[9] and to enfold their visits to Ramona-related places into their own lives in meaningful ways.

This book examines the practices of tourists at Ramona landmarks, the development of such Ramona-related attractions, and their impact on southern California's landscape as well as on "social memory" in southern Californian more broadly. Social memories (also called, with varying shades of meaning, collective, public, or cultural memories) link both individuals and groups to their group's relevant past, and to past events and

"Bee and Metta" were careful to record their visit to Ramona's Marriage Place through this photograph, circa 1928. Reproduced by permission of Taylor and Francis Publishing.

places. They serve to tie us to what is relevant today about our past—to make the past meaningful by the light of the present.[10] Grounded both by individual experiences and, significantly, by places, social memories link individuals to a collective sense of history, and often to their nation's perceived past. These aspects of social memory are particularly clear when the memories in question are held in the minds of those still living. Thus, for example, most who recall the terrorist attacks on the Pentagon and the World Trade Center on 11 September 2001 will explain *where they were* and *what they were doing* when they first heard of the attacks. Though not present at either the Pentagon or the Trade Center, in memory Americans link themselves to national tragedy through their personal, emplaced experiences of it.[11]

Further, the sites where social memories are inscribed retain cultural importance. Thus, the site of the World Trade Center, like Dealy Plaza, the Book Depository building, and the "grassy knoll" in Dallas (the location of the Kennedy assassination), along with significant sites not remembered for tragedies—Plymouth Rock or Ellis Island, to name just two—have become hallowed ground, important places of homage and remembrance.[12] And, while some such places are remembered in the lives of living individuals, because social memory ties us to narratives of the nation and ideas about national identity, that need not be the case: None who today look upon Plymouth Rock witnessed the Pilgrims' landing, but that need not diminish their experiences at such a site. What is significant instead is that the visitor/viewer shares national knowledge about that site (in this case, likely an American elementary education that taught the significance of the place of the Pilgrims' supposed first North American footfall).

So, too, such sites need not be grounded in fact to remain significant: as this book will demonstrate, fictional and/or mythic landmarks are no less important in conjuring and creating social memories simply because they are fictional. This is an important aspect of social memory, for unlike what is often understood as history, social memories need not be founded in fact in order to be perceived significant; rather they need only be shared by members of a group and be perceived to hold some level cultural significance for that group. As scholars of social memory James Fentress and Chris Wickham explain, the social meaning, the societal importance, of memory is little affected by its truth, and its stability lies not in its veracity but rather in its ability to adapt to present needs.[13] In the case of southern California's Ramona-inspired past, both tourists and boosters found a past they perceived as idyllic, one for which landscape traces could be found and/or built, one that suited their desires—representing premodern tranquility against a modernizing, industrializing, urbanizing nation.[14]

And, though social memories are sustained by countless individuals, unlike personal memories, social memories need not be the *actual* memories of any one individual; rather, they can be the shared ways of interpreting past people, places, and events that help define group membership.[15] Thus, most American schoolchildren can relate the story of young George Washington who confessed to chopping down the cherry tree: "I cannot tell a lie." While this tale is, in fact, apocryphal, its learning and repetition are an important part of American social memory—and national mythology.[16] Similarly, most American adults can repeat the words of Apollo 11 astronaut Neil Armstrong who, setting foot on the moon, proclaimed, "One small step for man, one giant leap for mankind." Just the same, nearly none who repeat the phrase were with Armstrong at the time, and many are not old enough to have heard it broadcast live on television. But as a significant element of American social memory, many Americans young and old "remember" those words and feel their cultural significance whenever they are repeated.

As these two examples highlight, social memories help group members in the present think about their shared past. The cherry-tree story teaches children of the forthright honesty of our founders and, by implication, of the importance of honesty today as well. Armstrong's words, on the other hand, remind us of an American Cold War victory over the Soviet Union in the race to the moon and speak words of silent praise for "American ingenuity" and technological prowess. Thus, social memories do not simply recount the past, they portray elements of the past in a way that holds meaning for group members in the present; they make the past relevant in our lives today and thereby link us to those who came before us as well as to those who will follow.[17] Though the two examples above demonstrate how words and deeds can evoke social memories, far more than words alone are imbued with social memory: landscape is one of social memory's most powerful conveyors.

Much of the meaning we as humans, as cultural beings, make in our lives is triggered by the objects and artifacts around us, by the landscape. Thus while individuals may be stirred by personal memories on a visit to their childhood home, members of a group can be stirred by social memories when visiting landscapes of cultural significance for the group. For example, visitors to Ellis Island may feel the strain of thousands of poor immigrants who dreamed of a better life on the shores just beyond. Or those visiting Plymouth Rock may recall the excitement of the Pilgrims upon landing. Landscapes such as these can evoke powerful cultural images such as the hopes of individuals or the promise of an entire nation. But, as in the case of Ramona-identified places, the social memories evoked by landscapes can be just as powerful when they evoke a fictional past: the experiences of those who, newspapers reported, swooned away on a visit to Ramona's Marriage Place were every bit as real as the experiences of those who feel goosebumps for the Pilgrims' promise, despite the fact that the fictional Ramona can have had no real-life marriage place. Thus, the significance of landscape in social memory leads far beyond what is immediately visible or flatly "true" or "false."

Landscape, for cultural geographers and for the purposes of this book, includes physical features such as hills and dales, streams and coastlines, but also those features created or influenced by humans: the cultural traces on the face of the Earth and their countless representations. The objects of landscape study exist on a myriad of scales, any or even all of which may be important. At one scale, this book explores southern California as a region, examining its landscape as a whole. At a much smaller scale, this book examines landscape elements as tiny as a tear in an altar cloth. But since cultural artifacts need not rely on size for their significance, it is important to examine landscape and landscape elements across different scales. Although not all the tourists who visited southern California during the seventy years of the Ramona myth's greatest popularity viewed the torn altar cloth at Rancho Camulos (said to have been mended by Ramona herself), for those who did, as this book will show, their pilgrimage to the Camulos chapel held meaning that in turn helped shape their interpretations of southern California as a whole. Thus, elements from a work of fiction became factual through the landscape and came to influence the way residents and visitors in southern California thought about their past—which is to say, they became part of southern California social memory.

Southern California has long been derided for its emphasis on the phony, for commemorations such as these, which appear to occur in the face of the region's lack of a tangible history. But this phenomenon is not unique to California, nor is there any reason to believe that it is more prevalent there. While some have claimed that California's lack of a material past necessitated the creation of a fantasy one, the popularity of Ramona and the "fantasy heritage" it represents can also be understood as manifestations of an attempt to bring what is past into the present, and also to project what is present into the past—to connect contemporary existence to what came before.[18] Indeed, landscapes of literature, be they factual or fictional, have drawn visitors for hundreds of years; one need only think of visitors to the Middle East who flock to biblical places. Nor must landscapes have a mystical significance, as monuments to Mark Twain's characters attest. Nor indeed is such commemoration only a part of the past: the 1990s popularity of Robert James Waller's *Bridges of Madison County* spawned a tourist industry based on the covered bridges near Winterset, Iowa, where the novel was set. Indeed, Californians need not be laughed at for their preoccupation with *Ramona*. Rather, we may examine what has come to be known as the Ramona myth as a cultural and landscape phenomenon that, even as it obscured other versions of the past, made one particular version of the past meaningful in the present, casting upon it a golden glow. *Ramona* shone fantasy on fact, and perhaps this is not something always to be dismissed or scorned, for surely our world is illumined by more than reality alone.

Indeed, this is what the prevalence of myths in different societies may suggest: myths can reflect the societal importance of stories whose veracity cannot be verified. In this case, the term "Ramona myth," which many authors have used to refer to the phenomenon that followed *Ramona*'s publication, is a regional vernacular term, a term that grew up out of the phenomenon itself. Its first use seems to have been in 1910 by Edwin H. Clough, who wrote that in southern California by 1887 "the Ramona myth had grown to be a palpable and living reality in the minds of men under the spell of a gifted woman's compelling genius."[19] Myths, like social memories, serve an explanatory role in society: they teach the society about itself. If we follow such a definition then, as I hope this book will show, the term "Ramona myth" seems appropriate.

Though it seems simple to discount the influence of unreality on our interpretations of the past, we can stop to think for a moment about the role of historical fiction.[20] The presence of known and verifiable fact in fiction lends the fictive elements credibility, while the familiarity of certain fictive elements in a work about the past serves to make that past live in the minds of the readers. Indeed, this was precisely author Helen Hunt Jackson's goal in writing *Ramona*: after her factual works on the Indians had failed to attract widespread attention she turned to fiction as a way to reach an audience that her dry analysis had missed, and sought to disguise the same poignant message of Native American mistreatment in the cloak of a compelling story. She peppered her tale of Ramona and Alessandro with actual incidents in the Native American history of southern California as well as meticulous details of landscape and life in the region.[21] The overall effect was sufficiently engaging that the whole of the story came to seem plausible as reality rather than fiction and, following Jackson's death in 1885, a search began throughout southern California for the real places and real people to which Jackson had referred—not so much, however, for the real Native Americans whose homes had been taken away by incoming Anglo-American settlers (with the exception of Ramona herself, of course) or the sites of former Indian settlements, but rather for the sites of the romanticized and fictive elements of the story.

Thus, it was not long before a debate began among journalists, promoters, residents, and visitors as to the authenticity of various claims to Ramona-landmark status. In an important way, such debates (and they continue to this day) serve not to overturn spurious claims on the parts of some, but rather to enshrine the fictional elements of the novel along with, or even above the factual ones.[22] Hence, even challenges to the accuracy of certain claims (the status of Rancho Camulos as the "real" Home of Ramona, for example) led only to more intense scrutiny of the novel itself and to further dickering. Such claims never left the swirling world of debates around Ramona landmarks, and thus the claims to reality of the whole were scarcely questioned. In other words, the very act of challenging details only solidified the position of that which was challenged, rather than overturning it, and debaters lost sight of the fact that, whatever lay behind it, the basis of the novel was Jackson's imagination, that *Ramona* was a work of fiction. By continuing such debates today we lose sight not only of the underlying fictionality of the original work, but also of a more productive avenue of inquiry: What were the elements of a work of fiction that spoke to (and continue to speak to) residents and visitors to southern California and why were they meaningful, rather than which is the real "Home of Ramona"? How did particular landscape elements enshrined in a work of fiction come to signify a romanticized past, and, in the landscape, take on the status of history? How did and do such landscape elements influence California social memory? Whom does such a landscape-based memory serve, and whom does it exclude?

By examining the debates over Ramona landmarks themselves I hope to turn these debates in on themselves, to step outside their swirling contention and examine the deeper cultural meanings that I believe the persistence of the debates and the prevalence of the Ramona myth indicate. Those are the goals of this book, which are similar to the goals of much recent work in cultural geography.[23] One aim of such works has been to critically examine landscapes for the rhetorical messages they convey, often unbeknownst to their viewers. Landscapes, we hold, can be "read," or interpreted, just as books are read and interpreted. Indeed, they *are* read every day by their viewers, as we, in the process of going about our daily lives, make sense of the ordinary landscapes around us, understanding particular places, for example, as welcoming or not—based upon landscape clues. Landscapes, like written texts, encode powerful social, cultural, and political messages that are interpreted by their viewers, whether we stop to question them or not. And it is not just the visible components of landscape that convey such messages. Often it is our ability to *link* what we see in the landscape to other images, other texts about our society, that allows us to interpret landscape imagery. For example, when visitors to the ghost town of Bodie, California, see the gabled false fronts of the buildings along Bodie's Main Street they are reminded of the Western films they have seen, and from there to the moralistic messages about American pioneering spirit that such films convey. Landscape elements in an abandoned town in California connect them, in their minds, to films they have seen, and from there to important cultural themes that help to define us as Americans.[24]

The false-fronted buildings of Main Street in Bodie, once a booming nineteenth-century gold-mining town. Photograph by the author; reprinted courtesy of University of Nevada Press.

What this points to, in part, is an important way of interpreting landscape. Clearly, the landscapes of human occupancy and use are physically constructed: buildings are built, mountains are leveled, rivers are dammed. But cultural geographers have attempted to understand also the ways in which landscapes are socially constructed: to understand the social and cultural symbols embedded in such landscapes, the elements of landscape that we use every day to make meaning in our world. It is from this perspective that this book explores the Ramona-inspired landscapes of southern California.

To understand the public's reception of *Ramona*, we will first explore the life of author Helen Hunt Jackson, her traumas as well as her robust literary career, and place her writing in its literary-cultural context. We next look closely at her novel, and her use of description, characterization, and plot, which compelled readers to attempt to identify the places and people Jackson described.

In the late nineteenth and early twentieth centuries, when Jackson was writing and when *Ramona* achieved its popularity, dramatic changes took place in American transportation and tourism. Rail and later automobile travel emerged as elite pursuits, and subsequently became accessible to middle-class (white) Americans. Domestic tourism, which began as an upper-class pastime mimicking the European Grand Tour, became a nearly obligatory ritual of American citizenship, through which "average" (white) Americans both understood and inscribed American national identity. In southern California, the novel and Ramona-related landmarks became important parts of those tourists' itineraries. Following the tourists and boosters to seven of the most important Ramona landmarks in the region allows us to see in detail how each was discovered (or created), touristed, and developed.

The most important, the most canonical of all Ramona landmarks is Ventura County's Rancho Camulos, the "Home of Ramona," and symbolic epicenter of the Ramona myth. Lived in until 1924 by descendants of its original grantees who were both helped and hindered by their rancho's Ramona designation, this working ranch and citrus farm was not intended as a tourist attraction, but its unequivocal connection to the novel forced it into prominence as a tourist site. Never sporting a gift shop, Camulos nevertheless found its way onto postcards, photographs, souvenir teaspoons, and other tourist memorabilia, and images of its iconic south veranda were printed not just on photographs and postcards, but also on citrus labels and cookbooks, until this one landmark spoke of the

By 1886, Rancho Camulos in Ventura County had been identified as the "Home of Ramona" and became the symbolic heart of the Ramona myth. Note the inscription on this postcard, circa 1906: "Have you read 'Ramona'?" Reprinted courtesy of the Association of American Geographers.

entire Ramona myth. Camulos's competitor for Home-of-Ramona status was the Rancho Guajome in rural San Diego County. Thought by experts of the time to be better situated in terms of the geography the novel described, and allegedly visited by Helen Hunt Jackson, some insisted that it was Guajome the author had in mind. But residents here originally rejected visitors, and a rail stop was never provided. Guajome remained in Camulos's long shadow, and Guajome saw neither the volume of tourist traffic nor the intensity of sentiment.

Another San Diego locale, the adobe home of the Estudillo family, came to be better known as Ramona's Marriage Place. Although it was abandoned by the family not long after *Ramona*'s publication, tourists soon flocked to the ruin to find a scene familiar from the novel. While souvenirs were sold nearby, it would be some twenty years before the building was restored and opened as a tourist attraction—now with a curio shop and wishing well built in. The most commercial of all Ramona landmarks, Ramona's Marriage Place charged admission and sold countless souvenirs; nearly everything imaginable could be purchased in Ramona's Marriage Place theme—from graphic tape measures that looked like yo-yos to holy-water fonts, from California-bear letter openers to orange-shaped coin banks. But despite its commercialization, Ramona's Marriage Place remained a meaningful place for many who visited—from those who left calling cards, or carved their names on door posts, to those who were married in the attraction's chapel.

Least known of the major Ramona landmarks was Ramona's Birthplace in a small adobe near Mission San Gabriel. Here tourists could purchase Ramona-related souvenirs after visiting the mission or seeing the Mission Play. Beyond those souvenirs little remains—either in the landscape or in archival traces—of this site, testimony to the elusiveness of tourist attractions of the past.

Several southern California women were identified as the "Real Ramona." One woman, a Cahuilla Indian named Ramona Lubo, had watched her husband's brutal murder just as Ramona had in the novel, and soon both guidebook authors and tourists were visiting her, purchasing her baskets, or taking her photograph. Hired by different organizations to promote their events, she was eventually buried near her husband, Juan Diego, under tombstones labeled "Ramona" and "Alessandro." Because of the power and influence of the story, her fictional identification eclipsed and outlived Lubo's own identity.

The Ramona Pageant in the remote Riverside County town of Hemet was the first Ramona attraction that could not link itself directly to a place or person described in the novel (though scenes in the novel were set in the nearby mountains), and the first Ramona attraction that relied not on trolleys or railroads but rather automobile tourists. The pageant has offered an outdoor dramatization of the novel every year but five since 1923, and to this day continues to draw thousands of tourists annually. Despite its lack of a direct landscape link to the novel, the pageant has been successful because it dramatized the popular novel outdoors, in a landscape that was, nevertheless, recognizable and identifiable from the text, and because it, from the outset, took advantage of the newly popular automobile tourism as a way to reach this remote location.

Another Ramona landmark's connections to the novel (allegedly a place where Alessandro had once tied his horse) were discredited as spurious, but it nevertheless sought deliberately to draw automobile tourists: Culver City's Ramona Village theme park. Planned in the 1920s by Robert E. Callahan, a man who also penned a "sequel" to the novel—his 1930 *Daughter of Ramona*—his ambitious project was opposed by Ramona Pageant officials as well as Los Angeles boosters as "the worst kind of a Coney Island."[25] Beset by the financial crises of the Great Depression, Ramona Village would eventually become instead the Mission Village Trailer Park.

Ramona spread beyond those important landmarks. Other landscape manifestations of the novel—towns, streets, and subdivisions—sprung up, as well as businesses (Ramona Roof Tiles, Ramona Pharmacy, Ramona Jewelry) that used Ramona's name to attract customers or credibility. The story of Ramona spread across the nation in other ways as well, particularly in songs and film. Film especially is significant, for filmmakers often sought explicitly to link their productions with the "real" landscapes the novel seemed to have described, something that began with D. W. Griffith, who shot at the Rancho Camulos for his 1910 *Ramona* release—and gave the first ever screen credit to a movie's location, so important had Ramona's landscapes become.

While boosters profited from Ramona's success, it was the practices of the tourists that willed Ramona attractions into being, inscribing the landscape with a fictional past meaningful to them in the present. Of course, southern California has long been derided for either lacking a history or possessing only a phony one. In fact, the region that came to be known as "Ramona's Country" is not the only place where the fake and the real intertangle. And, more important, such intertangling of fact and fancy is an integral part of social memory, as we, in ever-ongoing ways, seek to make the past relevant in each new present. It is my hope that *Ramona Memories* will engage anyone curious about California's past and how its present came to be.

CHAPTER ONE

A DETERMINED AUTHOR
AND HER NOVEL

> Father, I scarcely dare to pray,
> So clear I see, now it is done,
> That I have wasted half my day
> And left my work but just begun.
> —Helen Jackson (H.H.), "A Last Prayer"

Helen Hunt Jackson was, from the first, both spirited and independent. Letters from her mother describe a stubborn and willful baby and later a petulant five-year-old: "I think sometimes I might just as well catch a blue jay and lecture it as to talk to my Helen."[1] At thirteen, confronted with her mother's imminent death from tuberculosis, Helen remained determinedly irreligious, despite her pious mother's and preacher father's admonitions. As she grew older, her intense and vivacious personality drew admiration, and she frequently captivated others in a gathering, with one observer noting that she "magnetically attracted her opposites." A California acquaintance would describe these same traits in Jackson's later years: "From whatever side she is approached, she seems to defy classification; an independent being of the very highest sort."[2] Her close friend and literary mentor, Thomas Wentworth Higginson, wrote that she was

> the most brilliant, impetuous, and thoroughly individual woman of her
> time, one whose very temperament seemed mingled of sunshine and fire;
> a personality so unique and so fascinating that few could comprehend
> the curious thread of firm New England texture that ran through her
> whole being, tempering waywardness, keeping impulse from making
> shipwreck of itself.[3]

She was born Helen Maria Fiske in Amherst, Massachusetts, on 15 October 1830, a child of staunch Calvinists. Jackson's mother, Deborah

Waterman Vinal Fiske, had committed herself to the service of Christ as a young woman, professing religious convictions far stronger than those of her own father, successful businessman David Vinal. Jackson's father, Nathan Welby Fiske, too, had devoted himself to a life of proselytizing for Christ. He first sought a career in the ministry, but, when unsuccessful at making converts, he accepted a position as a professor of language and rhetoric at Amherst College. His convictions, too, were were far stronger than those of his father, Nathan Fiske, a subsistence farmer whose lack of piety was a source of humiliation for his son.[4] The Fiskes, Nathan and Deborah, were devoted to their religious beliefs and determined to impart them to their surviving children, Helen and Ann. Indeed, those strong Calvinist convictions were readily apparent in the list of books in nine-year-old Helen's library. Titles included *The Pastor's Daughter, The Child's Books of Repentance, A Child's Scripture Question Book* (two volumes), *Scripture Animals,* and the five-volume series Temperance Tales.[5]

If Jackson's early life was heavily colored by her parents' religious convictions, so too was it cast in the shadow of her mother's (and later her father's) illness. Deborah Vinal Fiske had lost her own mother to tuberculosis when she was but two years old and had felt a heightened sense of her own mortality from the disease her whole life. Always searching for ways to know the mother she could not remember, she was seized with a passion to leave behind enough of herself to provide her own two daughters with the maternal moral compass she had lacked. Throughout her adult life, Deborah Fiske wrote letters to family and friends that were explicitly intended for the edification of her two daughters after her death. Indeed, upon her death Nathan Fiske collected the letters (which their original recipients had been instructed to retain) and divided them between his daughters. Mrs. Fiske employed other means of instruction as well. But when young Helen proved such a challenge to her mother, and the future receipt of the letters could not counsel her daughter in the present, Mrs. Fiske began writing articles for the *Youth's Companion* magazine (to which her daughter had a subscription). These articles she wrote both in secret and under a pseudonym, and they featured a child Helen's age who constantly interrupted her Bible lessons with irrelevant questions and would not sit still.[6]

The goal of so intense a moral training was more than just piety; it was intended also to mold the Fiske children into submissive houseguests, as their mother knew they must inevitably become. Just as Deborah Fiske herself had become a boarder in the homes of others upon her own mother's death, she knew that since she shared her mother's illness the same fate would befall her own children, and she sought diligently to prepare the girls to meet the demands of boarding with obedience and cheerful submission. She admonished her daughters to be pleasant and helpful guests, suggesting they do things like "dust chairs, and take lamps down from the chambers, and carry away dishes" to repay the kindness of their hosts. And, for Helen she included a list of what not to do when in the home of another:

> Never talk when others present are speaking.
> Never occupy the rocking chair or the easiest chair in a room when any older person is present. . . .
> Never eat after all at the table are done but yourself.
> Never leave chairs out of place or push them up against the paper and paint when you set them away.[7]

From most of these lessons and admonitions the young Jackson seems to have remained relatively unaffected, refusing even in the face of her own tragedies to adopt her parents' devout religious beliefs and practices, preferring to keep her beliefs to herself rather than to practice her religion formally or publicly (although she would later join the Unitarian faith).[8] But just the same some aspects of her parents' lives were mirrored in Jackson's own, particularly her writing.[9] While her mother wrote either as a personal correspondent or a covert essayist, her father was an impassioned author and translator of works related to the scriptures and to moral philosophy.[10] Some of her parents' moral and philosophical beliefs carried on in Jackson, too, though, thoughtful as she was, she sometimes reversed the opinions or beliefs she'd inherited: neither she nor her parents supported abolitionism (indeed though for a time during her first marriage Jackson herself leased a slave as a house servant, she later became a devoted admirer of Harriet Beecher Stowe).[11] None in Jackson's family supported women's suffrage, and none found females appropriate for the lecture circuit, though Jackson eventually reversed her opinion on this matter.[12] Nevertheless, at a time when public lecturing was a popular form of both education and entertainment, and despite Jackson's devotion to the cause of Indian rights, she herself never lectured on the matter.

Helen Hunt Jackson was just thirteen when her mother died of tuberculosis and just sixteen when the same illness claimed her father. Sickness and death, it seemed, were foundational to her existence. But though much of her childhood was shaped by her mother's ever-nearing death (that of her father was less expected), death later would serve as the catalyst that would forever change her adult life.

The deaths of both of Jackson's parents left her a boarder in the homes of others. Moving between different temporary residences, not all of them accommodating to her temperament, she nevertheless determined to complete her education, attending both the Ipswich Female Seminary and New York City's Abbott Institute. In 1852 Jackson married West Point graduate and Army lieutenant Edward Bissell Hunt, an ambitious man with a promising career ahead of him. Before a year was out, a son, Murray, was born. When he died of a brain tumor before he was a year old, Jackson was deeply stricken, blaming herself for her son's death. The next year, however, a second son, Warren "Rennie" Horsford Hunt was born, and this second baby thrived. Mother and son grew very close, particularly during the frequent absences of Lieutenant Hunt, whom they saw often only in the summer months as he was frequently stationed in regions deemed unsuitable for the health of his wife and child.

Lieutenant Hunt was promoted to captain, then to major, and eventually secured a position in New York where he could be with his family. There, in the midst of the Civil War, Hunt worked on a secret invention, an experimental submarine he called a "sea miner." On the day of the invention's first testing, as Major Hunt descended into his vessel, poison gases left behind by the firing of munitions from the craft overcame him. He died three days later, just before his wife arrived at his side. Again, she blamed herself, insisting that she could have saved him had she arrived in time.

Stricken by her husband's death, Jackson persevered for the sake of her son. Within two years both she and her son lay ill with diphtheria. Jackson recovered, but nine-year-old Rennie did not. With his death, Jackson fell into a deep depression, blaming herself now for his illness, too. She shut herself in her rooms, refusing to see anyone but family.[13] It was in the depths of this darkness that Helen Hunt Jackson first turned to writing.

Jackson began by writing poems that expressed the sorrows of her loss. "The Key of the Casket" appeared in the *New York Evening Post* on 7 June 1865, not two months after Rennie's death, under the signature of "Marah." Soon there were others, and soon their topics ranged from death and loss to nature poems as well. In October of that year, her first prose piece, a descriptive regionalist essay, "Mountain Life: The New Hampshire Town of Bethlehem," appeared—now under the signature "H.H."[14]

"Mountain Life" was not only her first prose piece, and her first work of regionalist writing, it also marked another important transition for Jackson: it was the first printed writing for which she was paid. Encouraged by this success, she arranged for an introduction to Thomas Wentworth Higginson, an important literary figure of the time who would serve until her death as her mentor, critic, and sometimes literary agent.[15] Through her friendship with Higginson she gained entrée to a circle of New England intellectuals: poets, writers, and editors, and she began to write more and more. By the time of her death, she had published literally hundreds of poems, pieces of short fiction, advice essays, and travel sketches as well as more than twenty books (many of them compilations of her poems and travel pieces).

As was common for women writers in the nineteenth century, rather than use her real name Jackson wrote under various pseudonyms, among them "Marah," "Saxe Holm," "Rip Van Winkle," and the most famous of all, "H.H." By the 1870s her work was regularly published in various newspapers such as the *New York Independent,* the *New York Evening Post,* and the *Christian Union,* and as the 1870s led into the 1880s she reached out more frequently to intellectual journals such as *The Nation, Scribner's Monthly Magazine, Harper's Monthly,* and the *Atlantic Monthly.* Prolific in her output, she had become one of the best paid writers of her time, often driving hard bargains with her publishers. Buoyed by the early success of her poetry, and sustained by Higginson's encouragement, she had embarked on a literary career that would eventually combine child-rearing advice, poetry, travel writing, fiction, and nonfiction. Now an enthusiastic adventuress, she traveled New England, Europe, and the American West with commissions from leading magazines to write about her experiences.[16] Already in these early travel sketches she demonstrated the keen eye for detail and penchant for precise description that would serve her so well later in her career.

While in Colorado on one of her western excursions, she met banker and railroad developer William Sharpless Jackson. She married him in 1875, making her permanent home in Colorado Springs. But it was not her marriage to Mr. Jackson that would most dramatically alter the course of her life. Helen Hunt Jackson, despite her association with prominent "crusaders" of the day, had long avoided taking up any of the causes then fashionable in her literary circle such as abolitionism, temperance, and women's suffrage. In 1879, at a Boston lecture given by the Native American Chief Standing Bear of the Poncas tribe, and his interpreter Susette LaFlesche (also known as Bright Eyes), that all changed.[17]

Standing Bear and LaFlesche were on the lecture circuit working to raise awareness about the suffering of the Poncas who had been forced to relocate to Indian Territory, and to raise money for their upcoming lawsuit in the U.S. Supreme Court. The plea from this tribe of settled agriculturalists facing the "rapacious advance of American civilization" struck a deep chord with Jackson, who devoted the bulk of her energy and writing for the rest of her life to righting the wrongs done to Native Americans.[18] From this point forward Helen Hunt Jackson became a devoted crusader herself. Recognizing her newfound passion as somewhat of a departure for herself, she wrote to a friend, "I have done now, I believe, the last of the things I have said I would never do. I have become what I have said a thousand times was the most odious thing in the world, 'a woman with a hobby.'"[19]

Launching a one-woman campaign to document and draw attention to the wrongs done to Native Americans by federal policies, she began an exhaustive research project on the subject at the Astor Library in New York and immediately shifted some of her writing output to a new form, writing impassioned nonfiction articles, editorials, and letters to the editor, and placing them often in the prestigious *New York Tribune*. Expressing her collected research in book form, in 1881 she published *A Century of Dishonor*, a chronicle of these wrongs focusing on seven tribes (including the Poncas), laid out like a legal brief and appended with lengthy statistics as well as testimonials to Indian "character," and then sent a copy to each member of Congress at her own expense.[20] But the book was dull and attracted little attention: as Jackson herself, aware of the book's density and difficult message, later wrote, "I tried to attack people's consciences directly, and they would not listen."[21]

Still, despite her book's lack of success, her articles, letters, and editorials attracted attention to the cause, and her resolve strengthened. Thus, when offered a commission to write four illustrated articles for *The Century* magazine about southern California she readily agreed: traveling around southern California would provide ample opportunity for Indian research as well. She had first visited the state with her friend Sarah Woolsey (better known by her pen name, "Susan Coolidge") in 1872, but had traveled only to northern California. Even then, however, she had been interested in returning to write on the missions, and now those very missions were linked with her *cause celèbre*. Thus, the first of Jackson's three visits to southern California commenced in December of 1881.[22]

Jackson prepared herself well for the trip by researching California history at New York's Astor Library (even reading books written in Spanish by Jesuit historians), and obtaining letters of introduction that would admit her (a Protestant-turned-Unitarian) into the Catholic circles of southern California.[23] She hoped that the clergy, in turn, would be able to lead her to make contact with the descendants of California's Mission Indians. Reduced to just some 5,000 in number, the Mission Indians lived scattered mainly on isolated reservations, in small rural villages, and in slums at the edges of American towns and cities. Though the missions themselves had been secularized in 1834 under Mexican rule, and most of their lands had subsequently been granted as Mexican ranchos, a significant number of Mission Indians had remained at or near the missions with no choice other than to work for the new landowners.[24]

Arriving in Los Angeles, Jackson was at once struck by the "delicious aroma from the old, ignorant, picturesque times," which she felt still lingered strongly.[25] In all of her travels and her writings on the region Jackson remained, as she had in her other regional writings, strongly drawn both to seeking out and to writing about what she saw as the remnants of traditional life ways as they persisted amid the advance of Anglo-American industrialization.[26] In the case of southern California, that included not just Native American life ways but, significantly, Mexican ones as well.

Wasting no time, Jackson fell to her work immediately. Her letter of introduction to Bishop Mora of Los Angeles netted her another letter of introduction, this time to Antonio Coronel, a former inspector of the missions (under Mexican rule), a former mayor of Los Angeles (under American rule), a well-connected Californio, and a longtime advocate for the Mission Indians.[27] With an itinerary Coronel had planned for her, Jackson set out, in January of 1882, on a two-month circuit around southern and central California even before her illustrator had arrived.[28] When illustrator Henry Sandham arrived in April, Jackson continued her travels with him, and then in May she traveled as well with her close friend, the wealthy Abbot Kinney, as her Spanish interpreter.[29]

Committed to her work, Jackson made a point of visiting as many of the missions and Indian villages as possible; she was indefatigable, often roaming California's rough backcountry alone in an open carriage. She also visited a number of ranchos and made contact with some Californio families. Wherever she went in her travels, Jackson bought baskets and lace and Indian curios to be used as illustrations in her magazine articles, and to decorate the rooms of the hotels in which she was frequently a long-term guest.[30]

Helen Hunt Jackson.

Jackson, now in her fifties, was small, plump, and positively ebullient. Something in her nature seemed to set at ease many of the people whom she met, and she tirelessly collected their stories of injustices and trage-dies.[31] The tales she was told of the wrongs done to the Mission Indians were of such a grave nature that she was compelled to intercede. Back east for the winter she corresponded with Secretary Teller of the Department of the Interior and, in 1883, secured an appointment as a "special agent" to that department with the specific task of visiting the Mission Indians and "ascertain[ing] the location and condition of various bands."[32] This led to her second trip to southern California in the spring of 1883, where, with Kinney as her officially appointed co-commissioner she journeyed to many more villages than she had visited on her previous trip, and to some that were even more remote. The roads were treacherous but Jackson, ever dedicated to her cause, insisted, "I'll go if it kills me."[33]

Now Jackson's travels took on an even more definite purpose with her official government appointment, and her field research in numerous small villages compelled her even more powerfully than her previous archival research had. Native Americans in southern California had not fared well under the Spanish or Mexican conquests and colonial periods, with native populations plummeting due to imported diseases and often brutal mistreatment, their social structures devastated by missionization and forced labor, and their lands largely usurped. Now, during the American conquest, the southern California Indian population fell a further 80 percent.[34] But while the devastation wrought during the Spanish and Mexican conquests was for Jackson in the past, in much of southern California the American conquest was very much a thing of the present, literally taking place before her eyes. Seeing the threats to these people, peaceable agriculturalists, by illegally encroaching white settlers and ill-surveyed reservation lands, Jackson took action, drawing attention to the poor surveys, demanding the eviction of white homesteaders, requesting additional reservation lands, and even hiring a law firm (whose fees she herself guaranteed) to defend the Mission Indians' rights. Her fifty-six-page "Report on the Conditions and Needs of the Missions Indians," co-authored with Kinney and submitted in July of 1883, made such requests official and led to a bill before Congress the following year. In an effort to secure the bill's passage she further sent two hundred copies of the report, at her own expense, to prominent friends and acquaintances, hoping they would help influence public (and congressional) opinion. The bill, "Act for the Relief of the Mission Indians in the State of California," passed in 1891.[35]

With her report and the four *Century* articles (one of which described the Mission Indians' situation) completed, Jackson now sought a new way to drive her message home. As early as May 1883, upon the completion of her California fieldwork, she contemplated the idea of writing a "story" that dramatized the wrongs done to the Mission Indians, one set in the towns and villages she had just visited.[36] Back in Colorado in October she was awakened one night with an idea so clear it startled her: the entire plot of a novel flashed before her, and haunted her until the day she could begin to write.[37] Jackson traveled to New York City, where, in rooms at the Berkeley Hotel, she settled down with her "traps" as she called them—the baskets and weavings she had collected while in southern California—to write the novel she planned to call "In the Name of the Law."[38]

Never one to balk from lofty goals, Jackson made her purpose in writing the book clear from the outset. She wrote to the Coronels in Los Angeles, "I will tell you what my next work for the Indians is to be. I am going to write a novel, in which will be set forth some Indian experiences in a way to move people's hearts. People will read a novel when they will not read serious books."[39]

On 1 December 1883 Jackson began her work. Seizing her like a passion, she could scarcely put it down, often writing as much as three thousand words in a day.[40] To Thomas Wentworth Higginson she wrote, "What I have to endure in holding myself away from it ... no words can tell. It is like keeping away from a lover whose hand I can reach."[41] At 11 p.m. on 9 March 1884 she finished the work the world would come to know as *Ramona*.[42]

In a calculated effort to draw the most publicity and the widest audience in the shortest amount of time, Jackson sacrificed a larger fee in order to publish her novel first as a serial in the weekly newspaper the *Christian Union*, beginning in May 1884. The full work appeared in print in November of that year, published by Roberts Brothers under Jackson's own name with "H.H." added.[43] She wrote to superintending editor of the *New York Independent* William Hayes Ward about the novel, "if I can do one hundredth part for the Indian that Mrs. Stowe did for the Negro I will be thankful."[44]

Ramona was an instant success, selling fifteen thousand copies in its first ten months of publication (very high sales at that time), but most reviewers concentrated on her romantic portrayal of southern California life rather than on the Indian material Jackson had presented. Disappointed, Jackson wrote to Charles Dudley Warner, editor of *Harper's* magazine, "Not one word for the Indians; I put my heart and soul in the book for them. It is a dead failure."[45] Jackson, however, was not one to give up, and she began planning her next work for the Indians: a children's book written, as she explained to Warner, "to educate a few thousand children ... to grow up ready to be just."[46]

Already, however, she was terribly ill. After falling down the stairs in her Colorado Springs home and failing to recover from a badly broken leg, Jackson began to realize her predicament.[47] She traveled to Los Angeles, her third and final visit to southern California, in an effort to regain her health. Instead, her health worsened, leading her to believe she had contracted malaria, and she moved to San Francisco in another attempt to improve her health.

Now aware she was dying, Jackson was drawn to the task of setting her affairs in order. She wrote letters of farewell to all of her friends and wrote detailed instructions on the disbursement of her possessions (her manuscripts and letters were to be burned), but even yet her cause had not left her mind.[48] On 8 August 1885 she wrote to President Cleveland,

> From my death bed I send you message of heartfelt thanks for what you have already done for the Indians.
>
>   I ask you to read my *Century of Dishonor.*
>
>   I am dying happier for the belief I have that it is your hand that is destined to strike the first steady blow toward lifting this burden of infamy from our country and righting the wrongs of the Indian race.[49]

Her work, she hoped, would linger longer than she. Helen Hunt Jackson died of cancer on 12 August 1885 at the age of fifty-four, ever devoted to her cause and, at most, only dimly aware of what was to become of her most important work.[50]

THE NOVEL

"It was sheep-shearing time in Southern California; but sheep-shearing was late at the Señora Moreno's."[51] With those words, Helen Hunt Jackson began the first southern California novel, the novel that would be called "unquestionably the best work yet produced by an American woman," the novel whose love by thousands of readers over many decades would forever change southern California's landscape and social memory.[52] As its title implies, the novel revolves around Ramona, who is half Indian and half Scottish, with her mother's dark hair and her father's blue eyes. When Ramona is an infant, her sea-captain father leaves her with the aristocratic Hispanic woman he has long loved, but who had married another man while he was at sea. When that woman, too, finds herself at death's door, she passes the baby Ramona to her sister, and so it is that the

The "Tourists' Edition" of Ramona (1922) featured the by-then widely recognizable south veranda of Rancho Camulos on its cover. This copy is inscribed "To Mother; Christmas 1924; in honor of her Grand[d]aughter Ramona Zu Tavern."

beautiful heroine comes to live at the rancho home of the strong-willed Señora Moreno. Ramona, completely unaware of her ancestry and background, is raised as an ill-favored stepchild, but nevertheless a member of the Californio aristocracy.

Along with the other citizens of the former Mexican Territory of California, the Moreno family and their rancho have suffered with the recent arrival of the Americans. Extensive lands once granted the family after the secularization of Mission San Fernando have now been claimed by the newly arrived Anglos, and the Moreno rancho has been reduced to but a fraction of its former grandeur. Despite these losses, however, life on the rancho goes on much as before: Jackson depicts a largely tranquil existence in which California's winterless climate graces their primitive-but-elegant lifestyle with endless bloom and verdure.

When Ramona's weak and unassertive stepbrother, Felipe, falls ill, the annual sheep-shearing is delayed, since the domineering Señora insists on presenting the image that her son Felipe is in charge of the rancho. Alessandro Assis, head of a group of itinerant Native American sheep-shearers and son of a chief, nurses Felipe back to health, building him a bed to sleep on out-of-doors and playing for him softly on the violin.[53] Alessandro, like all on the rancho except the Señora, is immediately smitten by Ramona's Madonna-like beauty.[54] When they fall in love, the Señora forbids Ramona to marry this Indian, so far beneath the stature of the Morenos, and she reveals to Ramona her true heritage, showing her a chest of jewels left her by her father, which is to be hers if she marries well. But Ramona, nineteen and in love, forsakes the jewels and elopes with Alessandro even though he is at first reluctant to take this seemingly fragile maiden into a life fraught with uncertainty.

Alessandro's father has recently been killed and their village destroyed by marauding American settlers and Alessandro is left penniless. But Ramona is inspired by her sudden awareness of the Indian blood that runs through her veins and she proves stronger than anyone had imagined. They journey to San Diego to be married, and their romance, journey, and marriage are depicted as a sort of spiritual union, for the pious and devout Ramona never appears less virginal, even after childbirth.

Ramona and Alessandro settle down at another Indian village and their life at first is happy. Soon, however, their bliss is shattered by yet another group of invading Anglos. Fleeing to a more impoverished farm, they must leave their crops and many of their possessions behind. No sooner are they settled than they are again forced from their land, this time driven to retreat to the mountains where they can barely eke out an existence. Nearly perishing in a snowstorm, the couple and their child are saved by a family of American hillbillies, who become their good friends—simple people (their speech rendered by Jackson in dialect) who are virtually the only good-natured Americans Jackson introduces. Despite this friendship, however, the couples' troubles and hardships are far from over. Tragedy strikes when their first baby, Eyes of the Sky, falls ill, the American doctor refuses to come to see it, and the child dies. Grief-stricken and bowed down with hardship, Ramona sustains herself with her Catholic faith. But at this point, for Alessandro, the suffering of his people and now his own family is too much, and he becomes subject to strange paroxyms. One day, in a "state of cataleptic aberration," he accidentally rides home on the wrong horse.[55] When he arrives home to his wife and their new daughter (also Ramona), Ramona (the elder) immediately realizes her husband's fateful mistake. Before anything can be done, however, the white owner of the horse arrives and brutally murders Alessandro before Ramona's eyes. When the white man is acquitted in Alessandro's murder, Ramona succumbs to a brain fever and all fear she will die.

At this time the novel returns to Felipe, who, due to the Señora's death, has finally emerged from his mother's long shadow. Loving Ramona always—and not just as a sister—he searches for her ceaselessly and, finding her near death, brings her back to her home on the Moreno rancho. She recovers and briefly life returns to its old, idyllic state. Felipe proclaims his love and Ramona agrees to marry him, but even such landed aristocracy as they are not safe from the onslaught of encroaching Americans. Resolving to bid farewell to their beloved rancho, they leave for Mexico to start a new life, one more like the old Californio life before the arrival of the Americans. Flourishing in the new land, Ramona becomes the belle of Mexico City, and she and Felipe have many children—but their favorite and the most charming of all remains the young Ramona, daughter of the once-proud Alessandro.

THE NOVEL IN CONTEXT

Retelling Jackson's plot may help us to understand the structure of her novel, but it can do little to help us to understand why her earnestly felt call to aid the Mission Indians was not well heeded. For that we must look

Artist Henry Sandham traveled with Jackson and, after her death, drew illustrations for Ramona. *This one shows the moment before Alessandro's tragic murder (Monterey Edition, 1900).*

further. To be sure, Jackson's novel appeared at a time—more than five years *before* the battle at Wounded Knee and less than a decade after Custer's last stand—when Native Americans were still widely reviled, and even feared, by whites. So writing a novel that endeared the Native American cause to the dominant Anglo population would be a challenge at the very least. Just the same, another woman, Harriet Beecher Stowe, had accomplished no less with *Uncle Tom's Cabin* some thirty years earlier. But despite the fact that Jackson openly aspired to "do one hundredth part for the Indian that Mrs. Stowe did for the Negro," Jackson's work—her writing itself as well as her ambition—can better be understood in its own cultural and indeed literary context.[56] To do this will require a different glimpse of Jackson's biography, a different look at her novel, and some further understanding of literary-cultural developments in the late nineteenth century.

When Helen Hunt Jackson began her career as a writer in the mid-1860s, she entered easily into the sentimental/domestic genre then acceptable for women writers and popular among women readers. Publishing her earliest poetry as a relief from the pain of her son's death, she was soon also publishing home and child-rearing advice. Thus, along with the works of other women like Louisa May Alcott (*Little Women* was published in this period), Jackson's work fit immediately and comfortably into the domestic realm both widely popular and acceptable for women of the day to publish in. Though popular, these works were not, at the time, considered to have great literary merit. By the 1870s and 1880s, however, a new "culture of letters" was emerging in which women authors could hold higher literary aspirations and achieve greater literary recognition.[57]

Travel writing, and in particular stories about "rustic places," had already been an accepted form for women writers since the 1850s.[58] Even the top intellectual/literary magazines of the day (the *Atlantic Monthly, Harper's Monthly, Scribner's Monthly,* and its successor, *The Century Magazine*) consistently published travel pieces—about remote corners of the United States as well as even more exotic locales abroad—alongside their other literary offerings,[59] and Helen Jackson had eagerly launched into this new form. By the late 1870s, *Scribner's,* which had become a frequent outlet for her poetry, was publishing her travel pieces as well. With poetry as well as nonfiction travel writing appearing in *Scribner's* and the *Atlantic* (as well as New York newspapers) many times per year, and friends (like Thomas Bailey Aldrich, editor of the *Atlantic,* and Charles Dudley Warner, editor of *Harper's*) prominent in the publishing world, Jackson had become a known and recognized writer, well connected in the nation's top literary circles.[60]

At the same time that Jackson began to seek the local color she would need to write a novel fictionalizing the plight of Native Americans in order to endear their cause to readers, what emerged as a leading literary form, one available for women authors in particular, was the regional novel: Set in remote (but real) corners of the United States, this fiction featured colorful characters speaking in dialects, lavish and loving place descriptions, and nostalgic depictions of picturesque folkways and a life outside of modernity.[61] Regional fiction was, in the second half of the nineteenth century, the "principal place of literary access." With a few notable exceptions, such as Henry James, nearly every writer who became established during this period, like Mark Twain and Sarah Orne Jewett, did so by writing regional fiction.[62] With Jackson's fieldwork experiences from her *Century* articles on southern California as well as her travels with Abbot Kinney while preparing her report on the Mission Indians, she now had not only the writerly skill and the entrée to the top journals, but also the detailed knowledge of certain local conditions that would be required to write a regional novel set in southern California and dramatizing the Mission Indians' plight. Accustomed to writing fact-based travel essays as well as incorporating aspects of her personal experiences into her fiction, Jackson wove into *Ramona* descriptions of real places and real people, and dramatizations of real events (many of them previously told in her "Report,"), all merged in her imagination around the love story of Ramona and Alessandro and set in a regional context recognizable to readers but also richly created by Jackson herself.[63]

Regional writing, in addition to its ubiquity and widespread popularity in the late nineteenth century, served specific cultural purposes that, in retrospect, may have worked (along with Jackson's specific use of plot, characterization, and description) ironically to *distract* interest from Jackson's cause. In the late nineteenth century, regional fiction's appeal lay in its presentation of places and people who had remained outside of the advancing urbanization and industrialization of the rest of the United States, for these advances, despite their obvious advantages, had already become suspect. Regional fiction thus presented a "counterworld" to urban modernity.[64] Historian Jackson Lears has written of the "weightlessness" felt by Victorian Americans in their everyday lives due to the rapid changes in an urbanizing country, leading them to seek experiences that seemed more "real" than their urban lives.[65] Regional fiction, with its rich descriptions of rural life and provincial communities, proffered glimpses of seemingly authentic cultures as yet unaffected by modernism; the folk and folkways described by regional writers offered an escape into a nostalgic past captured in remnant form in the present.[66] But for those like Jackson, whose regional fictions carried calls to action, the popularity and ready reception of regional works served only to distract from that message. In Jackson's work, regional fiction's style transformed her potentially emancipatory cry to aid the Native Americans into a nostalgic glance *back* at the Californio and Indian cultures that once had been.[67] In order to understand this, it will be necessary to examine Jackson's use of description, characterization, and plot in the text of her novel more closely.

RAMONA'S LANDSCAPE, CHARACTERS, AND PLOT

Despite Jackson's devoted allegiance to many historical and landscape details, her desire to create a novel whose plot and characters would win readers over to the Indian cause dictated that she make some changes— not only in the historical events, but also likely in the novel's plot. While Jackson was struggling with her dalliances from historical accuracy, she wrote to Abbot Kinney, "Do you think it will do any harm to depart from the chronological sequence of events in my story? For dramatic purposes I have put the Temecula ejectment *before* the first troubles in San Pasquale. Will anybody be idiot enough to make a point of that?"[68] It was not, however, her departure from the chronological sequence of events that caused readers to become swept up in her characters and their story rather than Jackson's message. Rather the strength of Jackson's place descriptions, the romanticized and exotic nature of her characters, and their picturesque, un-modernistic folkways, as well as her allegiance to a plot capped by what has seemed to many a happy ending, one that dispelled readers' concerns for Native Americans, contributed both to her novel's phenomenal success and to its failure to bring about reform.[69]

Jackson's strength in the novel is in her descriptive passages where her fieldworker's memory for detail created scenes of lavish realism, enveloping her reader in the romance of the tale and its setting.[70] From the outset, Jackson's opulent southern California landscape descriptions signal a location foreign to her eastern and midwestern audience.[71] Early in the novel Jackson describes the Moreno rancho in great detail:

> Between the veranda and the river meadows, out on which it looked, all was garden, orange grove, and almond orchard; the orange grove always green, never without snowy bloom or golden fruit; the garden never without flowers, summer or winter; and the almond orchard, in early spring, a fluttering canopy of pink and white petals, which, seen from the hills on the opposite side of the river, looked as if rosy sunrise clouds had fallen, and become tangled in the tree-tops. On either hand stretched away other orchards,—peach, apricot, pear, apple, pomegranate; and beyond these, vineyards. Nothing was to be seen but verdure or bloom or fruit at whatever time of year you sat on the Señora's south veranda. (16)

If the gardens of southern California proffered superabundance, no less so the fields of wildflowers in Jackson's tale:

> The wild mustard in Southern California is like that spoken of in the New Testament, in the branches of which the birds of the air may rest.[72] Coming up out of the earth, so slender a stem that dozens can find starting point in an inch, it darts up, a slender straight shoot, five, ten, twenty feet, with hundreds of fine feathery branches locking and interlocking with all the other hundreds around it, till it is an inextricable network like lace. Then it bursts into yellow bloom still finer, more feathery and lace-like. The stems are so infinitesimally small, and of so dark a green, that at a short distance they do not show, and the cloud of the blossom seems floating in the air; at times it looks like golden dust. With a clear blue sky behind it, as is often seen, it looks like a golden snow-storm. The plant is a tyrant and a nuisance . . . it takes riotous possession of a whole field in a season . . . but it is impossible to wish that the land were freed from it. Its gold is as distinct a value to the eye as the nugget gold is in the pocket. (37)

Often her description of bloom and blossom are intermingled with that of climate:

> And the delicious, languid, semi-tropic summer came hovering over the valley. The apricots turned golden, the peaches glowed, the grapes filled and hardened, like opaque emeralds hung thick under the canopied vines. The garden was a shade brown, and the roses had all fallen; but

there were lilies, and orange-blossoms, and poppies, and carnations and
geraniums in the pots, and musk. (106–7)

Jackson's praise of southern California's climate is often nearly incidental,
but seldom subtle: "Father Salvierderra drew near the home of the Señora
Moreno late in the afternoon of one of those mid-summer days of which
California has so many in spring" (36).

If her descriptions of the region and its climate are lavish, they are no
less loving, creating for her eastern and midwestern audience compelling
images of an exotic locale:

> The billowy hills on either side of the valley were covered with verdure
> and bloom,—myriads of low blossoming plants, so close to the earth
> that their tints lapped and overlapped on each other and on the green of
> the grass, as feathers in fine plumage overlap each other and blend into a
> changeful color.
>
> The countless curves, hollows, and crests of the coast-hills in South-
> ern California heighten these chameleon effects of the spring verdure;
> they are like nothing in nature except the glitter of a brilliant lizard in
> the sun or the iridescent sheen of a peacock's neck. (36)

So too is the lifestyle Jackson depicts for Ramona's family exotic, and
her descriptions of intriguing folkways explicitly portray a vanishing culture. Here Jackson describes life at the Moreno rancho:

> The Señora Moreno's house was one of the best specimens to be found in
> California of the representative house of the half barbaric, half elegant,
> wholly generous and free-handed life led there by Mexican men and
> women of degree in the early part of this century, under the rule of the
> Spanish and Mexican viceroys . . . when . . . its old name, "New Spain"
> was an ever-present link and stimulus to the warmest memories and
> deepest patriotisms of its people.
>
> It was a picturesque life, with more of sentiment and gayety in it,
> more also that was truly dramatic, more romance, than will ever be seen
> again on those sunny shores. The aroma of it all lingers there still; indus-
> tries and inventions have not yet slain it; it will last out its century,—in
> fact, it can never be quite lost, so long as there is left standing one such
> house as the Señora Moreno's. (11–12)

Of course, though their lives and their culture would change with the
influx of Anglo-Americans to the region, the Californios (and Native

Americans) whom Jackson described in many cases outlived Jackson herself, but to Jackson both cultures appeared on the brink of extinction, and it was this message that she conveyed in her novel.[73] Indeed she is explicit that the lifestyle she depicts is fast disappearing but not yet vanished beyond retrieval, evocations typical of nineteenth-century regional novels.[74]

In the style of regional fiction, Jackson describes practices exotic to Anglo-Americans as common to the Californio culture of southern California. Beginning with a description of sheep-shearing time at the Señora Moreno's rancho, all the early chapters of the novel are devoted to description of life among the Hispanic Morenos, with purposely no hint of the Indian tale that Jackson intends to tell.[75] Presenting vivid images of exotic customs on the brink of disappearance, Jackson here describes the sunrise hymn:

> As the first ray [of the dawning day] reached [Father Salvierderra's] window, he would throw the casement wide open, and standing there with bared head, strike up the melody of the sunrise hymn sung in all devout Mexican families. It was a beautiful custom, not yet wholly abandoned. At the first dawn of light, the oldest member of the family arose, and began singing some hymn familiar to the household. It was the duty of each person hearing it to immediately rise, or at least sit up in bed, and join in the singing. In a few moments the whole family would be singing, and the joyous sounds pouring out from the house like the music of the birds in the fields at dawn. (47–48)

Jackson's characters themselves are no less exotic. When even the remoteness of a Spanish/Mexican Californio culture is not enough, Jackson evokes an image of the widowed Señora Moreno gliding toward the rancho's private chapel for mass from a more geographically as well as temporally distant and still more exotic culture:

> The Señora, with her best black silk handkerchief bound tight around her forehead, the ends hanging down each side of her face, making her look like an Assyrian priestess, was descending the veranda steps. (51)

Jackson's exoticized characterizations reach their peak in the half-Indian Ramona, a woman persistently described in ethereal and otherworldly fashions. Like the blithe spirit she is, Ramona customarily "flies" rather than walks or runs.[76] Her appearance is consistently described as saintly, described here as Father Salvierderra's eyes light on her as she approaches him through the field of wild mustard described above.

> She had looked to the devout old monk, as she sprang through the cloud of golden flowers, the sun falling on her bared head, her cheeks flushed, her eyes shining, more like an apparition of an angel or a saint, than the flesh-and-blood maiden whom he had carried in his arms when she was a babe. (38–39)

The religious overtones of Ramona's description pervade Jackson's narration: "The sunset beams played around her hair like a halo" (47). Alessandro, too, is smitten by her divine appearance: "She looked like a saint, he thought; perhaps it was as a saint of help and guidance, the Virgin was sending her to him and his people," and he says as much to her: "My [Ramona][77] is like one of the Virgin's own saints" (205, 207). After the birth of her first two children and Alessandro's murder these qualities in Ramona become only more emphasized in Jackson's description of her character: "There was a rapt look of holy communion on her face, which made itself felt by the dullest perception, and sometimes overawed even where it attracted" (355–56). And finally, as Ramona and Felipe sail for Mexico, "Ramona sat bareheaded in the end of the boat, and the silver radiance from the water seemed to float up around her, and invest her as with a myriad halos" (360).

Thus, before introducing issues of Native American mistreatment, Jackson deliberately creates an intriguing setting and exotic characters that will hold strong appeal for her audience. As she wrote to *New York Independent* editor William Hayes Ward, "I am at work on a story—which I hope will do something for the Indian cause: it is laid in So. California—and there is so much Mexican life in it, that I hope to get people so interested in it, before they suspect anything Indian, that they will keep on."[78] Thus, the Indian scenes come only later in the novel, and not until the lives and fates of the Mission Indians have been closely connected to the lives of the Californios—specifically to the lives of the Morenos.

For Jackson the problems faced by the Mission Indians were contemporary. While she was aware that the Spanish, Mission, and Mexican systems had not been without flaw, most of the problems she saw on her travels in southern California were those whose immediate cause was Anglo-American.[79] Whatever the cause, the solutions to those problems would depend not upon the regimes of the past, but upon the U.S. government and the American people in the present. By linking the fates of the

Missions, the Californios, and the Indians, Jackson left the Americans as the only oppressors, intending her work to become a rallying cry to right the wrongs done to the Mission Indians by Americans and the American government, and to therefore help to solve *contemporary* problems.

Early in the novel readers learn that, though the Morenos live an apparently opulent life, their lands and their fortunes have already been much reduced by the incoming waves of Anglo-Americans, leaving them with but a pauper's share of their once princely estate.

> [T]he Señora Moreno now called herself a poor woman. Tract after
> tract, her lands had been taken away from her; it looked for a time as if
> nothing would be left. . . . [They] took away from the Señora in a day
> the greater part of her best pasturelands. . . . No wonder she believed
> the Americans thieves, and spoke of them always as hounds. . . . Any
> day, she said, the United States Government might send out a new Land
> commission to examine the decrees of the first, and revoke such as they
> saw fit. Once a thief, always a thief. Nobody need feel himself safe under
> American rule. (12–13)

Although Jackson acknowledges that much of the Moreno land "had once belonged to the Missions of San Fernando and Buenaventura" (13), it is not the Californios who are portrayed as the pillagers of these mission lands, nor the missions the pillagers of Indian lands. Rather, the rancheros, the missions, and the Indians share the same fate: their lands are being pillaged by waves of incoming Anglos. Father Salvierderra, the former mission priest who presides over services at the Moreno rancho, laments these losses:

> The fairer this beautiful land, the sadder to know it lost to the Church,—
> alien hands reaping its fullness, establishing new customs, new laws . . .
> new tokens of the settling up of the country,—farms opening, towns
> growing; the Americans pouring in, at all points, to reap the advantages
> of their new possessions. (36)

And, while there are problems now, Jackson portrays a past, before the arrival of Anglo-Americans, when all was well—for mission padres, rancheros, and Indians alike:

> In [Señor Moreno's] time, while the estate was at its best, and hundreds
> of Indians living within its borders, there was many a Sunday when the
> scene to be witnessed there was like the scenes at the Missions—the

chapel full of kneeling men and women; those who could not find room inside kneeling on the garden walks outside; Father Salvierderra, in gorgeous vestments, coming, at close of the services, slowly down the aisle, the close paced rows of worshipers parting to right and left to let him through, all looking up eagerly for his blessing. (18)

Once the fates of the missions, the Californios, and the Indians are all placed in American hands, Jackson introduces Alessandro, son of a Native American chief: born at the mission grounds, raised as a Catholic, Alessandro serves to link the fates of not just lands and livelihoods but also characters and their souls, telling Ramona "tales of the old Mission days that he had heard from his father; stories of saints, and of the early Fathers, who were more like saints than like men" (110). Like the Señora Moreno herself, Alessandro grew up at a mission, and he had been known to Father Salvierderra "since he was a little fellow playing in the corridors of San Luis Rey, the pet of all the Brothers there" (65). Though Alessandro is not so unequivocally praiseful of the missions as are the Morenos, he and his people are nevertheless devout. "They were all good Catholics, every one of the Temecula men [Alessandro's sheep-shearers]" (68). In this way, Jackson domesticates Alessandro and the members of his tribe and gradually draws the Indians into the already linked plights of the Californios and the missions.

In placing Indian characters in the idyllic lives of the Californios, Jackson (accurately for southern California at that time and before) portrays Native Americans as a distinctly lower social class in California society. When the Señora Moreno forbids her stepdaughter Ramona to marry Alessandro, it is because he is an Indian and therefore beneath Ramona, who has been raised as a Californio (129). Summing up the position of Native Americans in the novel's Californio society, Señora Moreno tells her son Felipe,

Of what is it that these . . . [Indians] are so proud? their ancestors,—naked savages less than a hundred years ago? Naked savages they themselves too, to-day, if we had not come here to teach and civilize them. The race was never meant for anything but servants. That was all the Fathers ever expected to make of them,—good, faithful Catholics, and contented laborers in the fields. (88)

Though at the bottom of the social and intellectual hierarchy, Jackson's Mission Indians are neither fearful nor violent, but rather peaceable farmers content with their status and often portrayed through the trope of the noble savage, as illustrated here when Jackson describes Alessandro, completely outside of modern science, naively pondering the nature of the universe:

> The sky was like amber; a few stars still shone faintly in the zenith. There was not a sound. It was one of those rare moments in which one can without difficulty realize the noiseless spinning of the earth through space. Alessandro knew nothing of this; he could not have been made to believe that the earth was moving. He thought the sun was coming up apace, and the earth was standing still,—a belief just as grand, just as thrilling, so far as all that goes, as the other: men worshipped the sun long before they found out that it stood still. Not the most reverent astronomer, with the mathematics of the heavens at his tongue's end, could have had more delight in the wondrous phenomenon of the dawn, than did this simple-minded, unlearned man. (48)

And, true to the image of the noble savage, Alessandro is portrayed as equal or even superior in matters of the soul:

> Alessandro was undeniably Ramona's inferior in position, education, in all the external matters of life; but in nature, in true nobility of soul, no! Alessandro was no man's inferior in these; and in capacity to love,— Felipe sometimes wondered whether he had ever known Alessandro's equal in that. (169)

Ramona, for her part, even though half-Indian, is always recognized as above full-blooded Indians and must first redefine Alessandro as a non-Indian before she can fall in love with him,

> Ramona gazed after him. For the first time, she looked at him with no thought of his being an Indian,—a thought there had surely been no need of her having, since his skin was not a shade darker than Felipe's; but so strong was the race feeling, that never till that moment had she forgotten it.
> "What a superb head, and what a walk!" she thought. (75)

Once Ramona has fallen in love with Alessandro, the Señora's revelation of Ramona's Indian parentage only strengthens Ramona's love for him, for now she is "of his people" (133). Nevertheless, Ramona never becomes fully an Indian, and even the Indians recognize her ethereal divinity. When Alessandro temporarily leaves Ramona in the care of the Indian woman Carmena, who is in the cemetery grieving the loss of her husband at the hands of the Americans,

> [Carmena] felt for the moment lifted out of herself by the sweet, sudden sympathy of this stranger,—this girl like herself, yet so different, so wonderful, so beautiful. . . . Had the saints sent her from heaven to Alessandro? (214)

Alessandro, devastated and perplexed by the loss of his lands and the fate that has befallen his people, begins to lose his faith and comes to believe that the saints have abandoned the Indians. "And Father Salvierderra says, God is good. It must be the saints no longer pray to Him for us" (223). But he never believes that the saints have abandoned Ramona. "It is only for [Ramona] that the saints pray. They are displeased with my people" (249).

In fact, it is her saintly, undying faith—and thus her European Catholicism rather than her "Indian-ness"—that enables Ramona to survive the hardships she and Alessandro endure together even while Alessandro succumbs,

> There was no real healing for Alessandro. His hurts had gone too deep. His passionate heart, ever secretly brooding on the wrongs he had borne, the hopeless outlook for his people in the future, and most of all on the probable destitution and suffering in store for Ramona, consumed itself as by hidden fires. Speech, complaint, active antagonism, might have saved him; but all these were foreign to his self-contained, reticent, repressed nature. Slowly . . . his brain gave way. (312)

For Ramona, on the other hand,

> forces of fortitude had been gathering in [her] soul during these last bitter years. Out of her gentle constancy had been woven the heroic fibre of which martyrs are made; this, and her inextinguishable faith, had made her strong. (342)[80]

Even Aunt Ri, the kindhearted American hillbilly who befriends Ramona and Alessandro and nurses Ramona back to health after Alessandro's murder, notices Ramona's godliness. "I allow I donno but I sh'd cum ter believin' in saints tew, 'ef I wuz ter live 'long sider er thet gal. 'Pears like she wuz suthin' more 'n human" (348–49). But it is Felipe, not her religion, that rescues Ramona, "not so much from death, as from a life worse than death," and Ramona allows herself to be led away from the Indian life she has lived with Alessandro (348).

Once Ramona has forsaken her Indian side, her life nearly returns to normal, and Jackson's narration briefly returns to the lavish description of the opening chapters,

> Life ran smoothly in the Moreno household, —smoothly to the eye. Nothing could be more peaceful, fairer to see than the routine of its days, with all the simple pleasures, light tasks, and easy diligence of all. Summer and winter were alike sunny, and had each its own joys. (358)

But life is not as before. The wicked American presence is felt strongly even on the Rancho Moreno:

> Year by year the conditions of life in California were growing more distasteful to [Felipe]. The methods, aims, standards of the fast in coming Americans were to him odious. . . . He found himself more and more alone in the country. Even the Spanish tongue was less and less spoken. He was beginning to yearn for Mexico,—for Mexico, which he had never seen, yet yearned for like an exile. There he might live among men and women of his own race and degree, and of congenial beliefs and occupations. (359)

Thus, at the close of the novel, the previously indecisive Felipe determines to leave for a land he has never seen, but which he hopes will be more like his own land in the past. And Ramona herself becomes a creature of the past. Returning to her aristocratic Californio upbringing, she even loses the feeling of Alessandro's continual presence which she had carried with her "as one in constant fellowship with one unseen" (356).

When Felipe proposes marriage to her Ramona closes the door forever on her Indian self with one last glimpse of her dead first husband: "A strange look which startled Felipe swept across Ramona's face: it might have been a moonbeam. It passed. Felipe never saw it again" (362). For Ramona and Felipe there is a future: they return to their past in a new venue. But for the Indians there is none; there is no romantic escape into a land of the past, only death, which, since Alessandro's death is now already distant and remote, becomes, in the novel, a nonissue.

Thus, Ramona's marriage to Felipe and the apparently happy ending of an otherwise tragic tale serve as an anticlimax at the end of Jackson's novel. Ending with Ramona's marriage to Felipe provides "narrative closure

At the novel's close the widowed Ramona leaves behind the Indian life she led with Alessandro, marrying stepbrother Felipe and going with him to a new life in Mexico. Drawing by Henry Sandham.

around the reconstitution of the 'Great Spanish Household' rather than around the murder of Alessandro," and thus ultimately distracts from Jackson's Indian message.[81] Rather than a "naturally motivated conclusion" the marriage comes as a sort of "epilogue," crippling the novel's tragic elements, distracting from the painful plight of the Indians Jackson had hoped so hard to portray.[82] Moreover, by concluding with Ramona and Felipe's departure for Mexico after Alessandro's murder, Jackson suggests the inevitable demise of both the Indian and the Californio presence in southern California (one which, especially in the case of the Indians, was widely believed to be inevitable in Jackson's time). And while both are presented as a loss, it is the Californio culture that Jackson has more forcefully presented, and which, through her conclusion, leaves the lingering impression on the reader.

For the readers of regional fiction the loss of the picturesquely evocative Californio culture to the onslaught of American progress would come as no surprise, for this type of literature often served as a sort of "cultural elegy," memorializing a culture on the brink of its demise while creating, through fiction, a "mentally possessable version of [that] loved thing lost in reality."[83] As Linda Nochlin has observed, "Only on the brink of destruction, in the course of incipient modification and cultural dilution, are the customs, costumes, and religious rituals of the dominated finally *seen* as picturesque. Reinterpreted as the precious remnants of disappearing ways of life . . . they are finally transformed into subjects of aesthetic delectation."[84] Further, since regional fiction like *Ramona* presented intact, anachronistic, and encapsulated "historic" cultures as self-contained and belonging to the past rather than interactive and able to adapt in the present, such cultures, refigured in fiction, could be neatly contained on the page, and the political realities of these minority groups never addressed. The effect of this form of presentation, and thus the public function of regional fiction, was, therefore, more than a mourning of disappearing cultures; it was also the purveying of "a certain story of contemporary cultures and of the relations among them: . . . [it told] local cultures into a history of their supercession by a modern order now risen to national dominance."[85] Regional fiction—with its picturesque description and curious dialects—enabled a transformation of potentially disruptive political differences into quaint cultural differences; in Jackson's work it transformed her potentially emancipatory cry to aid the Mission Indians into a nostalgic glance *back* at the Californio and Indian cultures that had once been, for "[b]y narrating the distance between reader and regional figure as temporal, regional writing [could] posit the spatially distant region as 'ahistorical' and outside the time of industrial development" as well as outside the time and place of possible intervention in the problems of the region.[86]

With emancipatory goals disabled, one of regional writing's primary accomplishments (and significance) in the nineteenth century was to describe the "surviving elements of a local past" in order that they could then "infuse the present with new meaning."[87] One primary way that that meaning was sought was through the increasingly popular practice of tourism, for by presenting tales of exotic, primitive, and interesting remnant cultures, all nearly extinct but yet extant on the North American continent, regional writers stimulated Victorian (and later) urges to travel. Reading about such isolated places and picturesque peoples became linked to the ability and desire to travel there, and thus regional writing became a critical component in the rise of tourism in America.[88]

Contrary to Jackson's goal, *Ramona* would serve as a particularly keen example. By the close of the novel "[t]he reader was no longer moved to address the underlying issues, but, rather, to visit the 'real' sites and people who now served as a marker for the past and the fictional texts."[89] Helen Hunt Jackson's call to aid the Mission Indians was eclipsed by the rush of travelers to California, many of whom soon sought out the very characters and locations her novel had made so memorable.

CHAPTER TWO

RAMONA'S PILGRIMS: TOURISM
AND SOUTHERN CALIFORNIA

> Year by year the conditions of life in California were grow-
> ing more distasteful. . . . The methods, aims, standards
> of the fast incoming [Anglo-] Americans were . . . odi-
> ous. . . . The passion for money and reckless spending of
> it, the great fortunes made in one hour, thrown away in
> another.
>
> —*Ramona*, 359

By the late 1880s travelers in large numbers began seeking out the locations described in Jackson's novel, making what came to be called "pilgrimages" to places like the Home of Ramona and Ramona's Marriage Place and soon buying property on streets, in subdivisions, and even towns named for the characters in the novel. They did not do so in a vacuum, for the 1880s marks an important transition both in the history of tourism in the United States and in the history of southern California.

By 1884, tourism in the United States was changing. Before then, as in Europe, travel had been an expensive pastime, and tourism therefore an elite pursuit. Wealthy Americans, like the wealthy Europeans they admired, engaged in extended Grand Tours of Europe, visiting centers of culture, art, and business.[1] Domestic travel, like European travel, had been expensive enough to confine such excursions to the upper classes, but not until the late nineteenth century did it become popular to travel domestically. Thus, *Ramona's* publication coincided with a significant rise in tourism at home. By the late nineteenth century the nation's transportation network had grown significantly, and rail fares began to drop, making domestic travel accessible to more and more people until by the early twentieth century, tourism would be an established leisure pursuit for both the upper and middle classes.[2]

At the same time that domestic tourism became more popular, it also began to be viewed nearly as a patriotic duty. By the turn of the century campaigns like "See America First" would link domestic travel with the very notions of citizenship and the construction of America as a nation; domestic tourist experiences were part of what good Americans were made of.[3]

Writers and publishers, not slow to seize a growing market, sought to capitalize on this new demand, and, in so doing, created travel stories and tourist guidebooks whose effect was to canonize the sites and scenes of the nation, identifying what was worth seeing, and, moreover, what *should* be seen, creating for travelers a normative tourism geography. Individuals and organizations, from the authors of travel writing, to civic boosters, magazine publishers, railroad corporations, industries with vested interests (like automobile-related companies or hospitality-oriented businesses), and government agencies presented the public with books and articles, many available free of charge, that directed where and how Americans should travel. Hosts of guidebooks listed points of interest and detailed how to get there, while travel writing published in popular magazines portrayed particular places in evocative and often picturesque detail.[4]

Without the cultural and historical legacies of European destinations, American tourist attractions developed along lines that made them distinctly American, reinforcing notions of a distinctly American identity and, through tourist experiences, locating that identity in landscape. Natural wonders and places of sublime beauty like Yosemite and the Grand Canyon provided a geological time depth even Europe could not surpass, suggesting ancient roots for a nation with an otherwise seemingly short history. Further, such sublime scenery suggested a divine accomplishment that surpassed even the castles, cathedrals, great art, and scenery of Europe. By teaching tourists which scenery to admire and how, the guidebooks transformed natural vistas into landscapes—to be encompassed by the gaze, or transformed into art and photographs—rivaling anything to be found in the Old World. In guidebooks and articles such "scenic nationalism" framed a series of canonical landscapes as icons of the nation.[5]

Historical sections in many guidebooks detailed the exploration and colonization of the region, state, or place in question, concluding with Anglo-American apotheosis. The historical sites chosen for description often portrayed a particular narrative of triumphant American history, focusing on such sites as Revolutionary War battlefields. Making manifest a narrative of Anglo-American success, even, and especially where others had failed, guidebooks emphasized how Anglo-Americans had transformed the wilderness into an increasingly powerful nation, even featuring man-made technological marvels such as dams as tourist attractions. The presentations of historical sites dramatically underscored such themes, as in the elegiac tones used to describe both Native American and Spanish ruins. As California's missions melted into "crumbling piles," authors of articles and guidebooks eulogized the Spanish past when "California enjoyed its perennial siesta," thus leaving ample room for Anglo progress in the present. Idealized images of Native Americans as noble savages served to reinforce not only their domination by whites, but also themes of nature as refuge from modern society, while "domesticated tourist Indians" on display selling and making handicrafts at tourist sites demonstrated for tourists the ideal of a life close to nature, one that could be vicariously experienced and consumed by tourists as they visited Native American sites and purchased Indian souvenirs.[6]

Other sites declared notable by tourist guidebooks and travel articles were "literary shrines," landmarks both to American authors and their works that served to glorify the American culture of letters, linking it with the nation's landscape, thus presenting great literature as a "natural" outgrowth of the nation's dramatic scenery. Such literary shrines as authors'

Helen Hunt Jackson's grave on Cheyenne Mountain above Colorado Springs, Colorado, became a significant tourist attraction. Eventually, due to this traffic, her remains were moved to a cemetery in Colorado Springs.

homes and graves and the scenes their works made famous testified to the vibrant culture that Americans had created from the wilderness and provided visitors with sites where they could remember beloved works of poetry and fiction.[7] Thus, American tourist attractions—whether points of great scenic beauty, the sites of battles, Indian or Spanish ruins, the routes of explorers and colonizers, feats of technology, shrines to American literature and literary figures, or other sites—mapped the history of the United States, and Anglo-American progress, onto a tourist landscape newly popular and increasingly accessible around the turn of the twentieth century. For Anglo-Americans, domestic travel became a way to define America as a place, to take pride in its unique landscape features, and to model themselves as good Americans. Tourism was becoming a "ritual of American citizenship."[8]

If guidebooks listed literary landmarks among the nation's important attractions, other literature—travel writing and regional fiction—served both to encourage and to buttress their prominence as landscape attractions. Regional fiction, with its colorful characters and apparently all-but-extinct lifeways, served as a compelling inducement for Victorian (and later) Americans to travel. Travel writing—ubiquitous in the nation's top magazines—and regional novels, both literary forms in high demand, made such out-of-the-way places "visitable in print." Then, as first upper-class and later middle-class vacation practices turned to tourism, such remote places initially encountered on the printed page became, along with dramatic scenery and historic sites, ideal destinations, ideal spots for aesthetic appreciation—perfect places for tourism.[9]

Indeed, prominent Los Angeles journalist Harry Carr, born in a small town in Iowa, might never have come to California at all but for the tourist materials that reached his parents. Carr's lawyer-father set out first in the mid-1880s, while his mother entertained herself and the children, preparing them for the land to which they too would soon be headed, by reading them stories of "Spanish" ranches—reading to them from *Ramona*. Nor were the Carrs the only ones: Margaret Allen, writing in 1914, suggested that "eastern visitors" commonly "read *Ramona* as part of their preparation for a winter's trip to Southern California."[10]

Not to be balked at as the superficial pastime of undiscriminating travelers, tourism "played a powerful role in America's invention of itself as a culture."[11] In southern California in the decades surrounding the turn of the twentieth century, the travels of individuals as well as the campaigns of boosters played a critical role in defining, even in creating, the region.

SOUTHERN CALIFORNIA AND THE BOOM OF THE 1880S

By the time *Ramona* was published in 1884, southern California, for so long still somnolent compared to the Gold Rush–inspired turmoil and growth felt in the north, was on the brink of immense change. The city of Los Angeles itself had remained a Hispanic pueblo, its comparatively small population still dominated by the Californio elite (including the Anglos who had married into Californio families and taken on Californio life-styles).[12] But the first outside railroad, the Southern Pacific, had reached the region in September 1876, shortly before Helen Hunt Jackson's visits.

With the railroad came the first significant waves of Anglo-Americans, mostly wealthy tourists like Jackson herself, many of them engaged in American versions of the Grand Tour or seeking a more pleasant climate in which to spend winter months.[13] With books and brochures beginning to advertise not just the wonders of scenery, but also southern California's warm, dry air as healthful for invalids (particularly consumptives and others with lung diseases), a "sanitarium belt" grew up alongside the luxury resort hotels to cater to these newcomers' needs.

Agriculture, too was changing in the region. Once known as the "cow counties," isolated southern California had been dominated by Californio ranchos mainly devoted to cattle ranching, and later sheep. In the 1870s the introduction of the Bahia or Washington winter-ripening navel orange as well as the summer-ripening Valencia orange just a few years later led to a dramatic rise in citrus production, mainly on Anglo-held lands. By the mid-1880s California citrus was winning both prizes and attention nationwide, and oranges themselves could be used as a lure to draw visitors, with thousands of carloads of oranges shipped east. By the late 1880s, in places like Riverside and Anaheim, more than a million citrus trees were forever transforming a landscape once known primarily for its "cattle on a thousand hills."[14]

But change initially was slow, and the arrival of railroad competition (at first to nearby San Bernardino) in the form of the Atchison, Topeka and Santa Fe in the fall of 1885 would lead to the massive influx of tourists and homeseekers in what became known as the "boom of the eighties." This boom transformed Los Angeles–area population and power struc-tures and cemented the American conquest, forever changing the region that Jackson had visited and the picturesque landscapes and lifeways she had described.[15]

After some three decades of Anglo-driven change, the initiation of a railroad rate war sparked the boom, ushering in tremendous waves of new settlers and altering southern California nearly overnight. In March of 1887 the Santa Fe obtained its own roadbed into Los Angeles (it had previously leased a right-of-way from the competition) and was ready to take on the powerful Southern Pacific. The ensuing rate war centered on the price of a ticket from points in the Mississippi Valley, a destination already heavily the focus of boosterist advertising about southern California. In 1885, before the arrival of the Santa Fe, fares had fluctuated around $125, keeping transcontinental travel too expensive for most. No sooner had the Santa Fe entered the region than the fare dropped to $95. Once the Santa Fe acquired its own roadbed, what one historian called "the greatest railroad 'rate war' ever seen in America" was on. On 6 March the battle focused on one-way fares between Kansas City and Los Angeles. That morning the fare began at twelve dollars. It dropped to ten, then to eight, then to six, and finally to four dollars as each railroad company underbid the other. Briefly, just after noon, the Southern Pacific announced a fare of only one dollar. So low a price was not sustainable, and within four days the price had risen again to two figures, but for the better part of a year, rates from Missouri River points remained below $25, and they rose only slowly to their former heights. The Southern Pacific and the Santa Fe had cleverly used the rate war to draw the public's attention to the attractions of southern California, one of which was available land.[16]

With the sudden arrival of so many rail-sped visitors—in 1887 alone, when the boom reached its peak, Los Angeles, a city with a population still under 50,000, saw more than 120,000 tourists visit—southern California's hotels and rooming houses "filled to overflowing; the demand for quarters could not be met." Some came after having read advertisements or promotional materials and, once there, were able to promote the region themselves as they sent news of their travels back home. In Los Angeles, for example, the number of letters mailed out increased during the boom from 2,083 to an astonishing 21,333 per month. A combination of genuine interest and ballyhoo stimulated real estate sales as well: the price of property skyrocketed, and within only a few months real estate prices rose over 300 percent. In the words of one historian of the boom, "The general intoxication soon took on the proportions of a gorgeous spree. The little Spanish-American town, dozing in the sun but a few months ago, was a mad house. . . . California was living . . . in the actual realm of real estate lunacy."[17]

During the boom an estimated 2,300 real estate firms rose up within the Los Angeles city limits, all in a city whose population in 1880 had been a mere 12,000.[18] Great speculation took place in the realm of existing properties, but still more erupted in new subdivisions and lot sales. The grandest speculation of all, however, occurred in the "townsite." From 1886 to 1888 in Los Angeles County some 1,770 tract maps, subdivisions, and replats were filed.[19] From January 1887 to July 1889 southern California witnessed the laying out of over sixty new towns embracing some 79,350 acres or 500,000 new lots in all, until it seemed that new towns appeared "like scenes conjured up by Aladdin's lamp."[20] Although the city of Los Angeles itself was the economic epicenter of the boom as well as the arrival (and departure) point for many tourists and homeseekers, the main focus of activity—activity critical to the life described by Helen Hunt Jackson in her novel—concerned the "rancho-blanketed suburbs": the new lands being subdivided and sold *had*, after all, belonged to somebody.[21]

RANCHOS BECOME SUBDIVISIONS

The California rancho system, begun during the Spanish conquest, had been based on large land concessions or grants made mostly after the secularization of the missions during the Mexican period (between 1834 and 1846), mainly to a favored upper class of Californio society.[22] Though the majority of those living in California before the American conquest were small or subsistence farmers, through over 700 land grants, some of them as large as 100,000 acres, a few well-endowed Californios enjoyed wealth and power. With many Indian servants and workers (often former mission neophytes), as well as Mexican and *mestizo* cowboys *(vaqueros)*, ranch hands, and laborers, these Californios had in the 1850s been able to build lavish lives based on a Gold Rush cattle boom, lives that, years later, Jackson glimpsed in her travels and subsequently described at the Moreno rancho in *Ramona*. Living in single-story adobe homes built about a central courtyard with large shaded porches (as the Morenos' was), some rancheros were wealthy enough to be able to import exotic goods like furniture and manufactured goods from Europe and New England, or silks and pottery from the Orient. Focused on the hide and tallow export trade, before the American conquest most of these Californio rancheros were highly vested in cattle, secondarily in horses (to ride), sheep (for wool), and to a lesser degree (mainly for their own subsistence) in wheat and wine grapes.[23] Even as they were vested in cattle and cattle lands, most rancheros were, by American standards, comparatively casual in documenting and legitimizing their holdings. Theirs was a culture based not upon written documentation but verbal agreement. Despite the wealth of a few, for most there was little premium on education so the majority remained illiterate.[24] Further, land titles based on sketched maps included boundaries defined by relatively ephemeral or only semi-stable objects such as streambeds, rocks, or trees. Some Californios, whose titles had been granted in haste before the American conquest, possessed only the barest of documentation.[25] These two aspects of rancho society (dependence on cattle and ill-documented land titles) left those Californios with ranchos vulnerable to the forces of nature as well as to outsiders, particularly when those outsiders were aggressively interested in acquiring land.

In the late 1840s and into the 1850s, as the American conquest swept the region, many Californio rancheros lost valuable lands to litigation under the American regime with its new standards of land titling, while the lands of others lingered for decades in the litigational balance. Then, devastating drought in the 1860s brought widespread ruin even to formerly wealthy rancheros (including many of those who had weathered litigation). As cattle lay dying on sun-bleached hillsides—as much as 70 percent of southern California's cattle population was wiped out—many Californios were forced to sell their acreage in order to pay debts or even simply to make ends meet. Others were forced to mortgage property at staggering rates of interest and eventually lost or had to sell land to meet interest payments. So devastated was the area that the city of Los Angeles withheld tax assessment in 1863 and 1864; for a time even valuable downtown lots seized for delinquent taxes stood for sale at rock-bottom prices with no buyers. By 1870 the old California families retained barely one-quarter of the lands they had once held.[26]

Simultaneous with a loss of land and cattle came a loss in political power as incoming Americans took control. Eventually the Spanish- and Mexican-descended Californios lost their majority status as Anglo-Americans became the largest population group. Nevertheless, into the 1880s, many Californio cultural traditions persisted despite conquest, litigation, and drought. The multiday fiestas for which Californio families and communities were renowned went on despite mounting debts and rising Anglo populations to become, for many, even more important as symbols of an enduring Californio culture in an increasingly Anglo southern

California. Spanish was still prominently spoken, and Los Angeles (and southern California more broadly) still gave the appearance of being a Spanish/Mexican (or Californio) place.[27]

Thus, the southern California that Helen Hunt Jackson visited in the early 1880s, and the ranchero life about which she wrote so evocatively in her 1884 novel, was one still extant and yet simultaneously embattled. Indeed, though Californios would long outlive Jackson, it was not difficult for her to perceive their culture as a remnant, as a precapitalist, preindustrial lifestyle on the verge of eclipse by encroaching Americans. Such cultures held strong appeal for Jackson, whose earlier regional work had also featured cultural groups threatened by the rapacious march of American colonization and industry. Now the degree that Jackson portrayed ways of life of wealthy Californio rancheros as precariously picturesque made them well suited to the kinds of travel writing and regional fiction that her nineteenth-century audience expected.[28]

Although Jackson indeed wrote a work of fiction, she did not create her romantic-sounding portrayal of Californio life all alone. Her letters of introduction and other connections enabled her to meet with a number of figures once prominent in the Mexican period who, at the time of Jackson's visits, still maintained at least an appearance of their preconquest lifestyle. Possibly the most formative of these southern California acquaintances was Antonio Coronel, a former mayor of Los Angeles, and the leader of the Californio community. Remaining wealthy despite land loss, Don Antonio still lived at his adobe home, El Recreo, in what was then Los Angeles's western suburb.[29] Now familiar as the busy industrial corner of Seventh and Alameda, when Jackson visited, El Recreo was isolated from its surroundings, blanketed in orange groves and featuring what one reporter described as a "beautiful garden with graveled walks and a prodigal opulence of fragrance and beauty" imbued with the "dignified elegance and ease characteristic of the Spanish regime." The inside of the house and Coronel's person itself no less reflected the years gone by, for Don Antonio had an extensive antiquarian library, which he shared with Jackson, and surrounded himself with artifacts from the days of his prime. He dressed elaborately in the manner of the Mexican period, eagerly told tales of old, and, together with his much younger wife, was fond of playing the guitar, singing old songs, and performing old Mexican dances—his entire lifestyle reflected a glamorized and nostalgic view of his own past.[30]

As recent scholars have pointed out, such nostalgic portrayals served

Antonio Coronel, shown here with wife Marianna, was a prominent Californio, well connected to both the Hispanic and early Anglo elite, and one of Jackson's most important southern California contacts. Originally published in Davis and Alderson, The True Story of Ramona *(1914).*

Hispanic Californians not as uncritical reactions to the loss of what had been, but rather as a form of resistance and opposition to their displacement by invading Anglo-Americans, and as an appropriation of a romanticized history that could contest the otherwise often unfavorable attitudes of Anglo-Americans to "Mexicans." But to Jackson, such nostalgia helped her conclude that southern California's Hispanic population and culture were doomed to extinction, and such apparent clinging to the past, in ways that she found uncritical, helped lead her to portray Californio culture as charmingly backward. Despite, or more likely because of this, she found Coronel's lifestyle and the Hispanic Californio culture she encountered in southern California entrancing.[31]

About her first meeting with Coronel at his home Jackson wrote in one of her articles for *The Century Magazine,* "I went but for a few moments call. I staid three hours, and left carrying with me bewildering treasures of pictures of the olden time." Jackson would visit more than once, and eventually number the Coronels among her friends, writing, "Whoever has the fortune to pass as a friend across the threshold of this house is transported, as if by a miracle, into the life of a half century ago."[32] Jackson found the aura of that romantic Californio past as well at the ranchos she visited, and even in the city of Los Angeles more broadly. In one of her travel articles for *The Century* she wrote of Los Angeles,

> The city of angels is a prosperous city now. . . . But it has not yet shaken off its past. A certain indefinable, delicious aroma from the old, ignorant, picturesque times lingers still, not only in by-ways and corners, but in the very centers of its newest activities.
>
> Mexican women, their heads wrapped in black shawls, and their bright eyes peering out between the close-gathered folds, glide about everywhere; the soft Spanish speech is continually heard. . . . One comes sometimes abruptly on a picture which seems bewilderingly un-American.[33]

To Jackson, an urbanite Easterner familiar with the old American cities of Boston and New York, as well as with the western outpost of Colorado Springs, Los Angeles seemed thoroughly different, but it was a difference grounded in what she perceived as the quaint and primitive past, not one threatening in present or future. It was a difference, therefore, that held strong tourist appeal for Jackson personally, for the readers of her travel writings, and for the readers of her novel.[34] What Jackson could not have known was that the boom of the eighties, coming close on the heels of her death, would, with its rush of incoming Anglos, eclipse the culture she described.

The boom dramatically accelerated the Americanization of the region as more and more ranchos were divided and subdivided into Anglo farms and towns where Anglo-Americans "built trolley lines, founded banks, and irrigated orange groves."[35] But the extravagance and fast pace of the boom could not be sustained and by late 1888 it was over.

The boom caused a phenomenal change in the population and demographics of the region. The Los Angeles population had increased by 500 percent, and the vast majority of these incoming residents were Anglos. By 1887 the Spanish-speaking made up less than 10 percent of the population, and increasingly they were newcomers too, unfamiliar with the old ways and politics. Even the nature of the electorate had changed nearly overnight; Californios, once the ruling class, lost their political influence. And more than demographics and political influence had shifted with the boom. Chronicler of the Californios Leonard Pitt wrote, "The [cultural] mores changed equally radically. The type of consumer goods advertised for sale, the tastes in food and dress, the prevalence of English over Spanish in daily life and official conversation, the Gilded Age recreations, and the style of commerce—all changed rapidly and irreversibly" as the boom put an effective end to the dominance of Californio culture, thus cementing southern California's "Americanization."[36] After the boom collapsed, the lives and lifestyles of those same Californios would be adapted for a new use, as newly powerful southern California Anglos sought to maintain (or even increase) the regional growth and development initiated by the boom.

BOOSTERISM AND DEVELOPMENT

With the eclipse of Californio political power and once the Californio culture of Southern California receded from its position of dominance, that very culture was deified by those same Anglos who had been largely responsible for the changes. In the words of historian Leonard Pitt, "No sooner had [the Californios] died than the gringo practically immolated himself upon their graves. The 'Spaniards' went into apotheosis; 'Spanish California' became a cult." And not without reason: With the sudden collapse of the boom, "[t]he mass psychology of failure spread even faster than the propaganda of success."[37] For business interests it now appeared critical to conjure a new image for the region, one that suggested continuity, not the fragile ephemerality of the boom. Southern California's mission, rancho, and "Spanish" heritage, as represented by men like Don Antonio Coronel, and as portrayed in *Ramona*, were made to order, for they provided an apparent link to centuries-old "traditions," to the mission padres and their perceived opposition to material wealth for its own sake, and to a life of repose, an eternal holiday in the sun, or rather, in the shade of a southern California veranda. The colorful and "un-American" lives of those living in California before the boom, could, after the boom, be used to attract, to possibly even sustain, the inflow of tourists and homeseekers to the region, as southern California vested itself even further in place marketing.[38]

During the boom references to *Ramona* appeared in promotional literature. An advertisement in the *Pasadena Daily Union* in October 1887, for instance, attempted to attract interest in the distant new township of Linda Rosa by stating that it was "nestled in the far-famed Temecula Valley, the home of Alessandro and Ramona." But for the most part, the use of the novel to promote the region was coincident with the new post-boom publicity movement, spearheaded by a small group of extremely powerful men.[39]

By the time the boom collapsed, place marketing was, even for southern Californians, not new. Beginning in the 1870s with the rise of tourism itself, places in the United States and Canada had begun to market themselves. In southern California by the 1870s books like Charles Nordhoff's influential *California for Health, Pleasure, and Residence* had promoted the treasures of the golden state to the dramatically widening tourist audience in the East and Midwest, and (like Helen Hunt Jackson in her travel articles) among those treasures had included the "Spanish Californians."[40]

But for some businesspeople, post-boom southern California would need more than just tourist guidebooks, and they sought much grander publicity schemes. The Southern Pacific Railroad had been aggressively marketing the region since the 1870s, in part to sell train tickets and in part to sell the thousands of acres of land allotted to the railroad in return for laying track on the then recently completed transcontinental line. Southern Pacific land agent Jerome Madden penned pamphlets and brochures like "California: Its Attractions for the Invalid, Tourist, Capitalist and Homemaker," which emphasized the state's fertile and affordable agricultural lands, all easily reached on Southern Pacific rails. The Southern Pacific further launched its own magazine, *Sunset,* in 1898, explicitly to attract tourists to California. But since the Southern Pacific was headquartered in San Francisco, southern California's promoters found their region playing second fiddle.[41]

In October 1888 Colonel Harrison Gray Otis put forth a motion to the business community to found the Los Angeles Chamber of Commerce, a purely boosterist organization whose express purpose was the promotion of southern California, particularly to citizens of the Midwest. Colonel (later General) Otis and the Chamber he supported became some of the most important boosters of the city, and a romanticized imagery of the "days of the dons" and the missions like that described in *Ramona* became a central focus.[42]

Like most of the city's boosters at this time (and indeed most of its population), Otis was a recent arrival. A Civil War veteran well connected to other powerful members of his Ohio regiment, Otis had come to Los Angeles in 1882 to improve his lot. Acquiring the nascent *Los Angeles Times* newspaper, he therein created a powerful mouthpiece not only to express his often-inflammatory opinions, but above all to promote his version of the region's growth. From Los Angeles's somnolent pre-boom period, which Otis had arrived just in time to witness, the general soon envisioned for southern California a "mightier Pacific empire with a population numbering in the millions where we now see only thousands, and possessing a measure of wealth, civilization and power now inconceivable," and he lived to carry out these dreams.[43]

The key to success for Otis's *Times* was advertising: The *Times* carried more of it than any other western paper and, in fact, more than all the San Francisco dailies put together. Along with its copious quantities of advertising, the *Times* also ran what could be called pseudo-news stories that served to draw further attention to and to lend credibility to its advertisements. As early as 1886 the *Times* ran adds for a new townsite called Ramona: "Ramona: The Greatest Attraction Yet Offered in the Way of Desirable Real Estate Investment," and by 1887 the *Times* was featuring "news" stories on the locations and characters in the novel. For example, on 13 January of that year the headline, "Camulos: The Real Home of Helen Hunt Jackson's 'Ramona'" appeared with a story on page 2—*Times* and other newspaper coverage of *Ramona*-related "stories" continued to be characteristic of southern California newspapers for many decades. Of course General Otis himself had reasons, beyond the success of his newspaper, for promoting southern California. He and his heirs became some of the region's largest landowners, and continuing development enabled them to subdivide and sell their lands at astronomical profits. Otis's was an ideology of expansionism combined with a belief that "what was good for the men of capital was good for the community."[44]

Otis, the Chamber of Commerce, and the pro-business Merchants Association used *Ramona*'s romanticized imagery of what came to be known as the Days of the Dons to promote an image of pastoral stability in southern California, even after the memories of the boom's collapse began to fade. In 1894 the Merchants Association (which would later become the Merchants and Manufacturers Association) promoted the first Fiesta de Los Angeles, with its theme, "a period of wonderful interest, which has never heretofore been utilized in celebrations of this kind, the achievements of the Spanish pioneers in the Great Pacific west of North and South America, and the striking customs and life of the strange races which they conquered to be contrasted with the march of American civilization." By the following year the Fiesta's parade included floral floats entitled "Spanish Life" and "Missions of California," and the brochure featured "scenes" from the Home of Ramona (featuring Rancho Camulos) and even pictured a woman identified as "the Ramona" standing before a tule house.[45]

For Otis, being vested in a romanticized version of southern California's past was more than just a business proposition; he became personally vested in it as well. By the turn of the century Otis and his wife, Eliza, lived in a Mission Revival–style mansion on Wilshire Boulevard, its architecture inspired by the renewed interest in the missions that the romanticized portrayal of southern California's past had engendered.[46] The Otises had also bought one of Los Angeles' original adobes located in the foothills of Hollywood.[47] Eliza Otis herself had served on the organizing committee of the Fiesta and even wrote poetry about "the Old Missions." The general, for his part, joined the advisory board of the Landmarks Club, founded to preserve the missions and other tangible remnants of the region's "Spanish" past.[48] Far from remaining distant from the romanticized past his paper helped to project, Otis and his wife embraced this glowing new social memory for southern California, the region they championed. Others would do so as well.

In 1884 Otis hired a new employee at the *Times,* a man who was to become one of the region's most ardent boosters and, even more so than his boss at the *Times,* one who would become deeply involved in southern California's

Ramona-inspired version of the past. Charles Fletcher Lummis arrived in southern California on foot on 1 February 1885, completing his pedestrian journey from Cincinnati, Ohio. All along the way Lummis, a journalist, had wired accounts of his journey to the *Times*, until, by the time of his arrival, he was already somewhat of a celebrity. Otis himself walked out to Mission San Gabriel to meet Lummis, offering him the job of city editor at the *Times*, a position Lummis would hold for three years. Enthralled by southern California's Hispanic past, Lummis fashioned himself into one the region's primary promoters, viewing the missions as "next to our climate and its consequences, the best capital southern California has."[49] Working not just to promote the region, but also to preserve its past, in 1895 he took on the leadership of the Landmarks Club, a voluntary organization dedicated to maintaining the missions which were at that time, as Lummis wrote, "falling to ruin with frightful rapidity, their roofs being breached or gone, the adobe walls melting away under the winter rains." Raising thousands of dollars both from prominent business interests (like Otis and the *Times*) and from the individual memberships costing only one dollar, the club could eventually claim to have saved some half a dozen of California's missions.[50]

A tireless promoter of southern California, in 1894 Lummis took on the editorship of a new magazine, sponsored by the Los Angeles Chamber of Commerce and dedicated to publicizing the region, called the *Land of Sunshine* and later known as *Out West*.[51] Lummis insisted on full editorial control, making it an attractive little magazine, copiously illustrated in rotogravure and printed on glossy paper. It was a success from the outset, and Lummis could boast that the first issue had sold considerably more copies at Los Angeles's two leading newsstands than *Harper's, The Century, Scribner's, McClure's, Cosmopolitan,* and the *Overland Monthly* combined, even though the bulk of the copies would always be purchased by the Chamber and distributed free to eastern libraries. With many articles, book reviews, and columns written by Lummis himself (often under pseudonyms), he used *Land of Sunshine* to crusade for causes (preserving the missions, promoting the Southwest's Spanish past, arguing for Native American rights, fighting against racial intolerance) as well as a vehicle to advertise the region's climate, agriculture, and lifestyle.[52] Over the years Lummis published a number of articles about Jackson's novel, its characters, and setting, linking southern California's landscape to *Ramona*, which he had begun doing even before he took over the magazine.

Even more than Otis, Lummis was not *just* a southern California booster:

Charles Fletcher Lummis, a staunch advocate for Native American causes, was also an avid promoter of southern California and the region he termed "the Southwest." Courtesy the Braun Research Library at the Southwest Museum (which Lummis founded); photograph number N42477.

Lummis lived what he boosted, becoming so personally involved in southern California's Hispanic past that he attempted to become a part of it. He took calling himself Don Carlos. Even his dress and his eating habits were meant to be reminiscent of "Spanish" times. Most interestingly perhaps, his pursuit of things "Spanish" led him, a Protestant still married to his first wife, to attempt to marry into one of the most prominent Catholic Californio families, the del Valles, whose Rancho Camulos was already popularly known as the Home of Ramona.[53] Thus, while the region's boosters were certainly interested in financial gain, theirs was a project that was felt and indeed lived.

Just the same, with its tireless promoters and efficiently organized campaigns, southern California became what some claimed was the most widely promoted place on the planet, as a "mushrooming volume of propaganda" touted the glories of every new settlement as well as the region as a whole. But if the boosters and the publications they produced were key in drawing attention to the region, so were the visitors. Even as images of southern California's splendor were distributed in brochures, magazines, and newspapers, other similar images were disseminated by those lured to the region. Beginning with the wealthy rail-sped tourists of the late nineteenth century, visitors to the region spread words and images of southern California's splendor by postcard, letter, photograph, travel article, travel book, and word of mouth. Languishing in southern California's mild winters, viewing snowcapped mountains from amid orange groves, visiting the sites and scenes of the region's factual and fictional pasts, and all the while enjoying the benefits that the modern urbanizing and industrializing nation brought with it, tourists became essential to southern California's growth.[54]

TOURIST TRAVEL, THE WEST, AND SOUTHERN CALIFORNIA

Tourism, of course, has been critical to the development of the American West as a whole, not just to southern California. It was critical not just because it was practiced by members of the trend-setting elite, but because it became a mass phenomenon eventually understood as nearly an obligation of American citizenship.[55] In the late nineteenth century, as rail fares grew more affordable, cities grew larger, and simultaneously as leisure time grew more widespread, increasing numbers of Americans—not just upper- but also middle-class Americans—sought new experiences in the form of tourist travel at home.[56] Thus as the nation urbanized and industrialized, tourism enabled individuals to leave the demands of work and daily (city) life for leisure, and to do so without rejecting the positive aspects of modern living.

But the rails would also always limit tourist travel, confining excur-

sions to points readily accessible by train, tying travel to railroad-set itineraries and timetables, and formalizing tourism in the public spaces of rail
cars and the tourist hotels that served rail lines. To facilitate tourism, railroads built spur lines, bringing sightseers from the main lines to points
of tourist interest like the Grand Canyon, and constructed rail stops at
popular tourist sites—like the one built at Rancho Camulos, known popularly as the Home of Ramona—specifically to meet tourist demand. But
rail tourists could still not set their own schedules or pause to linger over
a favorite site.[57]

Just as rail travel became accessible to middle-class Americans, a new
form of travel became popular with the wealthy—the automobile. While
eventually automobile tourism would eclipse rail travel and make domestic vacations affordable to nearly all Americans, initially it was both expensive and daring. Early cars, handmade creations in wood, steel, leather,
and brass, were expensive but, despite their high prices, from the 1890s
until the early 1920s automobiles were also finicky and unreliable at best.
And since any automobile journey was liable to prompt the need for major
repairs, early travel was made still more expensive by the need for a driver
skilled in the vehicle's operation, repair, and maintenance.[58]

Early automobile excursions were in many ways more like expeditions
than like twenty-first-century vacations. Roads and signage were still
predicated on horse-drawn transport: the dirt roads were rough, rutted
and potholed when dry, impassible bogs when wet; signs, meant for those
traveling at a horse's walking speed, were hard to read from an automobile,
when they were there at all. The poor roads and inadequate signage of the
East deteriorated still further in the West, where roads themselves were
often simply nonexistent, and motorists had to travel on railroad rights-
of-way or even ship their cars on trains. Western traveler Hugo Taussig
and his companion, heading through Nevada in 1909, had to resort to following the stumps of old telegraph poles—the remnants of the country's
first transcontinental telegraph line and also once the route of the Pony
Express—across an otherwise unmarked and vast expanse of open range.
When they were completely lost, a local rancher on horseback was able
to lead them back to a road, but not before they had had to cut their way
through several barbed-wire fences and build themselves a bridge out of
borrowed corral lumber.[59]

But locals in most places were not able to be of much assistance. Because many Americans never left the immediate vicinities of their towns
or farms, even when road connections were available most individuals

were unable to give accurate directions to those who desired to pass through on long-distance journeys. And because cars were novelties, the arrival of automobile tourists often drew crowds interested in looking at or talking about the vehicles rather than helping speed the passengers on their way.[60]

Rubber technology, too, was in its infancy, making reliable tires a thing of the future: between the bad roads and bad tires, early touring cars often carried four spares, and many, no doubt, used them all before reaching a suitable repair garage. Thus, maintenance and repairs of all kinds were constant companions, but spare parts remained scarce, often leading to lengthy delays. Early travel guides advised motorists to pack, in addition to "several jacks," an ax, a shovel, and such handy tools and supplies as a spark plug wrench, splicing pliers, wire, a grease gun, and a sheet of cork for making gaskets.[61]

Travel by automobile was physically demanding and full of discomforts for passengers. Tossed about by the rough roads and poor tires, automobile travelers had to, in the words of a 1902 automobile enthusiast, "learn to ride the machine as [they] would a trotter," taking the bumps accordingly. Pervasive dust and dirt worked their way into even the most well-protected suitcases, permeating their contents. Since early cars were open, dust, wind, and weather could scarcely be avoided, making automobile touring (something we now think of as conveniently climate-controlled) strictly an outdoor activity. Neither was automobile travel fast: where rail-sped tourists could make the cross-country journey in four days, early automobilists spent over a month. Finally, with so few traveling by road, the tourist infrastructure we now rely on—the service and gas stations, restaurants, and hotels—were few and far between; thus many early auto vacations were camping trips as well, and early automobile tourists often carried enough food and gear to be self-sufficient.[62]

Despite these inconveniences, automobile touring provided a freedom not offered on the rails. And because of auto touring's travails, automobile tourists were able to style themselves adventurers and even pioneers. Travel by car became more and more popular.[63]

Initially, however, such excursions were limited to the wealthy: the automobiles were costly, the journeys time consuming, and the trips expensive. Automobilists traveling cross-country before World War I might spend between $50 and $150 on gasoline alone, while the cost of a rail ticket hovered around $20. Just the same, the number of private automobiles rose astronomically, as cars became increasingly mass produced, cheaper to buy, and, by the 1920s, not only enclosed and therefore more comfort-

Ramona's Marriage Place, "Old Town", San Diego, Cal.

Domestic automobile tourism offered flexibility and convenience, but also often a daring adventure in open, expensive, and finicky automobiles, as it did for these speedy visitors to Ramona's Marriage Place. Postcard circa 1915. Collection of Phil Brigandi; reprinted by permission.

able, but also better built and dramatically more reliable. Though only 8,000 private cars were registered in the United States in 1900, by 1930 there would be 23 million. Automobiles had reached the middle classes, and so had automobile touring.[64]

Closely behind the rise in car ownership came the spread of hard-surfaced roads, for it was the very companies most vested in the automobile industry (car and tire manufacturers as well as oil companies), along with automobile drivers and car and "Good Roads" clubs, who first demanded improvements in the nation's road network. The rough and rutted dirt roads of the early days of automobile touring would gradually be replaced, first by gravel- and oil-based macadam, then by brick (in some areas), and eventually by concrete and asphalt. In 1904, of 2,152,000 total miles of rural roads in the United States, fewer than 150,000 were macadam or gravel, and only 123 were brick. With the federal government taking the lead after World War I, the 1920s and 1930s saw major nationwide road construction efforts, and many roads, like California's famous coastal Highway 1, were constructed explicitly with tourism in mind. By 1949 some 200,000 miles of U.S. roads were hard surfaced, and over 55 percent of all rural roads had been improved.[65]

Automobile touring was taking over. Between 1921 and 1941 travel by rail dropped 22 percent, while automobile travel rose by a factor of six;

by 1935 some 85 percent of all vacation travel in the United States was undertaken by car. The new mode of transportation for tourists changed the nature of travel, democratizing touring, and moving more Americans than the railroads ever had. Vacationers now set their own pace, planned their own route, picked their own sights to see. Whereas in the early years of American vacation travel in the 1870s and 1880s tourists were looked to primarily as potential investors and home buyers—people who would discover the attractions of other regions by touring, and then decide to stay (and this had been a clear focus of southern California boosterism during the boom)—by the end of the 1920s tourists were just that, "tourists," and tourist industries became increasingly geared to those who would just pass through.[66]

Significantly for southern Californians, this automobile age would be the first time when large numbers of Americans could afford to visit the West, and western travel became a prime vacation destination, "drawing more attention from tourists than any other region." Indeed, California in particular became a destination in itself, for many tourists the ultimate goal of their western travel. By the late 1920s, with cheaper, more dependable cars, increased roadside facilities, and widening general prosperity, automobile tourism was reaching a broad audience of "native-born, white, upper- and middle-class Americans." This flow of tourists would not abate: in 1928, the year tourists to southern California were first counted, some 650,000 visited the region; by the early 1950s that number had risen to an annual total of nearly 4 million. Just as had been the case with the railroads, automobile tourism began as an expensive elite endeavor, but slowly trickled down to the middle classes, eventually accessible to nearly all.[67]

If the mode of travel was changing, so too was the very meaning of travel. Automobile touring was, from the outset, represented differently than touring by rail, which encouraged a reconceptualization of the tourist experience. Where railroads and rail-tourism-based boosters had developed brand-name tourist destinations, marketing the point of arrival as the goal of tourism, those promoting automobile tourism marketed the journey and the experience themselves as significant parts of the goal, conceptualizing touring as a process rather than a single destination. By engaging in that process, tourists experienced America—its landscapes and its people—as individuals.[68]

Organizations such as the Automobile Association of America, the Lincoln Highway Association, National Old Trails Highway Association, and the

Wheelmen promoted car touring and produced large quantities of guide literature that argued that automobile tourists, because of their flexibility and individualized (and family-based) itineraries, were able to experience the nation directly—as if the automobile itself did not also mediate their experiences. By moving into the landscape in their cars, such publications argued, tourists would gain intimate contact with American culture and such insights as these travelers gleaned would in turn shed light not only on the nation's present, but even on the nation's past. Writing in *American Motorist,* W. D. Rishel contended that through automobile touring (and not train travel), "one is brought face to face with past memories of conditions that are gone forever," precisely the type of past evoked in *Ramona.*[69] Indeed, in southern California such sights included not only the missions, but also the Home of Ramona, a featured stop, for example, on the Wheelmen's 1914 Studebaker automobile tour. In fact, guidebooks often recommended a Ramona-related visit quite prominently, like Ruth Kedzie Wood's 1915 *The Tourist's California,* which advised tourists arriving from the north to take a somewhat lengthier route to Los Angeles that they might avail themselves of a stop at Camulos, where visitors inspired by their recognition in the landscape of scenes from *Ramona* would "pause and sigh at every corner."[70]

By visiting such sites, and personally identifying with them through their travel experiences, tourists were thought better able to identify with the events of history, and thus they would be able to make that history their own.[71] Tourists, therefore, through the personal and individual experiences of automobile touring in particular, were actively involved in the processes of creating a new social memory for the region, one that could be gleaned from the landscape, one that was at least in part based not on fact but on fiction—on *Ramona.*

ATTRACTIONS AND MEMENTOS

As Americans took to the rails and later to their cars, as increasingly large number of Americans engaged in tourism, and as tourism reached the middle and even lower classes, America's very tourist landscapes changed as well. To be sure, the canonical attractions—Yellowstone, the Grand Canyon, Yosemite—defined by early elite tourists and guidebooks of the late nineteenth century, remained among the most important sites to see. But in particular, as more and more Americans took to the highways rather than the rails, the very landscapes along those highways that led to the attractions began to reflect the needs and desires of those who passed through, as well as the needs and desires of those who sought to prosper from the traffic.[72]

In the late nineteenth century, attractions that lured tourists on transcontinental journeys included elaborate fairs and festivals. Western states like California invested heavily in their exhibits at World's Fairs, like the World's Columbian Exhibition held in Chicago in 1893, or the Lewis and Clark Exposition held in Portland in 1905, where the elaborate California pavilions were built to look like missions.[73] Regional events like the Mid-Winter Fair held in San Francisco in 1894 and Pasadena's now-famous Tournament of Roses parade, which began in 1889, highlighted California's climate and sought to draw wintertime visitors, for winter was then California's peak season. Such fairs and expositions published numerous lavishly illustrated volumes that served as guides to the fairs as well as guides to the region. For example, the Mid-Winter Fair produced *The "Monarch" Souvenir of Sunset City and Sunset Scenes, Being Views of California Midwinter Fair and Famous Scenes in the Golden State,* which featured photographs by I. W. Taber, the fair's official photographer. The fair, and the state, were evidently so lavish that it took fifteen portfolios to document all that Taber found essential, and he did not overlook Ramona-related sites, describing, for example, "Ramona's Cottage" in Ventura County, and careful to note that the "picturesque old homestead" appeared "the same to-day" as when Jackson used it as the setting for her novel.[74]

After the turn of the century, historical pageantry became a popular attraction, and by the 1920s California had several, including the Mission Play and the annual Ramona Pageant, an outdoor dramatization of the novel. With the advent of automobile and bus touring, such pageants could be situated in remote locations away from rail or trolley service for tourists could arrive in their own automobiles or on buses provided by tour and transit companies. By the 1920s, too, the automobile was sufficiently dominant that attractions, like the proposed Ramona Village theme park in Culver City, modeled themselves on roadside convenience rather than rail connections. Ramona Village promoter Robert Callahan sought to draw investors by noting that his location on Washington Boulevard saw the passing of some twenty thousand cars per day. Since scenes in the novel described southern California locations that were both remote and far-flung, the automobile would become the perfect way to reach Ramona-related attractions.[75]

Catering to traveling motorists—to tourists—billboards crept across mile after mile of American highway, along with gasoline stations (which had developed chain identities linked to oil companies by the late 1920s), as well as restaurants, auto camps, motor courts, and later, motels until, particularly on the edges of cities, entire commercial strips emerged, hoping to lure the business of passersby.[76]

One reason for passersby to stop was the availability of souvenirs—the mementos of places and sights that served to remind their owners not just of the place visited, but also of the trip and the visit itself, of the giver of the gift, or of the events surrounding the item's purchase. Early in the nineteenth century railroad companies had begun to distribute illustrated albums and brochures drawing attention to sights along their routes. As the century progressed, new developments in printing technology allowed for the use of more sophisticated images in brochures and albums, as well as in newspapers and magazines. Initially images were produced in the form of woodcuts, but by the late nineteenth century lithographs and even photographs themselves—reproduced by means of the new halftone process—were able to be printed, enabling the reproduction of not only black and white but also intermediate shades of gray. Images became more realistic and at the same time more prevalent.[77]

By the late 1890s American manufacturers had also realized the lure of the souvenir and were producing commemorative items like the often lavishly embellished souvenir teaspoon, its bowl and handle engraved and/or cast in the likeness of the place visited, which became a common collectible. So important were such spoons as souvenirs that over a period of years Ramona's Marriage Place in Old Town San Diego would eventually see more than twenty different spoons.[78]

Souvenirs eventually came in all types, prices, shapes, and sizes. By 1910 the souvenir industry itself emerged as a mass-market industrial phenomenon, with items often no longer produced in the places they were sold, but centrally manufactured in large quantities by vendors such as Arrow Novelty Company of New York. From the "lurid pillow top" embellished with images of the place visited, like that of San Diego which included Ramona's Marriage Place, to salt and pepper shakers mass-produced in the shape of squirrels or cats peering out of top hats, with the local place name—Ramona's Marriage Place—silk-screened or stuck on later. While some items seemed superficial, others, like the framed images of the courtyard at Ramona's Marriage Place that held pressed flowers behind the glass, the holy-water fonts that included a crucifix and an image of

More than two dozen different souvenir spoons were made to commemorate Ramona-related attractions. Here, the top spoon depicts Ramona's Marriage Place in its bowl and other California attractions (giant sequoias and the state Capitol) on its handle. The middle spoon is devoted entirely to Ramona's Marriage Place (after restoration), showing the inner courtyard in the bowl and other prominent features (the Mexican caretta, outdoor oven, and pergola-shaded wishing well) on the handle. The lower spoon features a hand-engraved image of the south veranda of Rancho Camulos and the title "Ramona's Home."

that same courtyard, or even the sterling silver rosary case with the courtyard on its lid, were clearly more meaningful, particularly to those who, like Ramona, were Catholic. Other souvenirs were designed to be more practical, like the solid-copper letter openers, pot-metal coin banks, and sterling silver matchbox covers that all came embossed with the image and the name of Ramona's Marriage Place.[79] By the mid-twentieth century virtually anything could be made into a souvenir, and almost any souvenir imaginable was available with Ramona's name on it.

Despite the presence of so many options at hotel counters and souvenir stands around the country, in the early twentieth century the most popular souvenir by far was the postcard. Inexpensive to buy or to send and easy to transport, postcards provided evidence that the traveler had "been there." They were often elaborately hand-colored and retouched, making for images that tourists could not capture even when they had their own cameras. Before long postcards themselves—from all over the country and all over the world—became collectibles, traded and sought after.[80] In 1898, when U.S. postal regulations changed to allow for a brief message on the fronts of cards (where previously they could carry only addresses on their versos) an American postcard "mania" began, one that only accelerated in 1906 when messages were allowed on the address side of the card as well.

Statistics on postcard sales during this period demonstrate the importance in turn-of-the-century American culture of what is now often seen as a mundane or irrelevant form of expression.[81] In 1906 over 770 million postcards were mailed from points across the United States. By 1909 that figure had swelled to well over 900 million. During the craze one postcard manufacturer, the Illustrated Postcard Company, cited production figures of 3 million cards *per day*. For turn-of-the-century Americans, postcards symbolized status and an ability to travel, something newly accessible to the middle class and made possible first by the declining railroad fares of the late nineteenth century. But even for those who stayed behind, postcards were a way of seeing places, people, and things they had previously only read about, but had most likely never visited.[82] In this sense, the souvenir postcard also served as a surrogate for those unable to afford the firsthand experience, as they received and traded images of places they had not been.

Those visiting southern California had hundreds of postcard images to choose from, and scores of those related to the novel *Ramona*, its scenes, and its characters. Whether visitors bought images of the bells that rang at Ramona's wedding at Old Town San Diego, of the "Real Ramona" standing before her husband's grave on a remote Indian reservation, of Ramona's birthplace at Mission San Gabriel, or, most popular and iconic of all, of the south veranda at Ventura County's Rancho Camulos (though still a private residence, dozens of different cards featured the "Home of Ramona"), those who collected the cards could engage with ideas from the novel made real in southern California's landscape.

The Bells Which Chimed for Ramona's Wedding,
Old Town, San Diego, Cal.

Even relatively minor items with spurious connections to the novel were featured on postcards, such as "The Bells Which Chimed for Ramona's Wedding," postmarked 1907. (The novel's wedding scene does not include bells.)

Others, equipped with the inexpensive new amateur camera known as the Kodak, preloaded with 100 exposures of the new flexible-roll film, personalized their touring by making their own images. Heavily encouraged by Kodak advertisements—vacationing without "Kodaking," they argued, led to a vacation without memories—as if photographs were the only vehicles of memory a vacation provided.[83] Whether or not tourists agreed, photographs rapidly became essential to the tourist experience, as travelers photographed vistas, landscapes, and, of course, Ramona landmarks, often with themselves, or even later their cars, in the foreground. While many tourists snapped their own photographs, commercial photographs of popular tourist attractions were also available, like the set of thirteen views of the "Home of Ramona" available from photographer J. C. Brewster of San Buenaventura. These could then be kept by the tourists themselves, or given away as gifts, and Brewster suggested as much in his advertisement in the *Southern California Tourists' Guide Book* of 1888–89: "a good present to send East."[84]

But frequently too, photographs, postcards, brochures or other tourist literature, and souvenirs themselves, were assembled together with travel narratives in the albums and scrapbooks that tourists compiled to commemorate and remember their travels. Though such memory books were a newer form, travel narratives themselves were very old. Beginning in the

As tourists often did, this middle-aged couple posed with their automobile, here in front of Ramona's Marriage Place, circa 1927.

travel diaries of early explorers, by the time of the European Grand Tour, personal, written observations created a record of the traveler's actual and imagined journeys, and such journals often found a popular market interested in reading the accounts. From the nineteenth century, as domestic tourism expanded, until the late 1920s when automobile tourism became so commonplace as to lose some of its sense of adventure, many tourists found a publishing outlet for their travel narratives, and hundreds of such tales of adventure and misadventure were offered to a public curious about what the distant reaches and remote corners of the nation held in store.[85]

But for every tourist who managed to publish the tales of his or her travels, dozens more kept them to themselves. Often difficult to locate today, these unpublished accounts remain in the photograph albums, scrapbooks, and souvenir books compiled by individual tourists. Filled with postcards, brochures, photographs, ticket stubs, programs, maps, matchbooks, paper doilies, clippings, or pressed flowers, and often with many of the items and the experiences surrounding the items described, such memory albums documented personalized experiences with mass-marketed commodities and attractions and offer insight into the ways that touring was experienced and interpreted in the late nineteenth and early twentieth centuries.[86]

TALES OF TWO TRAVELERS

When writer Charles Francis Saunders and his wife, Sylvia, toured southern California in 1912 automobile travel was already popular enough that
the Saunderses sought a more unusual mode of transportation, "the little
driving trip"—and by driving they meant in a horse and buggy. Most
people, Saunders reported in his published account of their travels entitled *Under the Sky in California,* relied on southern California's extensive rail network, or simply had their automobiles shipped out and went
everywhere that way. But for the Saunderses, the "spirit of this land of
the afternoon" was best to be captured at the slow pace of a carriage.[87] It
was reading *Ramona* that had inspired him and his wife to embark upon
a two-week trip, so they laid their itinerary through the country "made
famous by that romance" in order to travel to the places about which they
had read (104). "[I]n harmony with the *Ramona* motif" they began their
travels in Santa Barbara with a hired carriage and strong, gentle horse,
and set out first for Rancho Camulos, by then already widely known as
the Home of Ramona (105). Along the way they were careful to recognize
details Jackson had described in the novel: the fields of wild mustard,
the crosses upon the hills, the positioning of the house, and the groves
of oranges and almonds. And upon arriving they sought out the south
veranda, speculating as to which window had been Ramona's.

Heading farther south and still seeking to follow the story line, they
passed missions San Fernando, San Gabriel, and San Juan Capistrano
to reach Mission San Luis Rey where Saunders's description seamlessly
mingled fact and fiction:

> on a little sunny knoll in the midst of a fertile farming country stands
> another Mission associated with *Ramona,* the Mission San Luis Rey.
> This, in its heyday, was perhaps the largest and richest—temporally
> speaking—of all the Southern California religious establishments of the
> Franciscans, and it was here that Alessandro's father, as will be remem-
> bered, was master of the flocks and herds and leader of the choir. (126)

Not far away the little party reached "the old Spanish rancho of Guajome" where Saunders (erroneously) explained Jackson had spent "some
weeks" "absorbing the atmosphere of Spanish-Californian home life which
is so livingly reproduced" in the novel. Demonstrating his intimate
knowledge not only of the novel but also of the controversy surrounding the scenes where it was said to have been set, Saunders explained that

Guajome was "indeed the original home of Ramona," for the geography of the novel could only be understood with Guajome as its setting. But, he continued, echoing the justifications of others before him, due to ill feelings between Jackson and the lady of the rancho, the novelist had chosen to describe the physical details of Camulos in her work instead, while leaving the broad geographical details linked to Guajome (127). With a lemon and a "sprig of rue" for souvenirs, the Saunderses departed, heading for the most poignant of Ramona sites, one so far from the beaten track it was seldom touristed (128). Their expert horse Gypsy Johnson pulled them onward across a countryside where "the *Ramona* student needs to divide himself in many sections to see everything at once, for this place of tragic memory is a veritable *Ramona* center" filled with sites all recognizable to readers of the novel, until at last they reached San Jacinto mountain "upon whose demon-haunted slope Alessandro met his cruel death" (132, 133).

Commenting on their trip, Sylvia Saunders, a watercolorist who had reveled in her opportunities to capture the crumbling missions, exclaimed, enraptured, "[W]hy go to Italy when there are sights like this and such days as these within the borders of our [own] country?" To which her husband responded that he minded not if others traveled to Italy, nor if they journeyed to California, only that, if, like so many tourists, but unlike the adventurous Saunderses, they never left the hotel, they not "lay claim to knowing something about California" for they "haven't seen the real California at all," something which the Saunderses, in their travels over the scenes of Helen Hunt Jackson's novel claimed they certainly had (129–30). The "real California" had become complexly intertwined with the fictional.

More than twenty years later, by August of 1941 when Ruby Faye Dennis and her new husband, Loran, set out on their honeymoon trip from Graham, Texas, to San Diego, California, in their 1937 Dodge, Ramona tourism was past its peak, but Ramona tourist attractions had long since become part of the tourist canon in southern California, among the list of must-see attractions. But where Charles Saunders published an account of his journey with his wife, Ruby Faye Dennis kept hers private, in an elaborate memory album she made that commemorated the journey. Photographs show Ruby and Loran posed before sites along the way, Loran with a covered wagon at the Continental Divide, Ruby Faye sporty in overalls at the "Arizona Welcomes You" sign or reaching to pluck an orange from a tree just over the California line. Postcards, the elaborately colored linen postcards of the 1930s and 1940s, record the canonical sights: the Grand Canyon, Petrified Forest, and Meteor Crater. And bits of ephemera mark the personal experiences, like the napkin upon which Ruby Faye noted that the carhops at the Waikiki Inn wore grass skirts, or the one from the Saratoga upon which she wrote that the "crooner sang 'Yours.'" Maps, with their route traced, detail the journey, matchbooks marked where they ate or where they stayed, ticket stubs recalled the concerts they saw, and snapshots from a photo booth in Hollywood portrayed "two moving stars."

But Loran and Ruby Faye did not ignore Ramona. On the contrary. Ruby Faye's album devotes two and a half pages alone to Ramona's Marriage Place in Old Town San Diego, compared to one page for Meteor Crater, two for the Petrified Forest, and nine for the Grand Canyon where they had stayed several days. And like Charles Saunders and so many other tourists before her, Ruby Faye Dennis in her visit to this Ramona landmark mingled the factual and the fictional in her account. She wrote of Ramona's Marriage Place, "In this building is the chapel and altar where Ramona married Allesandro." She went on to describe the "chair used by Helen Hunt Jackson while writing *Ramona*" and the wishing well "nearly full of pennies, nickels, dimes, quarters, etc." Making her story personal she added, "I made a wish too! But I won't tell—." Not missing the curio shop and the chance to purchase a souvenir from Ramona's Marriage Place, Ruby Faye saved even the bag her souvenir came in (it too was marked "Ramona's Marriage Place"), pasted it into her scrapbook among the colorful postcards she also purchased there, and on it wrote, "I bought a toothpick holder made out of California redwood." Commemorating their stay in San Diego, Ruby Faye included what some would see as a trite or tacky tourist souvenir, a million-dollar "Honeymoon Bond"—a full-color, foldout brochure featuring Ramona's Marriage Place and proclaiming that "The bridal couple is urged to visit Ramona's Marriage Place in historic Old Town, San Diego, there to find the romantic and colorful atmosphere of California's early days, so vividly portrayed in Helen Hunt Jackson's immortal love-story, 'Ramona.'" Clearly they did visit, but whether at the urging of the brochure, or some other, we know not. Either way, the young Mrs. Dennis included *Ramona* in her honeymoon, wrapping elements of the fictional story into factual travels she made with her new husband. Engaging the tourist commodities spun off from the novel, just as she did the postcards of the Grand Canyon, and personalizing them with her stories of songs sung and evenings spent, Ruby Faye Dennis's experiences of southern California were not complete without Ramona.[88]

As more and more middle-class, white Americans engaged in domestic travel, they reached out to commodified tourist industries, through brochures, travel guides, and souvenirs, but they also made their experiences their own, in photographs, sketches and watercolors, travel articles, books and diaries, and by enfolding the commodified souvenirs into their own personal scrapbooks and souvenir albums, inscribing both the personal and the commercial with their own memories of the Ramona landmarks they had visited. Tourism could offer the "paradoxical promise . . . [of a] one-of-a-kind personal experience as a mass-produced phenomenon," and Americans were eager to make it their own. The souvenirs, whether postcards or saltshakers, photographs or pressed flowers, allowed those who visited Ramona sights not just to "objectify their experience" but also to take the experience with them in a tangible way, and then to keep it with them after they departed.[89] All across America as tourists visited historic sites, whether real or fictional, tourism, and the images and the souvenirs tourists produced and collected, became integral to the creation of social memory. In southern California, *Ramona* and the romanticized images of the region's past that the novel presented became inscribed on the landscape and in the touring practices of travelers—and the fictional story of Ramona became an indispensable part of southern California's real social memory.

CHAPTER THREE

RANCHO CAMULOS:
SYMBOLIC HEART OF THE RAMONA MYTH

> The house was of adobe, low, with a wide veranda on
> the three sides of the inner court, and a still broader
> one across the entire front, which looked to the south.
> These verandas, especially those on the inner court, were
> supplementary rooms to the house. The greater part of
> the family life went on in them. . . . All the kitchen work,
> except the actual cooking, was done here, in front of the
> kitchen doors and windows. Babies slept, were washed,
> sat in the dirt, and played on the veranda. The women
> said their prayers, took their naps and wove their lace
> there. . . . The herdsmen and shepherds smoked there,
> lounged there, trained their dogs there; there the young
> made love and the old dozed. . . . [It] was a delightsome
> place.
>
> —*Ramona*, 14–15

If the focal point for family life in Jackson's novel was the veranda, one veranda in particular—the south veranda of Rancho Camulos in Ventura County—quickly became the focal point for the Ramona myth. Within two years of the novel's publication, and less than a year after Jackson's death, Rancho Camulos had been ensconced as the "Home of Ramona"— the first landmark to be identified with the novel. Camulos's status would eventually be challenged by another rancho (Rancho Guajome in San Diego County), though its place as the symbolic heart of the Ramona myth would never be overturned. But while Rancho Camulos achieved cultural significance in California through its association with a work of fiction, long before H.H. penned her prose, the house and the family who built it had laid their roots in fact.

In 1839, after the secularization of the missions, the Mexican government granted nearly eleven square leagues of land (some 48,000 acres) to

60 – Home of Ramona, Camulos Rancho, California.

Rancho Camulos was the first landmark identified with the novel, its south veranda widely reproduced in photographs and on postcards. Postcard circa 1906.

Antonio del Valle, a soldier in the Spanish and Mexican militaries and former mission administrator.[1] The land, known as Rancho San Francisco, part of which was identified as Rancho Camulos, had previously belonged to Mission San Fernando, the very mission that del Valle had overseen.

Upon his death in 1841 Antonio del Valle's property was divided among his heirs. Son Ygnacio inherited Camulos, a parcel in the Santa Clara River valley, along the present-day border of Los Angeles and Ventura counties, and defended his title against his Mexican and Indian neighbors, eventually securing it under the American regime. Ygnacio del Valle continued to increase his land holdings throughout his lifetime, acquiring at least partial title to ranchos El Tejon and Temescal as well. In 1851, after fathering an illegitimate son by another woman, Ygnacio married Ysabel Varela, then fourteen, with whom he would have eleven more children. By 1853 (in the American, not the Spanish or Mexican periods), Ygnacio del Valle had built on his rancho a U-shaped adobe home for his growing family. When Ygnacio died in 1880, he left everything to Ysabel. When Helen Hunt Jackson visited the rancho in 1882, Ysabel still presided as a figurehead, although her sons, first Reginaldo the eldest and then Ulpiano, had taken over stewardship. Jackson never met Ysabel del Valle, but, like Señora Moreno in the novel, Ysabel del Valle remained in mourning for her husband until she passed away in 1905. On her deathbed at her daughter's home in Los Angeles she longed to be at her husband's grave in the little

Camulos cemetery. When doctors forbade it, her son Ulpiano fetched his father's remains to have them buried with Ysabel's in one coffin.[2]

The del Valles carried out their lives at Camulos in an opulent manner and, like many landed Californios, had a penchant for conspicuous consumption. Members of California's Mexican aristocracy, they were leaders in government, church, and community. Even through the hard times engendered by the devastating drought of the 1860s, which had caused the collapse of some of the most established Californio ranchos, the del Valles managed to retain control of at least some of their landed holdings. At Camulos, as at other ranchos still in Californio hands, "even when the ranchos went into economic decline, the traditional rancho culture persisted stubbornly, in between mortgage payments." In keeping with custom the del Valles were lavish hosts, and it was not uncommon to find fifty guests at their supper table. Their household itself included many members of their extended family, as well as orphans adopted by Ysabel. In order to hold onto Rancho Camulos the del Valles had been forced to sell many of their other lands, including Rancho El Tejon, portions of Rancho Camulos itself, and to take out a mortgage on the remainder of Camulos, for which the interest alone accumulated at over $900 per month. Nonetheless, the family entered the 1880s with 1,340 acres of Camulos still intact and the rancho "exuded a deceptive air of well-being . . . considering its financial condition."[3]

Facing the changes head on, Reginaldo del Valle was positioned to succeed under the American regime. Well educated, he had completed law school in San Francisco and established a law practice in Los Angeles. He also had political ambitions and won a seat in the California State Assembly in 1880. In 1882 he was elected to the state Senate and then, at the age of just twenty-eight, he was elected president *pro tempore,* the state Senate's highest position. His brother Ulpiano attended Santa Clara College and returned to Camulos in 1886 to run the ranch. Together, the two sons converted the ranch from the no-longer-profitable cattle and sheep grazing (dominant in the Spanish and Mexican eras) to forward-looking intensive agriculture and viticulture, and incorporated the ranch with the siblings as stockholders. Ulpiano brought new ideas to the ranch, which included, for a time, the raising of blooded racehorses. Citrus and grapes, however, were Camulos's biggest successes. While raising oranges may not have had the romantic appeal of racehorses, at the turn of the century Camulos, as a fruit farm, was a showplace of the Santa Clara Valley.[4]

Members of the del Valle family of Rancho Camulos. Left to right: *Josefa and Ygnacio (junior),*
daughter Belle, eldest son Reginaldo, and Ulpiano, who managed the ranch. Courtesy Ventura
County Museum of History and Art; reprinted with permission.

This portrayal of the del Valle family as future-oriented, well-educated
innovators of agribusiness may seem to contradict Helen Hunt Jackson's
portrayal of the Californio lifestyle in *Ramona*, for which she had been
sent by Don Antonio Coronel expressly to Camulos. But the del Valles'

"whole hearted commit[ment] to finance capitalism and the new commercial ethic" went hand in glove with their own romanticized notion of
what Californio life should be, and indeed, how it should be portrayed,
notions they shared with Coronel and other Californios.[5] In addition to
Reginaldo del Valle's political ambitions, he held very distinct views of
his own heritage and its importance. In 1883 he was one of the founders of the Historical Society of Southern California; in 1887 he helped
found the "Ramona Parlor" of the Native Sons of the Golden West, and
in 1888 he was one of the founders, with Charles Fletcher Lummis, of
the Association for the Preservation of the Missions.[6] But beyond this
interest in the preservation of the past, the del Valles, even more than
other Californios, were swept up in the romantic deluge that accompanied
Ramona.[7]

After the novel's success and Jackson's death, southern California was
enveloped in a flurry of speculation as to where the actual locations in
the novel had been. Jackson's peregrinations in California and eye for detail
had enabled her to amass enough local color for her novel, but her descriptions of places, people, and events in the novel were at times so accurate that
subsequent authors were able to trace nearly everything in the novel to a
real-life counterpart. Since *Ramona* is, after all, a work of fiction, this
controversy could never be completely resolved, but most sources eventually came to agree that while the physical location of the Moreno home in
the novel corresponded best with Rancho Guajome in San Diego County,
the actual descriptions of the house, outbuildings, and environs could
only point to Rancho Camulos, which avid Ramonaphile George Wharton
James, writer of the authoritative guidebook *Through Ramona's Country*,
termed the "avowed and accepted home of the heroine."[8] Jackson, for example, describes the crosses that topped the hills surrounding the Moreno
property,

> [Señora Moreno] caused to be set up, upon every one of the soft rounded
> hills which made the beautiful rolling sides of that part of the valley, a
> large wooden cross; not a hill in sight of her house left without the sacred
> emblem of her faith. . . .
>
> There they stood, summer and winter, rain and shine, the silent,
> solemn, outstretched arms, and became landmarks to many a guideless
> traveller who had been told that his way would be by the first turn to the
> left or the right after passing the last one of the Señora Moreno's crosses,
> which he couldn't miss seeing. (14)

The Rancho Camulos, situated in a river valley, featured just such crosses on its surrounding hills.[9] Though Jackson spent only two hours at Camulos, her keen eye caught even the tiniest of details. The most widely described and most poignant for Ramona tourists was that of the torn altar cloth found in Camulos's small chapel. In the novel, when the altar cloth is accidentally torn, Ramona secretly and expertly mends it so that the Señora might not be angered (46). In fact, the del Valles' own altar cloth was torn, carefully mended, and even shown to interested parties after the novel's publication. Those who wrote about their visits to Camulos frequently commented on seeing the altar cloth, like one 1886 visitor who reported he had seen the "cloth, with the rent in it still showing, supposed to be the very one that Ramona mended."[10] In this way, possessions owned and used by the del Valle family themselves were soon viewed as Ramona-related objects, and as proof that Camulos was in fact the "Home of Ramona."[11]

Indeed, Rancho Camulos had acquired that appellation by 1886, just one and one half years after the novel's publication, and it would be a title that would both haunt and help the del Valles as long as they owned the property. In fact, the first known published account relating any place or any person in the novel to a factual place or person implicates Rancho Camulos. In May 1886, the *San Francisco Chronicle* published Edwards Roberts's article entitled "Ramona's Home: A Visit to the Camulos Ranch, and to the Scenes Described by 'H.H.,'" which was soon also reprinted as an appendix in many editions of the novel. Because this article appeared in so many copies of the novel, it authoritatively established Camulos as the "Home of Ramona," a claim that could never again completely be refuted.

Significantly, Roberts wrote in a tone that would be adopted by a whole genre of Ramona-inspired writers, sliding nearly seamlessly from factual description of Camulos to hallucinations on the scenes and characters in the novel:

> What I sought is this which I have found,—the Camulos ranch, the home of Ramona . . . in this house from which I write to-night. . . . Here, before the cool, shaded veranda on which I sit is the courtyard; here Felipe's room, and there Ramona's. . . .
>
> Taking "Ramona" in hand, one staying at Camulos can find almost every scene described. . . .
>
> All nature is fresh and fair; the season is that in which Ramona's new life began.[12]

Although Roberts does mention that the house was "built nearly thirty-one years ago" (which places Camulos's construction squarely in the American period, and not the Mexican or Spanish), this does not prevent him from calling forth a much earlier and more distant time and place:

> [O]ne can easily imagine himself in some foreign country. It is all un-American and strange. The heavy white walls of the house, the perfume of orange blossoms and roses, the organ chants and faint sound of prayers recited in Spanish, recall days in Spain where, as here, there was peace and quiet and an existence altogether romantic and poetical.[13]

In regional fiction like *Ramona*, such descriptions (of which Roberts's was only the first of many) exoticized the landmarks associated with the novel, thus heightening their intrigue. At a place like Camulos, the visitor could, after just a short trip from Los Angeles or Santa Barbara, experience an altogether different reality, one more like a romanticized past, and also indulge simultaneously in the fictional world of *Ramona*. In this way, at various Ramona landmarks across southern California, the past of fiction and the past of fact were becoming closely linked.

In 1887 Roberts went on to publish *Santa Barbara and Around There* in which he further established a link between Camulos and *Ramona* and between fact and fiction. He wrote of Camulos,

> If we are fortunate, we shall be shown the altar-cloth . . . that Ramona mended the day Father Salvierderra arrived. We shall have, in fact, the reality in place of fiction, a quaint, strange, utterly foreign reality, rarely found even in California, and now, thanks to "H.H.," given a coloring and an interest that has already made it a place of pilgrimage for the many readers of the gifted writer.[14]

Though Roberts seems to have been the first to publish, he was evidently not the first to make the connection between *Ramona* and Rancho Camulos, for even in 1886 he had been told by a member of the del Valle family that strangers would come to Camulos to "ask for Ramona and the Señora Moreno, and will not believe we are not the ones they wish to see."[15] It was, in retrospect, perhaps, a stroke of ill fortune for the family that Roberts happened to mention in his so-often-reprinted article that "[t]here being no hotel in this part of the valley, the Camulos is often filled with belated strangers or visited by those desirous of seeing what an old-time Spanish ranch is like," for soon their property would be overrun with Ramona seekers.[16]

For a time, however, life went on much as before. In March 1886, to mark
Ulpiano del Valle's twenty-first birthday, the family had occasion to throw
one of the fiestas for which they were famous. These parties—multiday
affairs filled with music and the abundant produce of the ranch—were
usually held two or three times per year and included as many as one
hundred invited guests.[17] One of those in attendance at Ulpiano's fete later
reminisced,

> We danced from morning until late at night . . . upon the broad *veran-*
> *dahs* surrounding the patio of the house. . . .
>
> [A long table had been erected beneath a vine-covered pergola.] When
> I picture that board groaning beneath its load of home-grown beef, mut-
> ton, pork, chickens, ducks, peacock, vegetables of all descriptions, flagons
> of the finest wines, aged brandy and everything to delight the heart and
> stomach of man, I regret that my present appetite is not as strong as it
> was then.[18]

Though the del Valles thus actively maintained Californio cultural traditions like fiestas, by the late 1880s many of those in attendance were Anglos.
One of them was Charles Fletcher Lummis. Lummis spoke Spanish flu-
ently and this small sinewy man from Harvard charmed the del Valles,
who affectionately called him Don Carlos. Most of all he had charmed
Juventino del Valle's seventeen-year-old daughter Susana Carmen and
by 1888 he wished to marry her. Lummis, however, was still married to
his first wife, Dorothea Rhodes Lummis, and his marriage was suffering
from difficulties, not the least of which was Lummis's philandering. Don
Carlos's plans in regards to young Miss del Valle were smashed, however,
when the family informed him that because of her Catholic faith Susana
Carmen could never marry a divorced man.[19]

Lummis's enthusiasm for the del Valles extended beyond his love
for Susana Carmen to a love for the rancho itself, leading him to become
"Camulos' leading exponent" and a man who "never tire[d] of singing
the praises of the del Valles and their ranch."[20] An avid photographer,
Lummis shot many pictures of the ranch and the aristocratic "Spanish"
lifestyle of the del Valles. His enthusiasm for the del Valles, however, also
embraced the rancho's connection to *Ramona*. In 1888 Lummis published
a book entitled *The Home of Ramona*, the first freestanding publication
relating a place, person, or event to the novel. Lummis's book consisted
largely of "photographs of Camulos, the fine old Spanish Estate described
by Mrs. Helen Hunt Jackson, as the Home of 'Ramona.'" Apparently eager

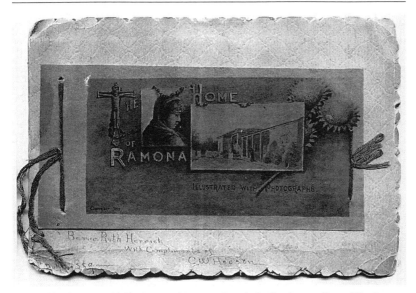

Charles Fletcher Lummis's The Home of Ramona *(1888), the first freestanding publication linking Ramona and southern California's landscape. Pageant Files, Ramona Bowl Museum; reprinted with permission.*

to fix Camulos as the Home of Ramona over the claims of other ranchos, Lummis wrote, "Shrewd landlords in other places have claimed for their property some connection with the book; but that Camulos is the spot portrayed as the home of the Morenos is absolutely established." Just the same, he also sought to distance his friends the del Valles themselves from the none-too-complimentary portrayals of the Morenos in the novel: "Camulos figures in the book simply as the chief scene. None of the characters were drawn thence; and possibly outside of the quaint old servants, there are no parallels in life there—certainly none of the weak Felipe or the pitiless Señora."[21] After this introduction Lummis waxes poetic on the role of Camulos in the novel, and, in the already established style, blends details from real life and romantic notions of the "Spanish" past (to which Camulos itself had never belonged) with the characters in the novel. His poem, entitled "Camulos," reads in part,

> The memories of Camulos,
>   How sweetly, sadly dear!
> Here Alessandro found his love,
>   Ramona's home was here;
> And here the great, warm woman-heart,

With others' sorrows filled,
    Dreamed out the story to whose fire
    A careless world has thrilled.

Still in the little chapel,
    Both proud and petty pray;
The torn and mended altar cloth
    Hangs in its place to-day;
To-day upon the circling hills
    The tall, white crosses rise
The staunch Señora planted there
    To point men to the skies.

The mustard hazes golden,
    The almond orchard's bloom,
The orange groves, the fleecy flocks,
    The saints, the Padre's room—
They all are here, as true and fair
    As in Ramona's day,
And hearts as gentle as her own,
    But happier always. . . .

Untaint by greed of riches,
    That is our modern shame;
Unchanged as in those far old days
    When Padre Serra came;
Its white adobes face the sun,
    Its myriad wood-doves call—
Its heart the heart of mother Spain—
    Of Spain before the fall![22]

Filled with blue cyanotype photographs and descriptions of scenes from the novel, in the book Lummis, even in his prose, blends the fictional life of Ramona with the actual lives of the del Valle family. For example, in his description of the south veranda, he details its importance to the del Valles but describes its location in relation to the Morenos: "Prominent among the many charms of Camulos is its south veranda. Here is the chief rallying point of the family in leisure hours—a sitting room half *al fresco*. It is about a hundred feet in length, and runs from the door of Father Salvierderra's room to that of Ramona's room."[23]

Though Lummis was the first, by the time his book was published

Camulos's tranquil isolation had already been changed forever by the arrival of the Southern Pacific Railroad in 1887. Despite a long-term political rivalry between Reginaldo del Valle and the owners of the Southern Pacific, the tracks were laid right along the back of the ranch house, and soon four to six trains a day passed Camulos.[24] When Roberts wrote his article on the rancho, just a year before, he noted that "no railroad has yet approached the premises, and only the heavy stage, drawn by four horses, and carrying mailbags and passengers, makes regular trips along the highway." Now the *Los Angeles Times* reporter who wrote "Camulos: The Home of Helen Hunt Jackson's 'Ramona,'" for the edition of 13 January 1887 could boast of the "new Southern Pacific extension from Newhall," which reached "the old Camulos rancho—a dream of quiet loveliness." The reporter also mentioned that a "station will be erected at Camulos, so that the quiet old place will soon become one of the common sights for travelers along the steel highway." Even without the convenience of rail access, so many tourists were already visiting Camulos that this author admitted that the quietude of the rancho had long since been broken by the rush of visitors, writing, "The owners of Camulos were long deterred from acknowledging the fact [that Camulos is the home of Ramona] owing to the nuisance of curiosity-seekers, who pestered them nearly to death; but they now admit it gracefully."[25]

Similarly, when Jackson's friend and *Harper's* magazine editor Charles Dudley Warner wrote for the *Times* on 24 May 1887, he could state, "The new railway passes [Camulos] now, and the hospitable owners have been obliged to yield to the public curiosity and provide entertainment for a continual stream of visitors."[26] Even with little publicity or boosterism, no gift shop, and only the most rudimentary carriage access, Camulos had become an important and popular place to visit.

The railroad so facilitated tourism for Camulos that Reginaldo del Valle wrote to Charles Crocker of the Southern Pacific to request that a station be built to accommodate the tourist flow. A small station house was soon erected.[27] The Southern Pacific's Camulos stop became quite an attraction indeed, as one rider on the train declared, "many take the trip purposely to see this interesting spot," adding that when the conductor called out "'Camulos—Home of Ramona!' . . . instantly there [was] a general craning of necks and murmurs of wonder and satisfaction among the passengers."[28]

By 1888 Camulos as a tourist attraction was worthy of mention in the *Southern California Tourists' Guide Book,* which pointed out that the rancho is "on the line of the S. P. Co.'s Railway." Already Camulos had become not just a spot to visit, but also a place where visitors became swept up in their associations with *Ramona*. The *Guide* noted that it is "quite a romantic spot. . . . Many there are who have read *[Ramona]*, and become somewhat smitten with its original romantic scenes."

If visitors were smitten, they would perhaps also be interested in souvenirs of their visit, and, though the del Valles themselves sold no souvenirs and Camulos itself saw no gift shop, the *Guide,* in its Camulos coverage, also featured an advertisement:

> For views of the Home of Ramona at Camulos, Ventura County, California, the spot of the founding of the story by Helen Hunt Jackson, call on J. C. Brewster, San Buena Ventura, California. Large and small sets of thirteen views taken on the spot. A good present to send East.[29]

Thus, within three years of the novel's publication, large numbers of tourists were visiting the site that became known as the Home of Ramona, seeking to make not only a personal journey there, but also to purchase souvenirs, either as remembrances of their visits or as gifts for those back home. Camulos, though not developed as a tourist attraction, was becoming part of the southern California tourist canon just the same, its visitors inspired by a work of fiction visitable in the landscape of fact.

But by October 1888 the "continuous siege" of Ramona-seekers had become more than just a nuisance for the del Valle family. Their Californio hospitality was getting the better of their pocketbooks. The situation had gotten so out of hand that Señora del Valle had "provided meals and lodging for about 2,500 people" in one year alone.[30] Finally Reginaldo wrote to his mother,

> Querida Mamá:
>
> Por más que treinta años hemos dado hospitalidad en Camulos a todos los que deseaban visitarlo, y ha a llegado a tal grado que los gastos son enormes, y si continuamos al paso que vamos, pronto quedaremos en la ruina. Los gastos del último año son mucho más que lo que produjo el rancho, y me veo obligado a poner el remedio antes que sea demasiado tarde.
>
> En lo futuro ninguno de nuestra casa tendrá el privilegio de invitar a nadie a Camulos. Los amigos íntimos nuestros saben que siempre serán bien recibidos.
>
> La generosidad con que se distribuyen por todas partes, y en todas direcciones, los productos del rancho debe limitarse también un poco.

Además los estrangeros que vienen con la curiosidad de Ramona, que se les dé aviso que no tenemos hotel, y no podemos hospedarlos solo en los casos que no se pueda evitar.

Hágame favor de leer y dar a leer esta carta a hombres y mujeres de nuestra familia.

Me veo obligado a dar estas instrucciones para proteger nuestros intereses y poder vivir tranquilos, porque de otra manera la ruina e infelicidad serán los únicos resultados.

Su hijo que la ama,

[signed R. F. del Valle][31]

His letter can be translated into English as follows:

Dear Mother,

For more than thirty years we have offered our hospitality at Camulos to all those who wished to visit it, and now it has reached such a degree that the costs are enormous, and, if we continue at the pace we are going, we will soon fall into ruin. The costs of the last year are much more than the production of the rancho, and I see myself obligated to impose a remedy before it is too late.

In the future, no one from our household will have the privilege of inviting anyone to Camulos. Our intimate friends know that they will always be well-received.

The generosity with which you distribute to all parts and in all directions, the products of the rancho, will have to limit itself too a little bit.

What's more, as for the strangers who come with curiosity for Ramona, please advise them that we do not have a hotel, and cannot accommodate them, except in unavoidable circumstances.

Do me the favor of reading this letter and giving it to the men and women of our family.

I see myself obligated to give these instructions in order to protect our interests and to be able to live tranquilly, because otherwise ruin and unhappiness will be the only results.

Your son who loves you,

[signed R. F. del Valle]

Despite Reginaldo del Valle's prohibition on hosting the strangers who came in search of Ramona, the torrent of pilgrims did not by any means abate, and even when it did not wear on their pocketbooks, it began to wear on the del Valles' patience. The following year, when two writers for the *Overland Monthly* visited the rancho they were offered an apology by one of the young del Valle women:

> "You must forgive me for mistaking you for more of those dreaded tourists, who insist upon seeing everything from the bed rooms to the sheep corral." . . . [She] went on to explain in her perfect English how much they had been annoyed by people coming at all times and hours to visit the home of the far-famed Ramona.[32]

Indeed, interest in visiting Rancho Camulos, the Home of Ramona, continued unabated. By 1893 the guidebook entitled *In Semi-Tropical California* featured a foldout map showing the Southern Pacific's Camulos stop and even included fare and timetable information.[33] In fact, the Southern Pacific ran tourist excursions to Camulos and featured their Camulos stop (with an image of the rancho's south veranda) in their brochures. In an effort to distinguish their service from that of the competing Atchison, Topeka, and Santa Fe Railroad, one Southern Pacific brochure wrote of the Camulos stop,

> Home of Helen Hunt Jackson's heroine "Ramona"; writer took for setting old Del Valle estate, known in book as Morena [sic] Rancho. House, surrounded by flowers and fruit trees, can be seen from train. Visitors admitted free to grounds. Camulos is served only by Southern Pacific rails.[34]

And, clearly, if the Southern Pacific preyed on the hospitality of the del Valles, so, in large numbers, did the tourists themselves. One visitor to Camulos wrote that some of the tourists went

> beyond the bounds of propriety and consideration. . . . One morning, before the family had arisen, a stout, florid-faced tourist, sporting sandy side-whiskers and an air of pomposity, rushed into a private apartment, threw up the curtains and exclaimed, "Where is Ramony? We want to see Ramony!"[35]

In *Ramona Illustrated: The Genesis of the Story of Ramona* authors A. C. Vroman (a well-known southern California photographer) and T. F. Barnes attempted to document, with photographs and quotations from the novel, many of the locations portrayed. Staunch supporters of Rancho Camulos as the home of Ramona over any other contender, most of their photographs depicted scenes at Camulos that corresponded quite precisely with the text of the novel and which were sometimes contrasted with scenes from Home-of-Ramona-contender Rancho Guajome to "prove" it was not Guajome that Jackson was describing. Despite the fact that their book would undoubtedly lure more tourists to Rancho Camulos, Vroman and Barnes were apparently sensitive to the del Valles' plight for they printed somewhat of a warning to tourists:

> So many people, [the del Valles] tell us, come unannounced and roam about without so much as a gracious acknowledgment of their presence on the premises; some even so rude and contemptible as to slip a spoon from the table into their pocket when hospitality is shown them and asked to join the family at meal time.
>
> We marvel at the patience of these good people when we are told that within nine months, actual count, more than eight hundred meals were served to strangers, much against their desires; but hospitality must never find an ending in old Spanish [sic] homes. No doubt it would be a great relief to them if some other place could take the honor of the "Home of Ramona."
>
> . . . [When visiting Rancho Camulos,] we must remember that we are on private, not public property; that we owe it to the many yet to follow us that we do our part well.[36]

Despite such admonitions, however, the del Valles continued to suffer under the tourist onslaught. Like his elder brother, Ulpiano del Valle was eventually compelled to take action. An article appeared in the *Ventura Weekly Democrat* that explained that because of a few "ill-mannered people . . . who abuse the privileges and hospitality" extended to them by the del Valles at this "Mecca of visitors, tourists and globe trotters . . . the innocent must suffer with the guilty, by being deprived of the pleasure, hereafter, of visiting the place and enjoying its far-famed hospitality." An announcement from Ulpiano del Valle was then printed in full:

> It is with regret that I am compelled by the law of self-protection to deprive pleasure seekers of seeing the home of Ramona, but patience has ceased to be a virtue. On the 12th inst., the Santa Barbara excursion train was delayed here for twenty minutes by an accident, and a mob a 300 of both sexes took advantage of the opportunity to raid the orchards as thoroughly and steal as many oranges as the time would permit, even invading the private grounds and apartments of the house. Entreaties by the one ranchman around did not avail to stop the disgraceful occurrences.
>
> As this is the third, and by odds, the worst invasion by such a lawless mob of marauders, of which the malicious behavior of a majority of its

members, would degrade professional tramps, I am obliged to state . . .
that while I am manager no other such band of loose excursionists will be
permitted to enter within the grounds of the Camulos Rancho.

U. F. Del Valle[37]

The del Valles had reached the end of their rope, but even in death, it
seemed, they could not shake their association with the Home of Ramona.
In 1905, when matriarch Ysabel del Valle died, the *Los Angeles Times*
obituary for her identified the "noted woman['s]" house as the "home of
Ramona."[38]

So widely known was Camulos as the Home of Ramona that the very
name *Camulos* came to take the place of the name of the heroine's fictional home in the novel. Film and theatrical productions of the novel
often referred to Camulos and not the Rancho Moreno (as the home of
the heroine is called in the book). An 1897 dramatization of the novel was
called *Ramona or, the Bells of Camulos*.[39]

In 1905 Virginia Calhoun's stage adaptation of the novel completely
conflated Camulos with the Rancho Moreno. As one newspaper described
the production, "the first scene is the old Camulos Rancho."[40] But beyond
just the setting, various characters in the play refer to the rancho as Camulos. For example, in act 2, scene 1, Ramona (played by Miss Calhoun
herself) protests the Señora's idea of sending her to a convent and cries,
"away from Camulos . . . I should die!" Leaving her home to elope with
Alessandro she bids farewell, "[A]dios! Dear Camulos! Adios!" Alessandro (played by Lawrence [later D. W.] Griffith) tells his wife in act 3,
scene 1, that he has been "dreaming of thee, and of that night at Camulos
one year ago." And in addition to photographs of many of the missions,
the program includes a picture of the south veranda of Camulos identified as the Home of Ramona and text identifying the rooms of Ramona,
Felipe, and the Señora.[41]

So established was Camulos as the Home of Ramona that this conflation
was carried out in filmic versions of *Ramona* as well. When D. W. Griffith
decided to film *Ramona* in 1910, the company shot on location at Camulos.
The film's promotional literature and title cards made a point of noting
this fact. Camulos had become so established as the Home of Ramona that
shooting there lent credibility and authenticity to the production.[42]

Reference to Camulos would continue to be important for filmic Ramonas. Though no surviving complete print exists, Clune's Studios 1916
production of *Ramona* likely shot on location there, and the program listed

"Camulos" (rather than the Rancho Moreno) as its setting for act 1.[43] When the 1928 production starring Dolores del Rio as Ramona was reviewed in the *Los Angeles Times,* the reviewer found the location significant enough to note that "[t]he natural settings, curiously enough, were obtained in Utah."[44] And for the 1936 Technicolor *Ramona,* an "exact duplicate of the [chapel] on the Camulos ranch" was built for the set.[45]

Similarly, early brochures for the Ramona Pageant highlighted their claim that the pageant itself, performed in the hills of Riverside County, was set in the area where much of the novel took place, but nevertheless identified the setting of act 1 as "The Camulos Ranch," even though Camulos was located far from the site of the pageant.[46] Indeed, Camulos had become so identified with Ramona that the 1929 cookbook entitled *Ramona's Spanish-Mexican Cookery* was illustrated with a picture of the south veranda on the cover and the caption "Ramona's Home, Camulos Ranch, California."[47]

By 1920 such sustained notoriety meant that the situation for the del Valles was still out of hand. With automobile travel already well established, an announcement was printed in the Southern California Automobile Association magazine *Touring Topics* carrying the headline "Ramona's Home Closed. Vandalism of Visitors Results in Sealing up of Doors of Historic and Romantic Spot." The short article read,

> Tourists and visitors to Ramona's Home . . . will be disappointed to learn that it has been rigidly closed to the public. . . . For a number of years this historical residence was open to everyone; but the continued and increasing tendency of sight-seers to distribute remnants of luncheon over its floors, pry off souvenirs from the walls and building, deposit wads of chewing-gum on the picture frames, and in divers[e] other ways to disport themselves with a happy abandon, compelled the owners to hermetically seal the entrance to the former domicile of Mrs. Jackson's celebrated heroine.
>
> "Tis a pity."[48]

Just the same, despite such incidents, and the general inconvenience to the del Valles, the del Valles themselves were by no means innocent victims of boosterist publicity or tourist desire, for they themselves used the Home of Ramona to their advantage. Their south veranda had become so familiar through countless postcards and photographs that they capitalized on it in the labels for their citrus and raisin crops and on their letterhead. "Home of Ramona Brand" became their trademark.[49] Even the staff capitalized on the rancho's notoriety. One reporter noted that an "Indian servant girl" had been "quietly collecting a considerable revenue by pretending to be the original Ramona, and selling the privilege of taking her snapshot."[50]

Members of the family also took an avid interest in preserving not only landmarks of Californio history, but also the romanticized past presented by the novel. Reginaldo del Valle was an ardent supporter of the marking of the supposed route of "El Camino Real" with mission-bell replicas, and, in fact, the "restored" route ran right past Camulos (which had its own bell marker until it was stolen), despite the fact that Camulos as such had not existed before the secularization of the missions.[51] Reginaldo, his daughter Lucretia, his sister Josefa, and his brother Ygnacio were all stockholders in John Steven McGroarty's romantic epic called the *Mission Play,* and Lucretia del Valle herself wore her grandmother Ysabel's gowns and rings in over 850 performances when she starred in the play as Josefa Yorba.[52]

Despite their dedication to preserving *Ramona*'s version of their own

The del Valle family was able to benefit from their rancho's Ramona-related notoriety to sell ranch produce under the "Home of Ramona" brand.

past, in 1924 the del Valles sold Rancho Camulos to August Rübel, a Swiss immigrant who was also interested in California's history and even more interested in developing the property's oil potential. The *Los Angeles Times* marked the sale by noting that "an era in the history of California closed yesterday. . . . The passing of the Del Valles is the passing of the old regime."[53] Immediately there was concern for the fate of the house, and, much to the relief of many, including Charles Fletcher Lummis, who urged the new owners to people the ranch with those of "Spanish" heritage and to hire Belle del Valle and her husband, Charles, as "resident caretakers of a glorious past," Rübel announced that the "ranch and the buildings [would be] held intact."[54] Despite this promise, the passing of the del Valles, so long associated with the novel, still heralded the end of an era, one likened, unsurprisingly, to the novel *Ramona:* Lummis wrote of the sale of the rancho in a letter to a friend, "I suppose the old days are gone forever—as bitter a tragedy as which Mrs. Jackson pictured in her novel concerning the Indians."[55]

August Rübel, and his family after him, proved true to their word, with Rübel educating his children in California history, the role of their rancho in the story of Ramona, and collecting a sizable library on the subject. The Rübels, like the del Valles before them, grew accustomed to having their meals interrupted by what they came to call "Ramona hunters." However, after August Rübel was killed during World War II, his wife's new husband was not so sympathetic. After Mrs. Rübel Burger's death in 1968, he closed the property to all visitors, notifying anyone desirous of visiting that he was not interested in publicity or in having his privacy invaded. The devastating earthquake that struck southern California in January 1994 and heavily damaged Rancho Camulos may also have caused Burger to have a debilitating heart attack. Upon his death not long later, the children of August Rübel regained control of the property, beginning a process of meticulous restoration of the building, their goal to establish Camulos as a museum, permanently open to the public.[56]

Interestingly, it was not the fact that Camulos is one of California's original adobe structures, or the significance of the del Valle family, that was key to the success of their application for National Historic Landmark status. Rather, the success of the application, upon which much potential funding for the future museum relied, hinged on the *fictional* role of the house as the Home of Ramona.[57]

Neither are the Rübel family and their descendants the only ones for whom the status of Rancho Camulos as the Home of Ramona continues to be important. One contemporary historian insists on continuing the debate about Helen Hunt Jackson's intentions regarding the home of her heroine, claiming to have uncovered new facts establishing Camulos as the unequivocal site.[58]

Thus, it seems that even today, over one hundred years after *Ramona*'s publication, the words of Eleanor Wiseman, who visited Camulos in 1899, still ring true:

> Noted as Mrs. Jackson has made it, through the charm she has thrown over it in her romance, and the little world she has created within its walls, no less interesting does it seem to us with its real living characters. . . .
> It was hard to separate the ideal of the story from the real that we had this day become acquainted with.[59]

Camulos, more than any other place, came to symbolize *Ramona* in the minds of the public. While few now make the pilgrimage on account of the novel, during the myth's greatest popularity (from the late 1880s to the early 1960s) Camulos *was* the Home of Ramona, and as such it was the key landmark for Ramona-seekers. In 1893 a young woman named Olive Percival compiled a booklet, which she titled *The Home of Ramona*. In later years she described her work as a "souvenir booklet made by me (young pilgrim not yet 25)." In it can be found a photograph of the south veranda of Camulos, quotes from the novel written in Percival's hand, and pressed flowers and plants. For each cutting Percival noted the precise novel-related location on the grounds of the rancho from which she plucked it, attributing the jasmine, for example, "in front of Ramona's bedroom."[60] The following year, a Mrs. C. B. Jones of Greenville, Texas acquired a copy of the 1893 edition of the novel. On the inside front cover she glued a handsome full-color image of Camulos's south veranda, and on the facing page, beneath her name, she chronicled a visit she had made to Jackson's grave four years previous.[61]

Beyond the plights or profits of the del Valles and the Rübels, Camulos had symbolic meaning to Ramona-seeking tourists. Created in fiction, the Home of Ramona was reflected back in tourist practices such as the sending of postcards, the purchase of photographs, the compilation of souvenir albums, the customizing of one's own edition of the novel, or the ever-popular pilgrimage to those hallowed halls. Rancho Camulos had become the Home of Ramona.

CHAPTER FOUR

A CLOSE SECOND:
RANCHO GUAJOME

A great wave of emotion swept over her. It was the only
home she had ever known.
—*Ramona*, 192

In November 1894, nearly a decade after Rancho Camulos became established as the Home of Ramona, *Rural Californian* magazine ran an article, "Rancho Guajome: The Real Home of Ramona." Leaping right into the controversy over the "real" people and places in the novel, the anonymous author cited the "latest research," claiming that this revealed not only that Ramona and Alessandro were not "myths" but that "the search for Ramona's home has gone steadily on and it has finally been located at Rancho Guajome."[1] Rancho Guajome was emerging as a competitor for Camulos's "Home of Ramona" title.

Just as the lands that later belonged to the Rancho Camulos had once belonged to Mission San Fernando, the lands that comprised Rancho Guajome had once been part of Mission San Luis Rey. After secularization Governor Pío Pico granted these lands to two former Indian neophytes of the mission, Andrés and José Manuel, in one of the rare grants of lands made directly to California Indians. It was not long before the brothers had sold their half square league (2,219.4 acres) to Don Abel Stearns, one of Los Angeles's wealthiest businessmen. Stearns, an Anglo-American, had married into one of the most prominent of Californio families, the Bandinis of San Diego. Juan Bandini was Stearns's business partner, and in 1841 Stearns, then already forty-three years old, married Bandini's fourteen-year-old daughter, Arcadia.[2]

Arcadia was not the only Bandini daughter to marry an Anglo.[3] Cave Johnson Couts, a native of Tennessee and graduate of West Point, arrived in California with his regiment in 1849, and apparently his destiny "literally fell into his lap." According to legend, young Ysidora Bandini was perched on the roof of the family home in Old Town San Diego watching the regiment ride past when she leaned too far over the edge and fell.[4] Lieutenant Couts, seeing the damsel falling, is said to have "made an abrupt charge, catching his lady in distress just in time." Whether or not this tale is true, Couts and Bandini were married in 1851 "amid a fiesta that lasted a week." One of the wedding gifts, from the bride's brother-in-law Stearns, was the 2,219.4-acre Rancho Guajome.[5]

Couts set about to improve the property, and through his appointment as local Indian agent he was able to obtain the services of some three hundred Native American laborers, likely as indentured servants he paid but little. Couts's crew built barns, stables, sheds, corrals, and the house, making the thousands of adobe bricks necessary for the construction themselves.[6] Most of the roof tiles were taken from nearby Mission San Luis Rey, then in disuse and a state of disrepair—Couts obtained permission for the use of the tiles from the bishop in charge and made a "substantial donation" to the church in return. In 1853 the twenty-two-room house, built as a square around a central courtyard, was complete and Ysidora and her first two children moved in (her other eight children were all born at Guajome).[7]

Though Couts, as Indian subagent, had written his superior that "these Indians are probably more advanced than any pertaining to your super-

Rancho Guajome. Photograph by George Wharton James for his book Through Ramona's Country *(1908).*

intendency," he was not always benevolent with his charges.[8] In fact, Couts was known to have a "violent temper" and was indicted twice in 1855 for whipping Indians with a rawhide *reatta;* one of them died as a result of his injuries. Couts was also twice indicted for murder, each time of a Hispanic, and both times he was acquitted, albeit on technicalities.[9] Leland Stanford summed up Couts's personality like this: "In this hero's shadow . . . lurked nepotism, arrogance, quarrelsomeness, questionable husbandry, and possible wrongful subjugation of Indian protégés over whom, as federal sub-agent for such natives in his area, he held autocratic power."[10]

Thus, it appears that Couts used his connections with the Californio and Catholic Church communities to obtain a considerable land grant, a sizable Native American labor force, and even building materials, all of which he oversaw with despotic fervor. Not only is this a dramatically different personality from that specifically described for the Moreno family in *Ramona,* but Couts's harsh and manipulative treatment of Native Americans and Hispanics certainly sets him apart from any of the Californios Helen Hunt Jackson so evocatively portrayed. While Jackson portrayed a romanticized and peaceable co-existence for Californio rancheros and Native Americans, Couts's example reminds the reader of the realities of Indian subjugation under not just the mission system and the American conquest, but under the Mexican regime as well.[11]

Despite (or perhaps because of) Couts's despotic side, he was an astute businessman. He invested early in livestock and reaped the benefits of the Gold Rush demand for beef. With his profits he was able to greatly expand his holdings, acquiring also the ranchos Buena Vista and Los Vallecitos de San Marcos until he owned over 20,000 acres. Couts's desire was to make Guajome the "grandest . . . of all the southern California ranchos." And even when the tides turned for the Californios after the collapse of the Gold Rush beef market and the devastating drought of the 1860s, Couts was able to remain solvent by liquidating some of his landholdings.[12]

Like the del Valles of Rancho Camulos, Couts was quick to shift away from his troubled investment in cattle ranching and turn to intensive agriculture. In fact, Couts was one of the first to plant orange trees in southern California (in 1854) and by the 1870s his vast orchards included, in addition to groves of oranges and vineyards, varieties of lemon, apple, peach, pear, apricot, plum, persimmon, pomegranate, quince, mulberry, almond, black walnut, and even more exotic tropical fruits such as the avocado, chicomoya, and marengo.[13]

With Couts's profits and his wife's prominent Californio standing, the Guajome ranch house was built and furnished in the most opulent manner. Despite the fact that the home would later be described as "the finest extant example in the United States of the traditional Spanish-Mexican one-story adobe hacienda," the house, built not during the Spanish or Mexican periods but actually after U.S. statehood, combined both American Colonial and Hispanic architectural styles.[14] Furnishing included what is said to be the first piano in California (imported from Europe and brought by Ysidora from the Bandini household). Walls were decorated with oil paintings while a polished crystal chandelier graced the parlor. In 1868 Couts added a personal chapel for his wife's convenience, reportedly obtaining special permission from the pope for its construction.[15] Finished out in this manner, the rancho verily boasted of the lavish lifestyle often associated with the halcyon days of California's rancheros about which Helen Hunt Jackson would write.

Guajome, rural in location, became a "mecca" for the social and cultural life of San Diego's hinterlands and was allegedly visited by famous passersby, among them Judge Benjamin Hayes and General Ulysses S. Grant. Guajome's reputation was indulged in by the family, who at times exaggerated the rancho's cultural prominence, claiming, for instance, that General Lew Wallace wrote a portion of *Ben Hur* while at the rancho, although Wallace historians insist he never even visited California.[16]

But not all went well at Guajome. Despite Couts's successes in agriculture, a law requiring the fencing in of all range lands forced him to sell his remaining herds at ruinous prices. By the time Couts died in 1874 his rancho's "carefree era of affluence" had ended.

Couts left full control of his property to his wife, Ysidora, who, like the Señora Moreno in *Ramona* and the Señora del Valle as well, never remarried. One of her last wishes was to be buried beside her "dear husband" when she herself passed away in 1897. Upon Ysidora's death the property passed to the surviving eight children, but it was the fourth child, Cave Couts Jr., who saw to it that the property remained intact, purchasing the interests of his brothers and sisters.[17]

Couts Jr. claimed he had been present in the spring of 1882 when Helen Hunt Jackson was a guest at the rancho and for many years a controversy raged regarding her visit. Jackson biographer Ruth Odell, who interviewed Couts Jr. in September 1936, wrote based on that interview that Jackson was a guest at the rancho for a period of three weeks, during which Couts was a "semi-invalid by reason of a scythe-cut leg, which kept him more or less a cripple in his hammock . . . [and made him] a logical Felipe" for

Jackson's novel, since Felipe spends critical scenes near the beginning of the novel bedridden (albeit not with a flesh wound).[18]

Whether or not Couts Jr. served as a model for Felipe, Jackson's very visit to Rancho Guajome has been clouded in a controversy centered on two interrelated issues: the nature of her relationship with the Coutses, and her intentions regarding her writing at the time of her visit. According to Odell's interview with Couts Jr., Jackson made a nuisance of herself by interfering with ranch routine and "constantly inciting the Indians to rebel against the work assigned them and to demand better food."[19] Whether or not Jackson was a difficult houseguest, the claims that she *was* have fueled arguments lauding Rancho Guajome as the Home of Ramona, for various authors have claimed that Jackson was at Guajome gathering material for *Ramona*.[20] In fact, authors Vroman and Barnes went so far as to claim that it was Señora Couts herself who gave Jackson the idea for the romantic kernel of her story when asked if she knew of any "elopement in the neighborhood."[21] Vroman and Barnes go on to claim that since Jackson irritated the Coutses, the two women broke their friendship, and that Señora Couts forbade Mrs. Jackson from using Guajome as the setting for her novel. Devastated, Jackson returned to Los Angeles, where the Coronels suggested she visit Rancho Camulos for the purpose of finding a new setting for *Ramona*. Such claims, however, cannot be sustained since, at the time of her visit to Guajome, Jackson was not gathering material for a novel—indeed, Jackson herself would later lament not having had the idea of writing a novel in mind during her visit to California. In addition, it cannot be proved that Jackson visited Guajome before she visited Camulos or that she actually visited Guajome at all.[22]

Nevertheless, similarities between Rancho Guajome and the Moreno rancho in the novel were readily apparent, and by the 1890s Guajome had become accepted as *a* "Home of Ramona."[23] As Guajome's proponents made clear, of particular power in emphasizing Guajome as *the* Home of Ramona (over Camulos) was the fact of its location relative to other avowed Ramona locations such as Old Town San Diego (where Ramona and Alessandro are married) and the Temecula area (where Alessandro's people lived before being evicted by Anglos, as well as to the hills of which region Alessandro and Ramona flee the Anglo invaders). The novel details aspects of local geography that appear, in this case, to disqualify Camulos and point instead to Rancho Guajome—points that writers about Ramona locales were quick to note. For example, Margaret V. Allen, in her 1914 book *Ramona's Homeland*, wrote that

If the Morena [sic] ranch had any definite existence outside the author's
brain, it must have been at Guajome. It is two days journey from San
Diego [it takes Ramona and Alessandro two days in the novel], a few
miles from [Mission] San Louis [sic] Rey [where the Padres all knew
Alessandro], and less then six hours by a "fleet pony" from Temecula
[referring to the trip made by one of Alessandro's sheep shearers to fetch
Alessandro's violin].[24]

Despite such lobbying efforts, however, just as at Camulos, various writers
claimed that the Couts family was reluctant to have Guajome identified
with the famous novel. After Señora Couts's death in 1897 the *Los Angeles
Times* ran a story claiming that it was only out of deference to Mrs. Couts
that the identity of the true Home of Ramona had never been revealed.
The reporter elaborated:

Ever since Helen Hunt Jackson wrote her famous novel depicting the
Spanish-Indian life of Southern California as it was before the enter-
prising New Englander invaded its peaceful domain, there has been a
world of speculation as to the identity of the heroine and the location of
the home where the tragic romance of Ramona and her Indian lover,
Alessandro, was worked out by the skillful pen of the novelist.

The original "Home of Ramona" is as numerous in Southern California as the stakes marking out town lots were during the real-estate boom
there a few years ago . . . the one oftenest referred to . . . is at Camulos . . .
it easily passes as the original but it is not.

Out of respect to the sensitive feelings of Mrs. Coutts [sic], however,
the public has been allowed to believe this innocent fiction, and Camulos
has borne the honors and thus diverted attention from the real scene of
inspiration—which was at the old Coutts [sic] Rancho at Guayjoma [sic].[25]

Others as well trumpeted Guajome's status. The author of *Rancho Guajome:
The Real Home of Ramona* declared, "now that there is no doubt as to the
true place . . . tens of thousands of tourists . . . will throng there yearly to
visit the scenes that so inspired Helen Hunt Jackson." In an important
move, this author also noted the precise location of the home, in the same
way that Edwards Roberts and others had done for Camulos, noting that
Guajome lay "one and one-half miles from the San Luis Rey Mission . . .
on the Santa Fe Railway."[26] Since Rancho Camulos, which had been
identified for nearly ten years as the Home of Ramona, was located on
the route of the Santa Fe's competitor, the Southern Pacific, the conten-

tion that Rancho Guajome was the *real* Home of Ramona established the Santa Fe's claim to a prominent Ramona landmark. In fact, the Santa Fe reissued the article, adding to the back cover this statement:

> The real home of Ramona is located on the line of the Santa Fe Route four miles from Oceanside, California.
> Tourists who wish to see the historic old Missions and other interesting scenes should take the Santa Fe Route.[27]

But while the statement that tourists would come by the "tens of thousands" was surely an exaggeration, like Camulos, even without a train station Rancho Guajome became a destination for Ramona-seekers. The reprint of the 1894 article, while it noted that Mrs. Couts still lived in the home, stated that the property was in the possession of an "Englishman" by the name of A. McWhirter, and that McWhirter "will be pleased to show the places made interesting by Helen Hunt Jackson's famous novel, to all tourists and pleasure seekers who may take an interest in the home of Ramona."[28]

And just as the del Valles of Camulos were personally involved in the promotion of their rancho as the Home of Ramona, so some of the Couts family attempted to profit from *their* rancho's notoriety. Cave Couts Jr.'s brother, William B. Couts, printed a pamphlet entitled "San Luis Rey Mission and the Home of Ramona," in which he offered his own services as tour guide to Guajome, listing eleven key features of the tour that corresponded to points in the novel such as "the south veranda" and "the chapel." Couts hedged his bets, stating, "The Couts family do not claim that Guajome, their home place, is the real Ramona's home, but tourists will have it that it is." He also guaranteed the satisfaction of those who took his tour, stating, "W.B. Couts will not take your money if you are not satisfied with your visit to the ranch."[29] And just as at Camulos, postcards and photographs appeared with Guajome identified as the Home of Ramona.[30]

While some writers, like Margaret Allen, were insistent that Guajome was the "real" Home of Ramona (she even claimed that "Mrs. Jackson never intended to make Camulos Ranch the home of Ramona"), others, like Charles Fletcher Lummis, considered Guajome a pretender to the throne.[31] In fact, Lummis, under the pen name Juan del Rio, claimed that Camulos was definitely the home of the heroine and that "it never would have been applied elsewhere but for the hope of inveigling money from

Ramona's Home, where Helen Hunt Jackson wrote her famous book.

Because of its location near many of the Indian scenes in the novel, some Ramona sleuths insisted that Rancho Guajome was the real Home of Ramona, but Guajome was never as widely touristed as Camulos. Postcard circa 1906. Collection of Phil Brigandi; reprinted by permission.

'Ramona tourists.'"[32] And other authors, like Vroman and Barnes, concurred with Lummis. They wrote,

> Of Guajome what [else] can we say than
> "Of all sad words of tongue or *pen*
> The saddest are these, *It might have been.*"[33]

Similarly, in *The True Story of Ramona,* authors Davis and Alderson agree that "[n]either Guajome, which [Jackson] had several times visited, nor any other Southern California ranch was referred to by [Jackson] in connection with the plot . . . for the romance of 'Ramona.'"[34] Even Ramona expert George Wharton James had to concede that Guajome was but a runner-up for the Home of Ramona title:

> Mrs. Jackson herself, who surely ought to have known what she meant to do, placed the fictitious home of her fictitious character at Camulos. . . . [But] Guajome is remarkably interesting, whether Ramona's fictitious home or not.[35]

Just the same, and just as with the del Valles at Camulos, it was not long before the stream of tourists seeking the Home of Ramona was more than the Coutses could enjoy—particularly since, as at Camulos, some of those tourists went beyond the bounds of propriety, invading the private parts of the house. George Wharton James wrote of Guajome in 1908 that tourists would even enter the kitchen,

> lift off the lids from the cooking-pots to see what is therein, offering as a lame excuse for their rudeness, with a sickly smile, "I thought it might be fryholes"—some call it *fry joles*—"cooking."[36]

Others, "camera fiends," were so desirous of a photograph of the rancho's enclosed patio that they climbed the roof, damaging some of the tiles, and necessitating repairs.[37] Not, apparently as patient as the del Valles were with such pilgrims, Couts Jr. himself soon posted a sign that read:

> Notice.
> Ladies and gentlemen calling here, in my absence, will kindly refrain from assuming liberties in and about these premises that would be objectionable to you if exercised by strangers in your homes.
>   This is private property and must be respected. Sightseers are only tolerated, Never wanted!!
>   Cave J. Couts, Owner.[38]

In a more cynical mood, he is also said to have written, "If you want Ramona, go to Hell N. Hunt."[39]

But Couts Jr. was faring poorly for more reasons than just the influx of tourists to his property. In 1897, not long before his mother's death, he underwent a bitter and contested divorce from his wife (whom he had wed in 1887), losing custody of his son, Cave Couts III. He further sustained financial problems and was unable to maintain the home in its former state of splendor. By the turn of the century Guajome was becoming dilapidated and the authors of the *The Genesis of the Story of Ramona* made note of it: "already in a neglected state it will soon be left out of the list of possible homes of Ramona."[40] Apparently, so improperly maintained a building could scarcely fill visitors' impressions of what the Home of Ramona should look like. In order to be associated with the novel, Ramona landmarks had to retain the air described of them in the original text or fall into ruin completely. A liminal state of dilapidation, implying that residents lived in relative poverty, was not well received. But the situation for the rancho only worsened. As another visitor who came to Guajome in 1910 wrote, picturesque ruins were one thing, but the state of Guajome was not acceptable:

The ruin of the Guajome seems more like the hideous decay of a mur-
dered body than the peaceful dissolution which sheds over most ancient
buildings, that peculiar charm we can all recognize. Cans, bottles, and
other refuse covered the floors and the broken chairs and tables of the
rooms we entered; the fish pond was slimy and defiled; the fountain dry
and shattered. But for a few flowers that bloomed in the dusty courtyard
I could discover nothing of attraction. It was a relief to turn our backs
upon the place.[41]

In a state of financial insolvency, Couts Jr. tried several times to sell the
property, utilizing its Home-of-Ramona notoriety in order to attempt to
attract a buyer. His first attempt was to the Guajome Fruit Colony in 1894.
When that attempt failed, he tried again, in 1902, to sell the house and
property, this time to the U.S. government, which sought land for a reservation for the Warner's Ranch (Mission) Indians, a plan that, like the first
one, was doomed to failure. The findings of the commission investigating
the possible sale read in part,

This rather famous rancho—one of the few old-style Spanish haciendas
left in California, and supposed by some to be the spot described by
Helen Hunt Jackson as the home of "Ramona"—lies near the Mission of
San Luis Rey. . . . The locality would be entirely unsuitable for Indians
born and bred in the mountains at an altitude over 7 times as great;
remote from the sea, and in an arid region.[42]

The most dramatic of all of Couts's plans, however, was that of 1904–5
for the Rancho Guajome Health Company. Architects Will Hebbard and
Irving Gill, already known for their Mission Revival designs, were contracted by a group of doctors to turn the rancho into a "combined uto-
pian colony and nursing home for semi-invalids."[43] But, like Couts's other
plans, this one also failed.

It wasn't until 1916 that the very one who was responsible for the
original grant of Guajome to the Couts family came to the rescue. Arcadia
Bandini Stearns de Baker, the remarried widow of Don Abel Stearns,
died, leaving nearly seven million dollars to relatives. Couts Jr.'s share was
enough to repay his debts and remodel the Guajome adobe. Attempting
to update his property, he added a new facade to the building: a row of
arches inspired by Mission Revival architecture. In addition, he built
guest apartments, bathrooms, and garages, and updated the electrical
and plumbing service to the house. With this influx of family money

Couts Jr. experienced a reversal of fortune and now "basked in his re-furbished reputation as the 'last of the Dons,' entertaining lavishly."[44]

Further, Couts Jr.'s Ramona-related celebrity rated him free tickets to the Ramona Pageant, which had begun in 1923. Pageant President Edward Poorman wrote him,

> Because of your intimate connection with the story of Ramona, and because the wonderful Rancho Juaome [sic] is still owned by the family with which the story is so closely connected, I am sure you will enjoy see-ing the play; and I know we will more than be honored to have you.[45]

Couts Jr.'s high profile also attracted writer Peter B. Kyne, who vis-ited Guajome and selected it as the setting for his 1921 novel *The Pride of Palomar*. When William Randolph Hearst filmed the novel in 1922, Guajome was used as a location. Intriguingly, however, since the house was partially undergoing remodeling at that time, some of the exteriors had to be shot elsewhere—and Rancho Camulos, connected to Guajome by its Ramona affiliation, was chosen as the second location. Camulos had already been declared the "avowed and accepted" Home of Ramona; now it interceded in Guajome's representation of Rancho Guajome in *The Pride of Palomar* as well. The identities of the two ranchos as Home of Ramona had become so interchangeable that on film the two became one, and Camulos could even tread on Guajome's ability to represent itself.[46]

Cave Couts Jr. died in 1943 at Rancho Guajome, in the same bed in which he was born, leaving the property to his longtime companion and housekeeper, Ida Richardson, with whom he had two children. Slowly, Richardson and her son Earl Richardson began to sell off some of the property, including the Couts family papers. In 1966 a real estate agent told the Richardsons, "We're up to our hips in history. . . . I'd like to put you into a place with all the modern conveniences."[47] But the Richardsons remained at Guajome. Ida Richardson died in 1972, and in 1973 the Coun-ty of San Diego acquired Rancho Guajome through condemnation pro-ceedings, paying to Earl Richardson the sum of $1,021,840.[48] Since then it has been open to the public (except during its restoration in the late 1990s) as a San Diego County park.

Throughout its career as a Home of Ramona, Rancho Guajome lived in Camulos's long shadow. Though southern California boosters promot-ing Ramona-related attractions most often awarded the Home of Ramona title to Guajome's competitor, George Wharton James was adamant in attempting to put the matter to rest. Confronted with claims for Guajome's Home of Ramona status, James wrote,

> Mrs. Jackson herself, who surely ought to have known what she meant to do, placed the fictitious home of her fictitious character at Camulos, on the coast line of the Southern Pacific railway. Her word is final. No amount of argument can possibly overturn what she herself has written, but if argument be needed, let it be said that with but one exception no error can be found in the descriptions and locations at Camulos, while there are several discrepancies when one endeavors to locate the scenes at Guajome.[49]

While James, a former minister, presented no evidence of Jackson's intentions in the matter, he did offer an explanation for Camulos's inconsistencies (which he identified as those of overall geographical location rather than any errors in description of the rancho itself):

> [I]t seems far more reasonable to me that the author deliberately and purposefully made discrepancies of this character apparent in her book, so that it would be impossible for any one to attempt to locate exactly the home of her fictitious character. Naturally she would want to throw people off the scent.[50]

But, with Jackson dead, the controversy was never fully resolved, and dedicated Ramona tourists, like writer Charles Frances Saunders and his wife, Sylvia—who toured Ramona-related sites in a carriage—insisted on visiting *both* Homes of Ramona. Beginning their tour with Rancho Camulos, they ended it shortly after their visit to Guajome. Claiming full allegiance to neither rancho, Saunders wrote, "Guajome is indeed the original home of Ramona and the geography of the novel in several particulars is intelligible only when we know this." So the little party made the most of what Guajome had to offer in the way of Ramona-relatedness: they enjoyed its familiar surroundings rather than seeking out the minute particulars (the crosses on the hills, the south veranda) as they had at Camulos.[51] Excited at seeing the places the novel had made familiar, Sylvia Saunders exclaimed,

> Breakfast in sight of San Luis Rey; dinner overlooking the barley fields and olive yards of Guajome; supper, I suppose, in the shadow of the Pala bell tower; why go to Italy when there are sights like this [all

related to *Ramona*] and such days as these within the borders of our ain countree?[52]

Though Guajome never reached the canonical status of Rancho Camulos, those who visited could still indulge in the richness of its *Ramona*-related imagery—visiting real places described in a work of fiction and, as ever, inscribing fantasy upon the world of fact.

CHAPTER FIVE

RAMONA'S MARRIAGE PLACE, "WHICH NO TOURIST WILL FAIL TO VISIT"

> Father Gaspara's house was at the end of a long, low
> adobe building, which had served no mean purpose in
> the old Presidio days, but was now fallen into decay;
> and all its rooms, except those occupied by the Father,
> had been long uninhabited. On the opposite side of the
> way, in a neglected, weedy open, stood his chapel,—a
> poverty-stricken little place, its walls imperfectly white-
> washed. . . . Everything about it was in unison with the
> atmosphere of the place,—the most profoundly melan-
> choly in all Southern California.
> —*Ramona*, 231–32

On 28 August 1887, a large front-page illustration of the decrepit Estudillo adobe in Old Town San Diego carried the title (in romantically stylized letters that looked like dripping wax) "The Marriage Place of Ramona." The unnamed author of the *San Diego Union* article wrote, "To sleepy Old Town [the house] is known as the Estudillo's, but the outside world knows it as the marriage place of 'Ramona.'"[1] The author's claim was based on Jackson's brief description in the novel. Although this was not as detailed as some of Jackson's other place descriptions, it had not been difficult for Ramona sleuths to determine that the Estudillo adobe was, in fact, "Ramona's Marriage Place." More accurately, it was the site where Ramona and Alessandro's names were entered into Father Gaspara's marriage records.[2] The actual ceremony, though not described in the novel, was performed in the chapel nearby.[3] Such details aside, the Estudillo adobe earned the title "Ramona's Marriage Place," which in turn led to several decades of tourist promotion of the building in this role.[4]

The house had been built between 1827 and 1829 for José Maria Estudillo, a distinguished and prominent Californio.[5] He and his heirs lived in the

In ruins by the time Ramona *became popular, the Estudillo adobe was the only one of the three main buildings associated with the novel that had actually been built in the Spanish colonial period. Lantern slide (circa 1890).*

house until 1887, when José Maria's grandson, Salvador R. Estudillo, vacated the property, leaving it in the hands of a caretaker. In that same year, one of the first articles identifying the house as the Marriage Place of Ramona (cited above) was splashed on the front page of the *San Diego Union*.[6] The *Union* headlined "The Marriage Place of Ramona" and the article included sections entitled "A Typical Adobe" and "Queer Architecture," describing the house's construction and condition of which the author noted, "all is a Pompeii of ruins." Despite, or perhaps because of, this state of picturesque decay, the author found that "[t]he whole scene is a dreamy one." Then, adopting the established style of mixing fiction and fact, the author indulged in a personal fantasy, an imagined encounter in which the fictional hero and heroine appear in the courtyard—a scene not in the least reminiscent of the somber nighttime wedding scene that Jackson describes in the novel:

Intuitively one sees handsome Alessandro reach up and pick the luscious fruit [of the fig tree] and offer it to Ramona, standing near. At the old well across the yard they may have stood, fair Ramona balancing her olla of water, Alessandro whispering words of love.[7]

Like so many tourists at Ramona landmarks, this unnamed reporter engaged in the world of the fictional in the landscape of fact.

Though this was one of the earliest published accounts of the Estudillo adobe as the marriage place of Ramona, the author was not the first to visit: "Scratched on a cemented wall near a door, . . . is the delicate lettering 'Alessandro.'"[8]

Once the Estudillo adobe was identified as Ramona's Marriage Place, a tourist attraction, and a spot of romantic reflection, it was not long before San Diegans realized that there was money to be made. The first, most likely, was the adobe's caretaker. Salvador R. Estudillo, who had hired him, later explained that this caretaker "sold the tiles, adobes, and the locks of the house and said it was the home of Ramona. . . . In the end the house was destroyed; the wood from the corridors, and the doors and windows were stolen."[9]

Just a decade later, in 1898, writer Polly Larkin spent a "few weeks . . . living over the story," which, she noted, "[n]early all of our Californians have read." Describing the Estudillo adobe she wrote: "All over the walls of the various rooms of the old ruin can be found the names carved or written of people from all over the United States. Not a single room is in good condition. . . . It is a picture of desolation that you leave behind you and a memory that you will ever carry with you." Already then, however, a nearby curio store catered to the desires of tourists, selling, among other things, hand-carved picture frames "containing the picture of the old adobe house . . . beautifully inlaid in the polished, rich, brown wood."[10]

Like Rancho Camulos, the Estudillo house was becoming an attraction not to be missed. The following year no less a figure than William Sharpless Jackson himself made a visit to San Diego and the *Union* reported that he intended "to visit the scenes made famous by his loved and talented wife," scenes that would include Ramona's Marriage Place.[11]

Then, in January 1906 the Estudillos sold the property for $500 to one Nat Titus, a representative of the San Diego Electric Railway Company, who subsequently transferred the property in 1907 to the company outright for the nominal sum of ten dollars.[12] The San Diego Electric Railway Company was owned by one of San Diego's biggest boosters, John D. Spreckles, who already owned the luxurious Hotel Del Coronado and vast tracts of real estate in the San Diego area. His goal was the development of San Diego, for, as his biographer later wrote, he "dreamed of seeing it become a real city." To this end he had acquired San Diego's horse-drawn and cable-operated car lines and converted them into "an entirely new, thoroughly up-to-date, and splendidly equipped system of [electric] street railways," which he continually extended and improved in order to promote the growth of the city. At the ends of two of his most far-reaching car lines Spreckles developed "attractions": Mission Cliff Gardens and Ramona's Marriage Place. Spreckles thus relied not only on a new mode of transportation to speed the city's development, he relied on the nation's newfound interest in domestic tourism to popularize his trolley lines.[13]

Already established as a tourist site when Spreckles's company purchased the "old tumble-down adobe homestead generally known as the marriage place of Ramona," it was "in a crumbled and dilapidated condition," but nevertheless, as the *San Diego Union* pointed out, was "visited by thousands of people yearly." Thus, despite the property's poor condition, it was already a viable tourist attraction, made so largely by the demands of the tourists themselves.

Confident of their building's Ramona credentials, the company declared they would restore the structure "to its original appearance," but simultaneously make "the entire place . . . appear as portrayed in the famous novel,"

By 1906 the Estudillo adobe had become so established as the Marriage Place of Ramona that the property could be bought, remodeled, and developed specifically as a tourist attraction. Postcard postmarked 1913 (showing the building after restoration).

a project involving somewhat of a contradiction since the building's fictional counterpart was not restored but decayed. Announcing their plans in the *Union* (a paper owned by Spreckles) the company also revealed plans for a curio shop within the building itself, that the building would even be leased to a curio dealer, and that these efforts on the part of the company would not only greatly increase the tourist flow, but would make Ramona's Marriage Place a spot "which no tourist will fail to visit."[14]

Toward these ends the company, in 1908, retained the services of architect Hazel Wood Waterman. Waterman had already designed a home for William Clayton, the Spreckles Companies' vice president and managing director, and it was he who hired her to restore Ramona's Marriage Place.[15] Before work began, Waterman "arduously pursued the task of researching how adobe structures were built during the Mexican period in California," which included visiting all the remaining adobes in the vicinity, taking notes on their construction, and conversing with Charles Fletcher Lummis, who was then already known for his work on the missions with the Landmarks Club.[16] Quickly, however, the company's plans to restore the original appearance of the structure were altered. Waterman, in her detailed "Specifications for Restoration of Typical Spanish California Dwelling Popularly Known as 'Marriage Place of Ramona,' Old Town, San Diego," wrote,

> These plans and specifications are not intended for the restoration of
> this particular building as it was originally, nor as it developed thru
> changes and alterations; the idea is to restore and preserve it as a typical
> old Spanish California dwelling. . . . It is desired to preserve the type and
> to restore without destroying the picturesqueness of the old work.[17]

Waterman had a specific look in mind for the structure: "As far as is consistent with permanent preservation, the old work will be retained and an appearance of age will be given to all new work. Restoration that gives a new and modern appearance would be uninteresting."[18] The finished product, thus, would convey an antimodern appearance of picturesque age, decay, and obsolescence. To attain this, Waterman was very exacting in her directions:

> All adobe brick should be both made and laid by Mexicans only. Americans do not understand throwing them up characteristically, and therefore, artistically. . . .
>
> The [roof] tiles should also be hand made, somewhat irregular in
> shape and thickness, either old or stained to look old, and should be laid

Architect Hazel Wood Waterman (shown here in 1921) researched adobe construction methods for the restoration of the Estudillo house, then added details from Ramona, *as well as a curio shop. San Diego Historical Society Photograph Collection; reprinted by permission.*

without special attention to alignment. The under tiles may be modern made. . . .

Timbers to be notched at ends as if drawn by oxen, and to be hewn on three sides as if prepared in the forest, and by hand. This material . . . [is] to be "weathered" by exposure and dipping in mud and water. . . . The idea is to "age" in appearance all exposed construction material, and that it shall have none of the marks of the modern mill work. . . .

Construction of roof to be as shown and to be "exposed" from the interior. . . . All [principal rafters, purlins, posts and braces] to be bound with rawhide thongs, tied while wet. No nails to be visibly used. Common rafters to be spaced unevenly, 10" to 16" O.C. [on center], averaging 16" O.C.[19]

Thus, the restored building was to have the patina of age as well as the "charm of the work of half-skilled Indian hands," as if in imitation of the building's presumed original builders. But not the entire building was meant to be as good as old: "The caretaker's wing . . . will be finished for occupancy by a caretaker, and in it modern conveniences of plumbing, electric lights, etc., will be installed." Likewise, both the fountain and the well in the central courtyard were to be "supplied with water from the City water system, and to have proper outlets." Further, and as proposed by the Electric Railway Company when the restoration plans were announced, Waterman's original drawings detail and identify what would become the curio shop.[20]

In other words, Waterman herself, from the time she was hired, set out to construct not a restored Californio adobe but a romanticized and commercialized tourist attraction. Nor, indeed, was she immune to the romanticizing effects of *Ramona,* many of which she desired to include in the restoration plans. She wrote, "The arrangement of the outer court is planned in order to use features, such as the grape arbor, well, oven, artichoke patch, bells, and chapel suggested by 'Ramona,'"[21] all of which, in the novel, were actually features of the Rancho Moreno, and not of the place where Ramona was married. And just as Helen Hunt Jackson before her had stirred facts into her fiction, Waterman now blended Jackson's interpretation of California history, the tale of Ramona, and the actual history of the Estudillo family. She wrote years later,

What was there to make the preservation of this pathetic ruin worth while? Was there only an incident in a novel, a legend? . . . What history, what purposeful and romantic past was there to stir the memories . . .?

> The unique drama of an olden time is the real heritage of this old
> house.... Rich ... in everything that made wealth in those days, lavishly
> generous, hospitable to friend and stranger, honorable and courteous,
> [the Estudillo]'s was the life of that California whose history is romance
> itself.... [I]ts story is more thrilling and fascinating than fiction.[22]

Though Waterman herself hailed from Alabama, she wrote, incorporating
a quote from the novel in her description of the Estudillo family, that as she
contemplated the Estudillo project she was "stirred by these memories, it
seemed to me that the Estudillo house should be restored as a typical aristocratic dwelling of Spanish and Mexican California, representing those
days *'when it had served no mean purpose'* a relic of that unique California
civilization nowhere else to be found and almost forgotten." In restoring it
as a "typical" dwelling, then, Waterman needed no longer hold herself to
the original floor plan, or indeed even the original look of the house, and,
in fact, she didn't. Her drawings indicate that she moved the positions of
various doors and windows in the building. She also added a fireplace in
the main *sala* (living room) as well as a *parilla* (outdoor oven) in the
north wing. Waterman herself later acknowledged knowing that a partial
second story in the form of a cupola and a balcony had originally been
part of the house and wrote, "I regret that this balcony was not included
in the restoration."[23] In *Ramona* the building is described with no reference to a balcony.

Much of what has been written about Waterman's restoration is culled
from a document she wrote in 1935, "The Restoration of a Landmark."[24]
It seems that in her later years (Waterman died in 1948) she rethought her
role in the restoration of the Estudillo adobe, which, by then, had long been
known as Ramona's Marriage Place. While most of the document employs
a romantic and nostalgic tone heavily influenced by *Ramona* (Waterman
quotes the novel directly several times),[25] at the end of the document her
tone switches to outrage:

> [O]ne morning, printed in large letters on the front of troll[e]ycars to
> Old Town appeared the placard "To Ramona's Home." The property had
> been leased. Upon the restored house of the Estudillos was painted in
> very large letters "Ramona's Marriage Place."[26]

Thus, years after the fact, Waterman portrayed herself as duped, despite
the fact that she herself had designed the curio shop and that many of her
original documents and drawings make use of the Ramona's Marriage

Place title. Just the same, even in her outrage, she did not fully divest herself of *Ramona's* influences on her work:

> I am not responsible for the remunerative magic of the "Wishing Well"
> but a well of drinking water was in the scheme, shaded by a brush covered ramada and approached by a rustic vine-covered trellis which, like
> the Señora Moreno's "led straight down from the veranda steps."[27]

Whether Waterman herself was pleased or not, Mr. Spreckles, at any rate, *was,* and Ramona's Marriage Place was opened to the public by 1 May 1910.[28] As per the Electric Railway Company's original plan, the property was leased to a concessionaire, one Thomas Powell Getz, who subsequently bought the property outright from the Electric Railway in 1924.[29]

Tommy Getz (as he was known) had been a "Thespian of repute." Getting his start in theater in 1873 in a minstrel show, he had come to San Diego around the turn of the century to stage benefit theater performances for the Elks Club. Contacted by William Clayton, vice president and managing director of the Spreckles Companies, and fellow Elk, in 1910 Getz took on the lease of the newly restored Ramona's Marriage Place. If the purpose of the restored attraction was to draw tourists interested in Ramona landmarks, Getz was an excellent choice, for it was said he was "possessed of the soul of loving reverence for the past and the memory of Ramona."[30]

Almost immediately Ramona's Marriage Place attracted a good deal of attention as a spot to reflect on the novel and its characters. The *Overland Monthly's* correspondent summed up the attraction, alluding also to Waterman's incorporation of features from other sites described in the novel,

> Romance and materialism rub sides together severely at San Diego, today, since the trolley car now carries us from the heart of the city to the very door of "Ramona's Home" in "Old Town." . . .
>
> The patio is being planted with flowers which, with nice walks and a fountain, will render it a restful spot in which to muse upon Ramona and her lover.
>
> As one of the landmarks of Mrs. Jackson's story of romance and love, it will last for generations to come, and in the popular mind it will continue to be both Ramona's home and her marriage place. . . .
>
> Ramona and Alessandro! In your footsteps we have trod for a few hours, and we feel that we have learned to know you better than ever before.[31]

Once restoration work was complete, "Tommy" Getz took on the lease for Ramona's Marriage Place and developed it into the most commercial Ramona attraction.

4182. Inner Court of Ramona's Home, San Diego, Cal.

The courtyard of Ramona's Marriage Place became a luxuriant garden with shaded pergola and wishing well—a common sight on postcards. Postcard (circa 1910) from the collection of Phil Brigandi; reprinted by permission.

And while tourists continued to flock to the attraction because of its associations with the novel, not all commentators were so smitten by the romance of Ramona and Alessandro. George Wharton James, the former minister who wrote *Through Ramona's Country* as a guidebook to the places associated with the novel, insisted upon a strict separation between fact and fiction in this case:

> The house at old San Diego, described in Chapter XVIII, is the one occupied by the priest on his visits there, and thousands of photographs of it have been sold as "the house where Ramona was married," and of "the bells that rang when Ramona was married." The old house is there, the chapel is there, and the bells are there, so why not make use of them? So the photographer has utilized them to his profit. But the purchaser of the pictures seems to have forgotten that Ramona was married only in the brain of Mrs. Jackson, and that therefore these real bells can scarcely have rung at a fictitious marriage of a fictitious Ramona to a fictitious Alessandro by a fictitious priest after a fictitious elopement from a fictitious home of a fictitious Señora Moreno.[32]

Nevertheless, Getz was a good promoter for his tourist attraction and curio business, making pamphlets that advertised Ramona's Marriage Place available on trains bound for California.[33] And Getz marketed not just the

Estudillo adobe's association with the novel, but the notion of Ramona's Marriage Place as a spot of romantic reflection more broadly as well. One pamphlet, published in many editions by Getz himself, contained on the title page a poem:

> There's a certain charm about it,
>   With its flowers and the bees,
> That seems to rest your spirit
>   And set your heart at ease.
> It brings back fond old memories
>   That time cannot efface,
> And you feel that God is smiling
>   On "Ramona's Marriage Place."[34]

One room, originally the dining room, was outfitted by Getz as a "writing room." Here, printed on a sign hanging from the wall, was the suggestion, "This is a good place to sit down and write a letter to mother."[35] Getz successfully sold postcards and postcard sets, and even stamped them with a round "Ramona's Marriage Place" stamp resembling a Postal Service cancellation stamp.[36] Proclaiming that "hundreds of post cards, letters, etc., all bearing the imprint from 'Ramona's Marriage Place' are sent daily to all parts of the world," far more postcards of Ramona's Marriage Place were produced than for any other Ramona attraction. The Ramona's Marriage Place imprimatur became a successful sales device for numerous souvenir items, including tape measures, matchbox covers, ashtrays and pin trays, letter openers, teaspoons, salt and pepper shakers, hand-painted ostrich eggs, rosary boxes, and even miniature mother-of-pearl tomahawks—all stamped, cast, painted, or embossed "Ramona's Marriage Place." For those who wished to bring a living part of the place home with them, Getz even sold flower seeds from the garden.[37]

Getz himself lectured twice daily on the missions and *Ramona*. Influenced by his twenty-five years in the theater, he ran a lively show. Beginning by walking across the room with an "exaggerated wobble," he then announced to his audience, "I'm not drunk, friends. . . . I have to walk this way because of the old tiling on the floor. This tile was made in 1770 and is the first work of civilized man in California." Not avoiding self-promotion, Getz's brochure described his lectures "on the history of the old house, with its memories of Ramona," as "a constant treat to all who enter [the building's] restored and beautiful walls." Reinforcing the connections between fact and fiction so often made at Ramona landmarks,

By the early twentieth century, virtually every souvenir imaginable was sold in Ramona's Marriage Place motif, including this sterling silver matchbox cover.

the building's lecture room featured a "cycloramic painting of California, showing the old missions and the geographical points covered in the story of 'Ramona.'"[38]

Getz further made a family establishment out of the place: his daughter Marguerite was married there.[39] In fact, any couple interested in taking their vows on the same spot where it was said that the fictional Ramona and Alessandro had taken theirs could arrange to do so. Many availed themselves of the opportunity, making Ramona's Marriage Place significant not just for its link to a work of fiction, but important also for its significant personal meaning in the lives of individuals. One chronicler of Old Town wrote,

> The family chapel [at Ramona's Marriage Place] . . . is frequently used for weddings by persons of all denominations . . . pastors and priests of the various faiths coming to officiate.
>
> When used for weddings, the chapel, gaily bedecked with fragrant flowers stands out in marked contrast to the somber setting in which Ramona and Alessandro plighted their vows, as it was described in Mrs. Jackson's romantic story.[40]

Like other Ramona landmarks, Ramona's Marriage Place became a popular tourist attraction, perhaps all the more so because here, unlike

The Chapel in which Ramona was married 144
Ramona's Marriage Place, Old San Diego, Calif.

The novel does not describe Ramona's wedding, but the "restored" chapel in the Estudillo house became known as the place where Ramona was married—and a place for many tourists to take their vows.

at Camulos and Guajome, tourism was encouraged and actively sought: Getz told of one Labor Day when 1,632 people paid the ten-cent admission fee.[41] Further, while at Camulos and Guajome souvenirs were not sold and seldom given away, many of those who visited Ramona's Marriage Place sought not just to take something home with them, but also to leave something of themselves behind. One visitor was

> amazed by the thousands of cards left there by people who reside in all parts of the world. On window-panes, posters and rocks names have been inscribed in honor of Ramona. There is no other place in all the world where one immortal has received such tribute, except the birthplace of Shakespeare.[42]

Tommy Getz himself became a well-known figure in the city of San Diego. When on vacation in Arizona in 1932 his exclamation that he'd "much rather be chasing butterflies at Ramona's Marriage Place" made the *San Diego Union.* In 1934 Getz's obituary made the *Union*'s front page. On the day of his death a light was lit for him on the altar in the chapel at Ramona's Marriage Place and kept burning constantly.[43]

After Getz's death, his daughter Marguerite Weiss continued to operate her father's business. Despite the lack of Tommy's flamboyance, Ramona's

Marriage Place continued to be a significant attraction. Weiss maintained many of the traditions her father had started. In 1938, as her father had done before her, she hosted the gathering of the "True Vow Keepers Club" for couples who had been married over fifty years. She raised the admission price from ten to twenty-five cents and suggested on a flyer, "Know your California heritage—visit Old Town this week—and start your tour with the most famous of all early buildings, Ramona's Marriage Place."[44]

Marguerite Weiss sold the property in 1964 for an estimated sum of $125,000 to the Title Insurance and Trust Company. Ramona's Marriage Place was subsequently purchased by prominent local businessman Legler Benbough, who then donated it to the state of California in 1968. Once again suffering from the neglect of time, during 1968 and 1969 the building was re-restored under the guidance of architect Clyde Trudell.[45]

On 2 December 1968 the front page of the *San Diego Union* lamented in a headline across all eight columns above the masthead: "Ramona Loses 'Place' in Old Town." The large painted sign "Ramona's Marriage Place," which had long adorned the side of the building, was erased and when the building reopened in 1969, coincident with San Diego's 200th anniversary celebration, it was renamed "Casa de Estudillo."

37A:—CORRIDOR, RAMONA'S MARRIAGE PLACE, SHOWING FIRST BUGGY AND FIRST HOTEL DESK IN SAN DIEGO.

PHOTO BY LEE PASSMORE.   AND WHERE VISITORS LEAVE THEIR NAMES AND CARDS.

Tourists at Ramona's Marriage Place sought both to take things with them (at first even pieces of the building) and to leave something behind (at first carving their names in the walls). Later they purchased souvenirs and, by the hundreds, left calling cards as markers of their visits. Postcard circa 1915.

The second restoration was every bit as painstaking as the Waterman restoration, but now the cupola that had once graced the front of the adobe, left out in Waterman's restoration, was returned. Of this restoration the California Department of Parks and Recreation proclaimed,

> Great care was taken during restoration to preserve as much of the original structures as possible. In making adobe bricks, for example, the original adobe that had washed off the walls over the years was reclaimed. Cast into new bricks, mortared into place, airgunned to round off the fresh edges, and sandblasted to give the appearance of age, the new bricks blend perfectly with the originals. Indeed, they *are* the originals—only the workmanship is new.[46]

The state, it seems, did not take into consideration the fact that many of the adobe bricks in the building at that time had been made during the Waterman restoration of 1910 (which had been even more extensive), and that therefore these adobes were, in fact, *not* the originals.

For a time the brochures published by the Department of Parks and Recreation attempted to obscure the role the building had served in the Ramona myth. Brochures for Old Town State Historic Park as well as those for the Casa de Estudillo itself printed in the mid-1970s omit reference to the building's association with the novel. For example, the brochure published in 1977 about the Estudillo adobe reads, in part,

> The house was occupied by other members of the [Estudillo] family until 1887 when Salvador Estudillo moved to Los Angeles. He left [the house] in the hands of a caretaker, who sold every remaining item including the roof and floor tiles. Abandoned to the ravages of the elements and time, the casa slowly fell into ruin.
>
> In 1905, the casa was bought by John D. Spreckles, who financed its restoration under the supervision of Architect Hazel Waterman in 1910.
>
> In 1968 it was deeded to the State of California by Mr. Legler Benbough.[47]

By the 1990s, the department was no longer so adamant about erasing the memory of Ramona's Marriage Place, and the sign at the entrance (for which admission was now free) could acknowledge the building's long identification with the fictitious heroine.

Back in 1910, coincident with the opening of the then newly restored Ramona's Marriage Place, journalist and editorialist Edwin H. Clough published a lavishly illustrated volume entitled *Ramona's Marriage Place: The House of Estudillo.* In his book, Clough tells first the romanticized tale of the Estudillo family, then superimposes this history with the fictional account of Ramona and Alessandro's marriage, and then finally layers atop that an account of Waterman's painstakingly "authentic" restoration. Clough wrote,

> With the passing of the real came the more enduring fabric of the unreal, and it is a splendid tribute to the marvelous realism of Helen Hunt Jackson, that as the story of the Estudillos faded into the shifting, uncertain mists of tradition, the legend of Ramona and Alessandro assumed form and presence as palpable as living things of actual history. . . . Thus the romance colors the old chronicle and weaves itself on the fabric of fact until it is impossible to discriminate the true from the false, the real from the unreal. And what matters it, after all?[48]

Indeed, in the case of Ramona's Marriage Place, the actual history of the Estudillo family and their adobe had been so eclipsed by that of the fictitious Ramona that for a time the Estudillos were nearly forgotten. At Ramona's Marriage Place the commercialization of the Ramona myth reached its peak, with the dozens of souvenirs available in Getz's curio shop and myriad postcard images of the landmark mailed all over the nation.

By the early twentieth century Ramona's Marriage Place was so prominent an attraction that domestic tourists included it in their itineraries, alongside attractions that today might seem more significant. In 1937 four girlfriends embarked upon an automobile tour around the United States, stopping at prominent tourist sites all along way, taking photographs of themselves at those sites, as well as purchasing postcards that one of the four would later compile into an album. Along with the unnamed creator of the album, Geneva, Marion, and Gert began their cross-country journey with a stop at the Lincoln Memorial in Springfield, Illinois, after which the four stopped at Carlsbad Caverns, old downtown Albuquerque, Arizona's Petrified Forest, the Grand Canyon, Boulder (now Hoover) Dam, and then Ramona's Marriage Place, before swimming in the Pacific Ocean in Santa Barbara, visiting the (newly opened) Golden Gate Bridge, Stanford University, Yosemite, the Great Salt Lake, Yellowstone, Devil's Tower, the Rapid City Dinosaur Park, Mount Rushmore, the Badlands, and finally Starved Rock State Park back in Illinois.

In the album that documents their expedition, in between postcards of Abraham Lincoln's family home and Old Faithful, the album's creator saw fit to include four postcards from Ramona's Marriage Place, including one of the "Chapel in which Ramona was married" and the "Wishing

Though it was the most commercial of all Ramona attractions, Ramona's Marriage Place became a meaningful part of tourists' itineraries. Now known primarily as Casa de Estudillo, it remains a tourist attraction today. Postcard circa 1935.

well." While most of the photographs and postcards warranted no textual explanation, a few did, such as "Gert driving across the Great Salt Desert." One caption detailed the age, diameter, height, and girth of one of the giant sequoias they visited near Yosemite. For Ramona's Marriage Place, above the postcard of the Wishing Well (which had been constructed during the Waterman restoration) the album's author wrote out the text of the sign seen hanging next to the well on the postcard:

> Quaff ye the waters of Ramona's well
> Good luck they bring and secrets tell,
> Blessed were they by sandaled friar,
> So drink and wish for thy desire.[49]

Ramona's Marriage Place, the most commercial of all Ramona sites, had entered the tourist canon and taken its place alongside the nation's most important natural and historical sites, to be included, with those sites, as important parts of tourists' domestic travels. Though today known as Casa de Estudillo, Ramona's Marriage Place remains a tourist attraction.

CHAPTER SIX

RAMONA'S BIRTHPLACE:
ELUSIVE REMNANT OF AN ATTRACTION

[Ramona] could not quite fancy life without a veranda.
—*Ramona*, 250

N ot all of the sites associated with *Ramona* received as much promotion or left as great a legacy as Rancho Camulos or Ramona's Marriage Place. Indeed, far less is known of Ramona's Birthplace, but it was a touristed attraction. Its elusiveness today lingers as a testimony to the challenge of understanding tourist attractions of the past.

According to the novel, Ramona was born at or near Mission San Gabriel, and postcards of the late nineteenth and early twentieth centuries depict her place of birth near the mission: at a small adobe building that also housed a gift shop. According to George Wharton James, it was "appropriate" that Ramona's birthplace be near the mission, for it was not far from there that Scotsman Hugo Reid had lived, the man said to be the model for Ramona's father (and upon whose daughter's own Scottish and Indian parentage Ramona was said to have been based).[1] By the turn of the century the mission and the small cottage were easily accessible both by Santa Fe trains and by Pacific Electric trolley cars, making the attraction a convenient excursion for tourists visiting the Los Angeles area.[2]

Adjacent to the building that would be built as the Mission Playhouse, where John Steven McGroarty's *Mission Play* would be performed for many seasons (from 1912 to 1929), located near the corner of Ramona and Mission streets, and nearby Mission San Gabriel itself, the small adobe likely had no trouble attracting tourists.[3] Indeed, the play may have been sited at this location expressly because of the property's already demonstrated attraction for Ramona tourists. Souvenirs, in addition to postcards, were available for the adobe, like an oversized (three-inch-diameter) "Indian Head Penny" inscribed on the verso with "Ramona's Birthplace."[4]

Ramona's Birthplace may have been the first commercialized Ramona attraction. This card's sender (Ellen) writes, "I saw this house or adobe last week, every one goes to see it who can but it does not look romantic a bit."

Other postcards note a "Giant Grape Vine" located at "Ramona's Birthplace, San Gabriel, California." Some claim that this grapevine was the oldest in the state, and the one from which mission padres made their wine.[5] One tourist guidebook account notes that visitors to San Gabriel could pay ten cents to enter "Ramona's Home" and view the grapevine.[6]

Of course, the small adobe near Mission San Gabriel was never seriously touted as Ramona's home, and never even came close to competition with the ranchos Camulos or Guajome for this title. Rather, as seems to have been the case with the San Diego trolleys bound for Ramona's Marriage Place, the title "Ramona's Home" had likely become a kind of regional shorthand for a *Ramona*-related landmark of any kind.

Despite this confusion (whether deliberate or not), other sources kept the distinction between Ramona's home and her birthplace clearer. The program for Virginia Calhoun's 1905 stage production of *Ramona* noted Mission San Gabriel "Fifth Station on El Camino Real" as "The Birthplace of Ramona."[7]

The adobe lasted through much of the twentieth century. As late as 1941 the guidebook *Los Angeles: A Guide to the City and Its Environs,* compiled by members of the Writers' Program of U.S. Works Projects Administration in southern California, noted that at the corner of Mission Drive,

Ramona's Home   San Gabriel, California

This building, adjacent to the theater built for John Steven McGroarty's "Mission Play," was long identified as Ramona's Birthplace. Postcard circa 1920.

adjoining the Mission Playhouse, was a building called the "Grapevine Adobe." But the guide described a "sign [that] advertises it as the Birthplace of Ramona, vying for attention with a neon dine-and-dance sign set incongruously over the deeply recessed door in the adobe wall."[8] By then, in San Gabriel, Ramona was vying for attention with more contemporary attractions.

Today the small adobe is gone; it no longer stands near the re-restored mission. But the connection to Ramona lives on. As late as 1986, a gold panning tool on display at Mission San Gabriel noted on its descriptive tag that it was from "Ramona's Birthplace." Whether the reference was to the small adobe or to the mission itself is no longer clear. And, though in recent years the roadways in front of the mission have been rerouted, the street corner remains that of Mission Drive, Junipero Serra Drive, and Ramona Street.

The mission retains its connection to Ramona as well. One woman who visited in 1894 noted on the back of a photograph of her party taken there, "Ramona once worshipped in this Mission."

CHAPTER SEVEN

"REAL" RAMONAS

For serious study or for deep thought [Ramona] had no
vocation. She was a simple, joyous, gentle, clinging, faithful nature, like a clear brook, rippling along in the sun.
—*Ramona*, 34

It should come as no surprise, considering the search for Ramona landmarks, that a thorough investigation was conducted by late nineteenth-
and early twentieth-century Ramonaphiles into the origins of the character Ramona herself.[1] Of course, Jackson's book was first and foremost a
work of fiction, but like many writers the author wove descriptions of actual people, places, and events clearly (and purposefully) into her tale. Just
as there was no "real" Ramona's Home or Ramona's Marriage Place, there
was no one "real Ramona," but those insisting on finding the sources for
Jackson's inspiration could point to several. A strong claim could be—and
for more than one hundred years has been—made that the character of
Ramona was a composite of several living persons, blended together in
the author's imagination. As George Wharton James put it: "a score of
isolated and unconnected incidents in the lives of a score of different
individuals are brought together, and all attributed to the one fictitious
character Ramona."[2] But such seemingly simple explanations did not stop
the search for the one Real Ramona.

Perhaps, one friend of Jackson's argued, the author found her vision for
the heroine in the picture that she is said to have kept on her desk while
writing the novel. Sarah Woolsey, under the pen name of Susan Coolidge,
wrote in her introduction to the two-volume Monterey edition of *Ramona*
that on Jackson's desk stood

an unframed photograph after Dante Rossetti,—two heads, a man's and
a woman's, set in a nimbus of cloud, with a strange and beautiful regard

Romanticized imagery was used to represent
Ramona on product labels, advertisements, calen-
dars, and sheet music, as this version of the song
"Ramona" from a 1903 edition shows.

and meaning in their eyes. They were exactly her idea of what Ramona and Alessandro looked like, she said.[3]

Certainly such a romantic, pre-Raphaelite image is consistent with Jackson's description of the character of Ramona. But in addition to such comparatively lofty inspiration, after Jackson's death those interested in the novel (tourists, boosters, and others) found a plethora of local people who resembled Ramona in one way or another. Numerous aspects of the character's life made a number of women contenders for the title of the "Real Ramona," whether they simply bore the name, had similar parentage, or had any of a number of life incidents that mirrored those of the heroine in the novel.

Some traced Jackson's inspiration to use the name Ramona to Ramona Place Wolf, the part Indian, part African American wife of Alsacian Louis Wolf, owner of the Temecula store (which also figures in the novel). Jackson met Wolf on her travels in southern California and carried on a correspondence with her after leaving the state.[4]

Others maintained that it was at the residence of Mr. and Mrs. J. De Barth Shorb of San Marino that Jackson heard and became smitten with the "liquid sound" of the name Ramona. Shorb and his father-in-law, Benjamin "Don Benito" Wilson, were prominent developers, and the Shorbs, in the late nineteenth century, were among the most prominent southern California families.[5] Don Benito, an Anglo-American, had married the (Californio) daughter of Don Bernardo and Doña Ramona Yorba of the Rancho Cañon de Santa Ana (in what is now Orange County) and had served as U.S. Indian Agent for southern California in 1852. According to Shorb biographer Midge Sherwood, Don Benito Wilson's work had been influential to Jackson, and the Shorbs still had Don Benito's papers in their possession when the Coronels arranged for Jackson to meet them. But, as Sherwood tells the Shorb story, during Jackson's visit their seven-and-a-half-year-old daughter was unable to contain her curiosity about the "famous author" and so entered the room where her parents were entertaining. Jackson asked the child her name and, upon learning it, gleefully remarked, "Ramona—what a lovely name! . . . I have been searching for a name for the heroine of my next book, a novel about Indians. Ramona she shall be!" Unfortunately, since Jackson was not yet seriously considering an Indian novel, Sherwood's claim cannot be true.[6] Just the same, if the meeting itself did in fact occur, it *is* possible that Ramona Shorb was the source of the heroine's name.

One woman, Maria Ignacia Reid, had the half-Scottish, half-Indian parentage that Ramona had in the novel. Like Ramona, Ignacia was also the daughter of a Scotsman and at-least-sometime sailor—in Ignacia's case, it was not Angus Phail but Hugo Reid. Reid, so it was said, had had an ill-fated love affair in Mexico and then subsequently married the first woman he found with the same name as his former beloved (Victoria), this time an Indian "princess" raised at Mission San Gabriel. Another account of Reid's life, one more likely based in fact, contends that Reid (first a shopkeeper, only later a seafarer) fell in love with Victoria Bartolomea, the daughter of a Gabrieleño chief, though she was married to another man. Amid a flurry of gossip, Reid left for Mexico, but returned a year later upon hearing that Victoria's husband had died. Marrying the widow, Reid and his bride then settled in San Gabriel where, like Ramona, their daughter Ignacia was born.[7]

Another woman, Blanca Yndart, was said to be the granddaughter of a seafarer and had been left at Rancho Camulos to be cared for by Señora del Valle—just as Ramona was left at the Rancho Moreno. Both of her parents, however, had been of Spanish origin (it was another young girl in the care of Señora del Valle, Guadalupe Ridley, who shared Ramona's Native American parentage). But, in addition to being left to be cared for at a southern California rancho, Yndart was like Ramona in another key respect: for many years Señora del Valle secretly kept for the girl a chest full of jewels, rebozos, and damasks (referred to in the Ramona-related literature as the "Ramona jewels"), which had been collected by her grandfather and, as in the novel, were to be kept for her until she married.[8]

Just as the del Valles of Camulos could claim a "Real Ramona" on their property, so could the Couts family of Rancho Guajome, who claimed that Ramona was based on an Indian girl once in their employ named Matutini, who had eloped with another Indian, forsaking the civilized comforts of Guajome to return to what was termed the "wild life of the hills." Jackson, who may have stayed at Guajome and was alleged to have met Matutini before her elopement, was said to have been fascinated by the strength of the girl's love.[9]

And there were still others who staked claims to Real Ramona status. On 7 June 1897 the *Los Angeles Times* reported that while "it is popularly supposed that the original heroine of the book is dead . . . this is not so. 'Ramona' yet lives and graces the beautiful home of her American husband, a well-known lawyer in San Diego."[10] But no further identification was given for the woman or her husband.

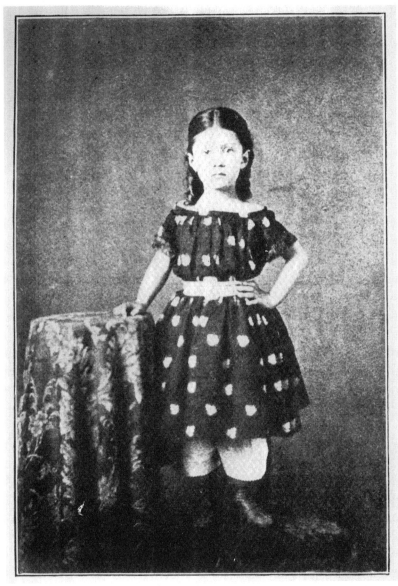

Blanca Yndart, indicated by some to be the "Real Ramona," shared aspects of Ramona's own story, including a chest of jewels. This photograph appeared in The True Story of Ramona *(1914).*

In the midst of so many claims, one might guess that the volume published in 1900 entitled *The Real Ramona of Helen Hunt Jackson's Famous Novel* would be the best authority on the matter and might actually clear up some of the mystery. Instead, however, D.A. Hufford's little book serves not only to add to the confusion about the real identity of the heroine, but adds also to the negative racial stereotyping of Native Americans against which Jackson had labored. Hufford asserted that the Real Ramona was a woman by the name of Lugardo Sandoval, wife of a Native American named Ramon Corallez who had been shot for horse-stealing, just as Alessandro was in the novel. In the fourth edition Hufford included five different images of the woman he identified as "Mrs. Machado" or "Ramona" (she remarried after Corallez's murder), but they are unmistakably four different women. Drawing both of the widely heralded Homes of Ramona into his story, Hufford claimed that Mrs. (Corallez) Machado (then Miss Sandoval) had been in the service of the Coutses of Guajome and was transferred to service at Rancho Camulos where, during sheep-shearing time, she met Corallez. As Hufford put it, the couple went on to experience "all the pitiful episodes that Ramona and Alessandro experienced."[11]

But Hufford went further in his claims, asserting that he had had the good fortune to interview his "Ramona," describing her as *greasy and slovenly.* According to Hufford, this Ramona was not only unattractive but also inarticulate (at least in English), for after a "generous donation" from Hufford of tobacco, rolling papers, handkerchiefs, and beads, Mrs. Machado spoke to him about her life: "I trouble much have, heap suffer."[12]

Of all those identified as the "Real Ramona," only one seems to have actually made some money from the title.[13] Ramona Lubo was a Cahuilla

Ramona Lubo shared a tragic part of the fictional Ramona's life: the murder of her husband before her eyes. Postcard circa 1910.

woman who married a Native American man named Juan Diego.[14] Like Alessandro, Diego was a sheep-shearer known for periodic episodes of madness. As in the novel, one of his spells drove him to accidentally take the horse of a white man, one Sam Temple (the fictional character's name in *Ramona* is Jim Farrar). And, as in *Ramona,* Temple followed Diego to the humble home he shared with Lubo and their small children and there he shot Diego several times before Lubo's eyes. Temple later claimed Diego had a knife, but Lubo insisted he had none. Since Lubo was Indian, however, she was not invited to testify at Temple's hearing. Temple, who claimed self-defense, was found not guilty.

For his own part, Temple was never particularly repentant about the killing. Once his fame as "the man who killed Alessandro" spread, he even planned to make appearances at the World's Columbian Exposition in Chicago in 1893 and at the Louis and Clark Exposition in Saint Louis in 1904. In the end, Temple, realizing that his fame was the result of negative publicity, changed his mind. The gun he used in the killing, however, did make the trip and was displayed at the Chicago fair.[15]

Helen Hunt Jackson, for her part, had known of Juan Diego's murder for she described it in her *Report on the Condition and Needs of the Mission Indians.*[16] In a letter to the editor of the *Atlantic Monthly* Jackson had written, "A Cahuilla Indian was shot two years ago exactly as Alessandro is—and his wife's name was Ramona and I never knew this last fact until Ramona was half written. What do you think of that for a coincidence?"[17]

After Diego's death Lubo continued to live in Cahuilla, eventually near the cemetery where her husband was buried. The children she and Diego had all died young, but she later had a son, Condino, with a white man named Hopkins to whom she was apparently never married. Living in relative destitution, Lubo earned her living washing clothes, weaving baskets, and working in the local apricot harvest. Because she was the wife of Juan Diego, "Alessandro," and therefore, in the eyes of many, the Real Ramona, soon tourists and reporters were visiting her often enough that she could use her affiliation with fiction to supplement her income.[18] The *Hemet News* reported in 1913 that sewer contractor J. F. McMullen had purchased her baskets at a "fancy price"—one demanded not only by her basketmaking skills but also her Real Ramona reputation.[19] Despite this, Lubo, along with many other Cahuillas, lived an existence far different from that of the aristocratic fictional heroine, always teetering on the brink of poverty.

Most of those who wrote of their encounters with Lubo, though, were disappointed in her manner and appearance, expecting her to look and act more like the beautiful and graceful young woman described in the novel. Though today their comments on the poverty- and tragedy-stricken Lubo sound offensive, at the time it likely seemed important to distinguish her from the romanticized images encountered in the novel. For those who visited Rancho Camulos or Guajome, the financial troubles plaguing these families most often went unseen and the fictional world of *Ramona* could easily be indulged in and sustained during the visit. An encounter with Lubo, however, did not allow the traveler to sustain such a romanticized notion and so had to be separated from it. Those who wrote of their encounters did this by insisting, in racist manner, that it was Lubo's full-blooded "Indianness" that was her downfall—Ramona in the novel, it will be remembered, was only half Indian and was raised by and later returned to an aristocratic "Spanish" family. Ramona Lubo had no such "good fortune." Typical of these hostile accounts of Lubo, the *San Diego Union* reported in 1898 that

> those who have read Helen Hunt Jackson's *Ramona* will be interested to learn that the heroine of that story is a resident of Cahuilla. . . . Ramona herself is about as ugly a looking squaw as one accustomed to visiting rancherias ever sees, in spite of the romantic robe of refinement super-kindly thrown over her squatty shape by Mrs. Jackson. *Ramona* rests gracefully on the finest tables in the most gorgeous homes of the land, but Ramona would rather sit on the ground in a scant calico dress of the unwashed pattern and sip frijoles and cheap coffee.[20]

Another reporter, this one writing for the *Riverside Morning Enterprise* just one year later, sought not only to distinguish Ramona Lubo from the character in the novel, but, in fact, to make her seem generally lowly. The reporter wrote,

> The other day I saw Ramona—the real Ramona— . . . of the story. She still lives at Cahuilla. . . . Her home is a poor, wretched, wooden shanty, looking more like a large-sized dilapidated dry goods box than a human habitation. . . . While it may shock many of the preconceived notions of those who expect this Ramona to fully comport with the ideal Ramona of "H.H.'s" novel, it is only truth to say that neither in person, face, mentality or morals is Ramona Lugo *[sic]* the being we have learned to love. That such ideal characters are found among the Indians, twenty years of close study and observation of many Indian tribes compels me to believe. They

are just as common as are the ideal characters of novelists among the white race. But, alas, the Imogens and Evangelines, and Little Dorritts and David Copperfield's Agnesses, and Diana Vernons, and Lauras and Beatrices and Sir Galahads are not every-day characters in the sphere of action of most white people, any more than ideal Ramonas are so numerous as to be plucked from every Indian genealogical bush.

No, alas! The real Ramona of this portion of the tale, the wife of Juan Diego, has the squat, plump, shapeless body of a wellfed, but coarse and vulgar animal. Her face expresses neither fine feelings, refinement, culture (not even a rude Indian culture) nor morality.[21]

Just as contemporary commentators described Lubo in this derogatory and negative manner, neither did they see it as clever on Lubo's part to supplement her income by her notoriety; rather, to them, it made her opportunistic. The *Los Angeles Evening Express* reported on 29 February 1892, "[T]he heroine [of *Ramona*], an Indian squaw, who still lives and makes her living by letting her picture be taken by the photogravure process, is a dissolute old hag, toothless and wrinkled."[22]

Indeed, pejorative comments about Lubo's appearance were the norm, and the fact that she charged photographers for taking her picture only further solidified these reporters' derogatory portrayals. One, writing for the *Los Angeles Times*, commented,

> The heroine of that splendid novel which has already become a classic still lives around one of the Indian villages. She is a big, fat squaw.
>
> She is intensely proud of the fact that she is the original Ramona and has to "be seen" financially before she will allow her photograph to be taken.[23]

If Lubo herself was able to capitalize on her fame in connection with the novel, so did others capitalize on it for her. Lubo's image appeared on several different postcards, featuring images of her in front of her tule-reed cabin, or even of her kneeling on the ground in the Cahuilla cemetery weeping before her husband's grave.[24] While it is not known whether Lubo benefited financially from these postcard images of her, she *was* hired to promote various enterprises with her persona. The *San Jacinto Register* noted on 23 January 1908,

> Ramona, the heroine of Helen Hunt Jackson's book of that name, has completed the term of her engagement with Captain Antonio Apache, at the Indian Village at Eastlake Park, Los Angeles. . . .

Ramona weeping at her husbands grave, Cal.

Ramona Lubo became so thoroughly identified with the fictional heroine that she was able to supplement her income by having her photograph taken (though postcards like this one, from 1909, likely did not earn her royalties).

Apache had her hired for exhibition at the Indian Village and her presence was widely advertised by posters and by streamers on the street cars of the city, as well as in the papers. While many were skeptical as to her being the genuine Ramona, of Helen Hunt Jackson's book, she proved a drawing card for the Village and thousands of people went there to see her.[25]

Beyond advertising events in other parts of southern California, Lubo became an agent for local publicity in her area as well: the *Hemet News* announced,

Hemet—"The Heart of Ramonaland"—will have a notable and unique booth at the Southern California Fair next week. . . . The chief exhibit is to be the original Ramona, now about 75 years of age, and a resident of the Cahuilla reservation. Another Ramona, intended to personify the Ramona of forty years ago, will be Miss Rose Costo.[26]

Though Lubo is said to have requested that someone accompany her in the exhibit, since her appearance had not been entirely pleasing to others, the Hemet Chamber of Commerce (which was in charge of the exhibit) may not have been willing to take the chance on Lubo's appearance alone, and so added Miss Costo to the exhibit. The *News* reviewed the exhibit a few days later:

The original Ramona is attracting general interest at the Hemet booth. . . . Mrs. Ramona Diego is the Indian woman about which the sentiment and romance of the great novel centers, and it was a fine conception of the committee to have her at the fair. Little less in interest is the personification of the Ramona of the Helen Hunt Jackson period by Miss Rose Costo of Valle Vista. Miss Costo is a striking type of Indian beauty, and there is much favorable comment on this feature of the Hemet booth.[27]

Lubo also appeared in the Hemet booth at the San Bernardino National Orange Show in 1922; this was her last public appearance. Her son, Condino Hopkins, told a reporter from the *Los Angeles Times* that she "took sick" after being exhibited at the show. Tragically, Lubo never recovered from this illness, and she died on 20 July 1922. Lubo was buried at the small Cahuilla cemetery near her husband and both graves were marked by small wooden crosses, as were other graves in the cemetery.[28]

Despite her death, interest in Ramona Lubo continued. And now, because of her death, she could be interred in the landscape as another Ramona

Ramona Lubo, posing as "the original Ramona," beside the young Rose Costo, the "personification of the Ramona of the Helen Hunt Jackson period."

landmark, visitable by tourists, without the contradictions previously felt by her appearance and living conditions.

Organizers of the Ramona Pageant, an outdoor dramatization of the novel, which commenced its annual performances in 1923, had hoped to be able to use Lubo's notoriety to advertise the pageant. Local resident Irwin E. Farrar, chairman of the Committee on Publicity and Public Relations, wrote in his typescript autobiography that "many of the early means of gaining publicity were novel and out of the ordinary" and that it was he who had engaged Lubo to work the Orange Show "largely to advertise the play."[29] Lubo's untimely demise prevented the pageant from exhibiting her for publicity during the pageant's actual run, but in 1931 the Ramona Pageant Association announced plans to erect suitable monuments to Lubo and Diego at the Cahuilla cemetery replacing the "weatherbeaten wooden crosses." The Los Angeles Times reporter who covered the story noted that "each year during the pageant season, hundreds of Californians interested in historical episodes of the Ramona story make pilgrimages to the reservation to see the graves of the Indian heroine and her ill-fated lover."[30]

Letters from memorial plaque and stone makers arrived at pageant headquarters from across the country. J. C. Deagan, Inc., makers of Deagan Tower Chimes—The Memorial Sublime, wrote to suggest the "dignity of golden-voiced tower chimes pealing forth Spanish love" at various times during the day and even suggested that "[t]he song 'Ramona' would be especially appropriate rendered on the Chimes."[31] Despite cooperation from members of the Cahuilla tribe (who were given free tickets to attend the 1931 opening performance of the pageant) in the project, President of the Ramona Pageant Association Edward Poorman responded to the various memorial companies that the project would have to be deferred since "contributions to [the] fund have not been as great as . . . anticipated, due possibly to the financial depression."[32]

Interest in marking the graves did not flag, however, and on 10 April 1938 the Los Angeles Times headlined "Ramona Honored at Unveiling of Monument on Reservation." The headstone, designed and carved by local residents and topped by a large, stone cross, read simply "RAMONA. DIED JULY 21, 1922." The grave of Juan Diego, however, was not marked by a stone until 1956. His stone, one without a cross, now reads "JUAN DIEGO. 'ALESSANDRO.' RAMONA'S MARTYRED SPOUSE. DIED MARCH 24, 1883."[33] In death, Diego and Lubo's real lives were virtually erased to allow the fiction of the novel to flourish in the minds of those who journeyed to the remote site.

Years after Ramona Lubo's death, and decades after that of her husband, Juan Diego, new monuments were erected over their graves, memorializing them as the fictional characters Ramona and Alessandro.

By 1973, however, tribespeople at the reservation announced that the graves and the cemetery would be off-limits to the public: overzealous visitors had been "chipping away bits of the gravestones as souvenirs." In this Native American cemetery, as at other locations designated as Ramona landmarks, some members of the public were hardly respectful.[34]

Both during her lifetime and after her death, Ramona Lubo's notoriety extended to her son Condino Hopkins as well. On 8 March 1907 the *Los Angeles Times* headlined, "Bridegroom Is Ramona's Son. Wealthy Youth Takes a San Jacinto Bride." The article that followed stressed both Hopkins's Indianness as well as his success in the Anglo world, something that could not be claimed for Lubo. Describing Hopkins as a "stalwart Indian youth aged 20, and whose form reflects the sinewy strength of life in the wild," the accompanying photograph showed him in fine (Anglo) formal wear as if dressed for the wedding. Despite emphasizing "instruction" Hopkins received from his "foster father," one "Judge Hopkins," in "ranching and stock raising" as well as the fact that he owned "several gem mines" and a copper mine, the article still spoke of him in a condescending tone, noting that "if Condino attends to business he will be as well-to-do as his white neighbors."

After his mother's death, Hopkins grew weary of hearing of publicity for the Ramona Pageant without sharing in the profits and, in 1927, he wrote to the San Jacinto–Hemet Chamber of Commerce,

> I have noticed in the papers that the exhibition known as the Ramona Pageant is to be presented again in what is called the "Ramona bowl," near Hemet, during this present spring. Although this pageant is supposed to be in honor of the Indian woman who was immortalized in Mrs. Jackson's famous story, it is well-known that it is primarily a publicity scheme on the part of the real estate interests in your locality. I am the son of this famous Indian woman, and I wish to call your attention to the fact that the use of her name in connection with this enterprise is entirely unauthorized by me. In view of the fact that her name is thus commercialized, with the proceeds of this exhibition netting thousands of dollars each season, it would seem to me that it would be no more than right and proper for her heirs to share in such receipts.[35]

Despite his attempts to share in the pageant's receipts, Hopkins appears to have been silenced by the response of Edward Poorman of the Chamber:

> For your information I would say that the Ramona Pageant is put on . . . for the purpose of preserving the history and romance of California, and creating an interest in the beautiful Indian history that we have here, thus calling the attention of the outside world to the fact that the scenes of Helen Hunt Jackson's immortal book *Ramona* were laid in this section.
>
> The Ramona Pageant is produced by the Chamber of Commerce and is a non-profit vehicle in all its details. There has been more money invested in producing this beautiful play than has ever been received from it. Therefore, from a financial standpoint, it becomes a liability to the people of this valley, rather than an asset.[36]

Though Hopkins was not able to glean any financial benefit from his matrilineage, he was interviewed about his mother's life. Speaking to the *Los Angeles Times* in 1922, soon after his mother's death, Hopkins sketched Lubo's biography to resemble as closely as possible that of the fictional Ramona. For example, he claimed she was born near Mission San Gabriel (as was the fictional Ramona), that she lived with a family named

Moreno, and had a horse named Baba (like the fictional Ramona). He first introduces Lubo's husband as Juan Diego but already in the same sentence as Diego's introduction begins referring to him only as "Alessandro."[37]

When Hopkins was interviewed again twenty years later, his mother's biography had changed considerably. He now stated that his mother's life had become "hopelessly entangled with fiction." He now insisted that she was not born at San Gabriel, or married at Old Town San Diego, and that she never had any jewels or wealth. Hopkins's revised biography of his mother did include one new point of correlation with the novel: he claimed that the Felipe of the novel was, in fact, his father, Mr. Hopkins.[38]

When Condino Hopkins died in 1951 the *Los Angeles Herald Examiner* saw fit to report the "death of the last living child of the heroine of Helen Hunt Jackson's novel, *Ramona*."[39] Even "Ramona's son," it seems, could not entirely escape the fictional past that had come to eclipse his mother's life.

CHAPTER EIGHT

THE STAGING OF A NOVEL

[It was] the afternoon of one of those midsummer days
of which California has so many in spring.
—*Ramona*, 36

On Friday, 13 April 1923, when the Ramona Pageant opened at the Ramona Bowl natural amphitheater outside the remote Riverside County town of Hemet, spectators trudged up the steep hillside, finding a place to sit on the "soft side of a rock," to witness the first outdoor dramatic incarnation of Jackson's novel.[1] It was to become an annual event. But where ranchos Camulos and Guajome had been reached mainly by rail, and Ramona's Marriage Place and Birthplace were accessible by streetcar, the Ramona Pageant would build its business by relying on the new tourists, those in their automobiles.

The idea of presenting the pageant in the San Jacinto Valley had arisen as early as 1906, and in 1913 the *San Jacinto Register* announced that the pageant would take the place of the valley's annual carnival, an event that had itself been superseded by the Riverside County Fair. Residents of the valley had long recognized that Helen Hunt Jackson laid many of the Indian scenes of her novel here (those taking place after Ramona's elopement), and the notion of a pageant, it was hoped, would capitalize on this fact, drawing Ramona-seekers from all over the nation. The 1913 promoters even envisioned bringing the "original 'Ramona'" (Ramona Lubo) to the pageant for the "curiously inclined" to see, but Lubo's death less than one year before the pageant's opening prevented that from becoming reality.[2]

It was in 1922, near the end of a booming era for outdoor pageantry, that members of the Hemet Valley Chamber of Commerce began to discuss the idea of an annual Ramona Pageant in earnest.[3] Late that year they enlisted the services of renowned pageant author and director Garnet Holme. With such pageants as the Hollywood Pilgrimage Play, the Desert

A large crowd gathers to watch the Ramona Pageant, circa 1931. Pageant Files, Ramona Bowl Museum; reprinted by permission.

Play, and the Mountain Play already under his belt, he was now hired to adapt *Ramona* to pageant form.

Attempting to avoid the excessive costs incurred with the large cast needed for a pageant, and to cultivate support in the community, Holme proposed that the cast of the pageant be made up, as much as possible, of local actors—provided this did not weaken the production by, as Holme put it, "including those who are not skilled enough to bear the principal roles." A tradition soon developed that only the roles of Ramona and Alessandro would be played by paid professional actors from outside the area: with over one hundred roles to be filled (a number that would swell to over four hundred by the end of the century), plus crew positions, a sizable volunteer corps was built up from the Hemet and neighboring San Jacinto communities.[4]

Much of the preparation for the first pageant involved making the selected site, called the Ramona Bowl, look like the scenes from the novel. Since all the action and all the scenes had to take place outdoors, the setting and scenery were critical. Helping in the effort, the Boy Scouts of Hemet cut trails and cleared brush while members of the American Legion erected a large cross, resembling the ones at the fictional Señora Moreno's home, on a hill above the bowl. And for the centerpiece and focal point of the "stage," pageant staff built a replica, not of the home of the Morenos as described in the novel, but of Rancho Camulos. So established was Camulos as the Home of Ramona by the 1920s that reference to the set in the pageant brochures could describe "Act One: 'The Camulos Ranch,'" omitting any reference to the fictional Rancho Moreno of the novel without confusion.[5]

In 1923, shortly before the opening of the first pageant, the Chambers of Commerce of the two rival communities of Hemet and San Jacinto united as one in support and promotion of the pageant and the mutual benefit they hoped would be derived from it. Attracting visitors to this rather remote location in the mountains between Los Angeles and San Diego in a time before mass automobile tourism was a challenge the Chambers were up to, at times using what Irwin E. Farrar, chairman of the Committee on Publicity and Public Relations, referred to as "novel and out-of-the-ordinary" publicity techniques.[6]

Out of the ordinary indeed: The newly united Chamber of Commerce

Publicity has been key to the Ramona Pageant's success, including novel means like the oxcart shown here featuring placards promoting the pageant on its sides and a young woman appearing as "Ramona" inside, distributing handbills. Pageant Files, Ramona Bowl Museum; reprinted by permission.

built a "mission ox cart" which, according to a newspaper article, toured the streets of southern California towns and cities. The cart was drawn by two oxen and carried a young lady who waved at passersby. The display was said to evoke "awe and admiration" in its viewers who were "fully convinced that it [the cart] must be at least one hundred years old" despite its large placards advertising the pageant.[7]

In 1923, the first year of publicity for the pageant, the cart passenger was none other than Rose Costo, the same young Native American woman who had exemplified "the Ramona of the Helen Hunt Jackson period" along-side Ramona Lubo in the Hemet exhibit at the National Orange Show. Her job was to "impersonate the famed Ramona" while passing out handbills as she rolled along in the cart. The following year Alberta Raynor rode in the cart, accompanied by her father, Burdette Raynor, head of the Chamber of Commerce, and ox driver Luke Therault.[8]

As the cart rolled slowly through the region, newspapers from all over southern California covered its progress with headlines like "Romance Follows Trail of Ox Cart Trio Through City." The accompanying articles emphasized the romantic and historic image of the vehicle: "Yesterday afternoon the oxcart with its lazy oxen dragged into town bringing with it a breath of old Spain."[9] Other reports were more detailed:

> Bringing the atmosphere of the old romantic days of California history with them three travellers arrived in Fullerton yesterday. . . . [I]t was [their] mode of travel that carried the essence of romance and attracted hundreds of Fullertonians. They were travelling in an ox cart . . . of the type used in the old days when natives travelled the rough rutty roads of Southern California between missions. . . .
>
> The trip through Southern California is an annual pilgrimage for the trio. Raynor is the secretary of the Chamber of Commerce in Hemet California, his daughter is his assistant and Therault is said to be the best oxen driver in the entire state. It is said that he can make a team of oxen do anything with the exception of playing cornet duets.
>
> The travellers have been making a tour of Southern California in behalf of the Ramona Pageant to be present[ed] at the Ramona Bowl near Hemet.[10]

The team toured cities including Riverside (where a lengthy stop with photo opportunities was made at the Mission Inn), Los Angeles, Santa Monica, Pasadena, and Long Beach. However, even expert driver Therault could not stop the hoof-and-mouth-disease epidemic that struck southern California in the spring of 1924 and forced the cart's quarantine at Glendale. The use of the ox cart as a means of publicity was discontinued after 1924.[11]

Other means of publicity were less unique but also less problematic for pageant promoters. The publicity staff developed close ties with major area newspapers like the *Los Angeles Times,* whose reporters were given complimentary passes to the pageant in return for free publicity. In 1930 one of the pageant staff (who was also editor of the *Hemet News*) wrote to *Times* columnist Lee Shippey,

> Thanks a lot for your very generous mention of the Ramona Pageant in your column last week.
>
> I hope it will be possible for you to bring your family and friends to the play this year and it will be a pleasure for me to take care of you in the matter of tickets if you will let me know your requirements.[12]

The *Times* staff was most cooperative in promoting the pageant. *Times* columnist Harry Carr (whose family had first studied California by reading *Ramona*) wrote to pageant staff during the depths of the Depression, "As you know without my saying so, I shall be always only too glad to help you in any way possible to put over the Ramona Pageant. It is one of the most valuable things that California has to offer the tourist."[13]

The *Times* was able to help the pageant through some difficult straits and pageant staff did not hide their gratitude. Ramona Pageant Association President Edward Poorman wrote to *Times* publisher Harry Chandler,

> We wish to take this opportunity to express to you our thanks and appreciation for what you and the *Los Angeles Time[s]* did in saving the Ramona Pageant from financial loss this year.
>
> Due to heavy rains and postponed performances, we were in a fair way to lose heavily, but the publicity given to us through the Times was the means of getting the news of the postponed performances to the people of Southern California. . . .
>
> [W]e feel that the *Los Angeles Times* just wants to have us succeed.[14]

But the pageant staff did not rely on the *Los Angeles Times* and the oxcart alone. Posters, handbills, and flyers were sent in large quantities to the Chambers of Commerce of numerous southern California communities for distribution with accompanying free passes for Chamber staffs. In 1936 the pageant's cover letter to "Secretaries of Chambers of Commerce of So. California" read in part,

*Attractive and colorful posters advertised the pageant, such as this one from 1928.
Pageant Files, Ramona Bowl Museum; reprinted by permission.*

Dear Friend,

This letter is to call your attention to the thirteenth annual Ramona
Pageant. . . .

The Ramona Pageant has gained world-wide recognition for its
beauty and simplicity, for its interesting legendary-historical story of the
Indian people who lived here and for the magnificent setting of the bowl
where it is presented.

. . . [I]t has been the splendid cooperation given us by the many organizations of Southern California which has resulted in our enterprise
being so successful.[15]

The various Chambers of Commerce responded enthusiastically, offering
to place window cards and distribute leaflets for the pageant. Secretary
Myers of the Glendale Chamber's response, though perhaps a bit colloquial,
is typical:

Dear Sir,

Mighty glad to learn that you are going to put on the pageant again this
year and anything we may be able to do as a help you may rest assured we
shall be pleased to do.[16]

Located in a remote area with very limited rail service, the pageant relied on the increasing popularity of automobile tourism, as well as on support from local mass-transit companies who were willing to operate bus
service during pageant weekends. In order to reach large numbers of newly
arrived motor tourists, the pageant secured mention in the guidebook
published by the All Year Club of Southern California's which, by 1932,
was distributed free of charge by state officers at the border to "[e]very
out-of-state motor car entering southern California for a vacation stay."[17]

The pageant also relied on the solid support of the Automobile Club
of Southern California.[18] Each of the thirty-four branch offices displayed
window cards and distributed folders and postcards. Issues of the club
magazine *Touring Topics* ran articles on the pageant, and the club, known
for its maps, distributed location maps of Hemet to southern California
papers for their use, helping to make the pageant's location more easily accessible to automobilists. The return for these services was the customary
complimentary tickets for staff members—though they sometimes had to
be asked for—the manager of the news department wrote to the pageant's
Los Angeles publicist,

The girls in the office have become so interested in the publicity on the affair that they are all anxious to attend, and I think they would feel well rewarded if you would send along some evidences of appreciation in the form of complimentary tickets so that they could give their beaux a party—they furnish the tickets if the beaux furnish the auto and gasoline.[19]

Even southern California residents like the Auto Club office staff were drawn to Ramona-related attractions, and the automobile made many of them both accessible and attractive. But despite the "girls" at the Auto Club and their access to cars, in the 1920s not all in southern California were so privileged. Perhaps one of the most valuable connections for the pageant was that with Motor Transit Company and Pacific Electric Railway Company. Both operated bus and trolley service between various southern California points and the pageant, running special trains and buses on pageant days. Without this support the pageant likely could not have survived, but the transit companies did well too: Motor Transit purchased pageant tickets at a cut-rate price and sold them to tourists as part of a special excursion fare that included the bus ride on a Motor Transit coach.

Both companies adorned their trains and buses, inside and out, with posters advertising the pageant and also distributed free folders and post-cards on board. In 1930 Motor Transit distributed 20,000 folders for the pageant. In 1934 two hundred Pacific Electric cars carried pageant banners, and each banner also bore the inscription "Go via Pacific Electric or Motor Transit." In addition, Pacific Electric, at its downtown subway terminal, displayed the "Ramona book," a nine-foot-tall, rotating advertisement for the pageant.[20]

Much of this publicity sought to tie the San Jacinto Valley region to the novel as closely as possible. By the 1920s so many places in southern California had become accepted as Ramona landmarks that acknowledging such connection lent credibility to the young pageant.

The 1925 pageant program described the "sister cities of Hemet and San Jacinto" as lying in the "center of 'Ramonaland' where hill and valley are full of memories of the two lovers." This label of authenticity was heightened by the pageant's location in a region where, at least in pageant publicity, not just individual landmarks, but the entire area claimed an association with the novel: "The Ramona country of Riverside county in which the play is staged is a mecca for sightseers the year round and few localities on the globe offer so great a field for the lover of romance of the days of the past."[21]

If not claiming general or specific references to the novel, publicity for the pageant (and thus for the sparsely populated Hemet–San Jacinto area in general) could at least allude to the novel's (and the region's) romantic evocation of the past. According to the *Arrowhead Magazine* (distributed free on all Union Pacific trains),

the presentation of the pageant is unique in that, while the audience enjoys the comforts of a modern concrete amphitheater, no artificial properties of any kind are used in the presentation and the spectators are given the illusion that they are really seeing events of decades ago transpire before their eyes.[22]

Though the novel actually mentioned real locations in the Hemet–San Jacinto area (Saboba, Temecula, and Mount San Jacinto), newspaper reports and promotions about the pageant often exaggerated these connections and the pageant staff, in the early days, allowed such erroneous reports to flourish unchecked.[23] The *Los Angeles Times* reported, "The production . . . has particular significance because of the fact that it was in old San Jacinto that Helen Hunt Jackson wrote the greater part of her romantic novel of California Indian and Spanish life."[24] In fact, of course, Jackson had written the novel entirely in New York City.

Other spurious claims for the pageant and its location involved elements of the novel itself. Another reporter insisted,

Mildred Brewster, widely known dramatic artist, who has been brought here to take the role of Ramona, will wear quaint and colorful costumes, the exact duplicates of those worn by the original Ramona in the early days when she was the accepted queen of the Indian villages from San Diego to Monterey.[25]

One article even promised that visitors could see "two peach trees planted by Ramona [which] annually bloom as of old."[26]

The pageant staff themselves did not present a much more accurate portrayal of events. Ramona Pageant Association President Edward Poorman wrote to the news department of the Automobile Club of Southern California about some of the valley's attractions in the hopes that they would be included in a future radio broadcast by the club,

Some of the places I think will interest you are: . . . the ruined home of
Ramona and Alessandro, the graves of Ramona and Alessandro, the
grave of Aunt Ri [and the] site of Aunt Ri's home in old town San Jacinto
where a great part of the story Ramona was written by Helen Hunt
Jackson.[27]

It was acknowledged by pageant staff, however, that with all the controversy surrounding the details of the novel, the very question of accuracy
in relation to *Ramona* had become a sticky one. Chairman of Publicity
Mrs. James H. Welch acknowledged to the Auto Club's News Department,
"Thank you for your desire to give the Pageant the correct historic publicity. It *is* difficult, with everyone claiming Ramona."[28]

Confusion or no, the press from the beginning responded with "rave
reviews" of the show and attendance from the outset was strong. Official
figures for the first (1923) season showed 3,023 persons in attendance and
the pageant cleared a profit of over $300 once all expenses were paid. De-
mand for seating continued, and in 1925 the pageant was extended to two
weekends. By 1927 the pageant was held on three weekends, and concrete
seating had been installed in the amphitheater. With the rise of automobile tourism, pageant managers recognized their primary audience,
and (also by 1927) provided improved vehicular access to the many now
arriving in their own automobiles. By the dawn of the 1930s the pageant's
success seemed assured, with attendance climbing to 14,000 per year.[29]

The 1931 season saw another novel publicity idea: patrons and patron-
esses of the pageant. Prominent citizens were invited to become patrons
and in return their names were listed in the 1931 pageant brochure. Not
surprisingly, these names included political figures such as then-Governor
James Rolph Jr., but the list also featured Californios whose families had
been drawn into the story of Ramona such as "Mrs. Ysabel del Valle Cram,
of Camulos Rancho" and "Mr. Cave J. Couts, Rancho Guajome, Vista California." So closely connected to the fictional landscape of the novel were
the real-life residents of the "Home[s] of Ramona," that their names could
bring attention and credibility for the pageant.[30]

Despite the Hemet–San Jacinto region's proclaimed status as a "mecca"
for tourists, the effects of the Great Depression were felt and, after a loss
in the 1932 season, the 1933 pageant was canceled altogether. The production resumed, however, in 1934 and, other than a four-year hiatus during
World War II, has continued to be presented annually ever since.[31]

Although over the years the pageant has attracted a large number of tourists to the Hemet–San Jacinto region—by the late 1980s over 38,000 per year attended six shows—surveys conducted by researcher James A. Cheney in 1972 found that only 7.5 percent of Hemet *residents* were introduced to the town by the pageant.[32] Thus, while the pageant succeeded in attracting tourists, and has served as a tremendous stimulant to the local economy, it has largely failed as a means to promote local real estate and attract permanent residents to the area. Perhaps those who came to Hemet with the curiosity for Ramona left satisfied—but with no desire to remain in the area.

As the years passed, the town of Hemet established itself not only as the site of the pageant but also as a trailer- and mobile home–based retirement community. In the 1960s, residents' average age was 63.4 years. With dropping real estate prices in the 1980s and increased commuting times for southern California residents, Hemet has more recently become home to "younger and more ethnically diverse families," bringing growth and its accompaniments, traffic and crime, to the valley.[33]

Although the pageant has attracted a relatively small number of home-seekers to the San Jacinto Valley it has helped to propel a few of its participants to careers beyond the valley. Most notable was "straight 'A' student" Raquel Tejada of La Jolla, who starred as Ramona in 1959. Tejada achieved international renown in later years as Raquel Welch.[34]

Just as the population of the Hemet–San Jacinto Valley has changed over the years, so has the script itself. In the course of over seventy-five years of production of the pageant, both the script itself and the pageant publicity have been adapted for the changing times, an issue that itself became popular in pageant publicity articles. The *Los Angeles Times,* in promoting the 1995 pageant, insisted that the era of multiculturalism and political correctness had not brought on a "Ramona Revolution," but that the pageant's director did seek increased historical accuracy, particularly in its depiction of "Native Americans" and pointed out that the pageant now included a blessing in the Cahuilla tongue.[35]

In 1993, after seventy years in production during many of which the pageant was the only major annual outdoor theater production in the state, the Ramona Pageant was declared by the California State Legislature the official "California State Outdoor Play."[36] Though it may seem, therefore, that the pageant's position is permanently established, the early twenty-first century, unlike the early twentieth, has not been a big era

Perhaps the best-known Ramona was Raquel Tejada, who starred in the role in 1959 and later became famous as Raquel Welch. Pageant Files, Ramona Bowl Museum; reprinted by permission.

for outdoor theater. In addition, the majority of those in attendance at this time are of retirement age. Thus, as the staff of the pageant face their twenty-first-century future, they will face a time when pageant audiences were not steeped in the Ramona myth as past generations of Californians

and California tourists were. While the Ramona Pageant is the most deliberately constructed successful landscape link to *Ramona*, what remains
to be seen is whether the pageant will hold continued appeal to those for
whom the phenomenon of Ramona is not a part of their daily conscious-
ness but rather hidden deep beneath the surface of the region's identity,
representation, and social memory.

CHAPTER NINE

RAMONA VILLAGE, FROM CONEY ISLAND TO TRAILER PARK

[I]t was the least bad place of its kind.
—*Ramona*, 217

As a boy, Robert Elmer Callahan was deeply influenced by *Ramona*. He later described how he "read and re-read the book and believed Ramona had really lived. Everywhere I went my eyes swept the faces of those around me in the hope that I would glimpse the sweet, soulful face so vividly portrayed in the story."[1]

Callahan's fascination with the novel did not abate. In 1930 he published a novel, *Daughter of Ramona*, intended to pick up where Helen Hunt Jackson's story had ended.[2] So compelled was Callahan that, in the foreword, he wrote that it was "inevitable that . . . I should write a story concerning Ramona." He went on to describe how he

> sought and had interviews with a score of persons who claimed they
> knew all the characters in the book . . . ; who claimed they had seen
> Ramona, had talked with her; but none of them told the same story, and
> as I visited the many interesting places described in the story, I became
> more curious and often wondered what a son or a daughter of Ramona
> might have been like.[3]

Though Callahan remained unconvinced by these tales, he was not driven to his own search for Ramona until after he had had a most intriguing experience:

> [W]hile hunting in Mexico, I came upon an old hermit wandering through
> the forest. Feeble, exhausted and unable to walk, after I carried him to
> camp, saved his life and gained his confidence he unfolded a tale about
> Ramona that seemed too strange to be true.[4]

The hermit, doubtless grateful to Callahan, allegedly told Callahan of a woman named Rita Gonzales who lived, with a "few artistic friends," in the "Valley of Youth," and that if Callahan could enter into *her* confidence Gonzales might "make a revelation about Ramona."

This left Callahan so intrigued that the very next day, as soon as the "sun had peeped over the bright canyon walls," he set out for the valley. There he found a cluster of mission-style buildings, which he presumed to be the work of an "artistic Indian tribe now extinct." In the largest adobe lived Gonzales, who, though "ninety-seven if she was a day," had "lustrous dark hair and the twinkling eye of youth." Much to Callahan's disappointment, however, Gonzales, despite her cultured intelligence on many subjects, was totally unwilling to have any discussions about Ramona.[5]

But Callahan persevered and gradually gained her confidence, until one day he experienced "the revelation of [his] life." Gonzales led him into a little sanctuary at the end of her living room, where she opened an old trunk filled with jewels, shawls, rebozos, and an altar cloth. "They are the real Ramona jewels," she told him, the ones that, in the novel, were held for Ramona by Señora Moreno and which Ramona had to forsake to marry the Indian Alessandro but which her stepbrother Felipe later returned to her. As if this was not astonishing enough for Callahan, Gonzales, turning to face him, explained "in a tone of supreme dignity," *"I am the real Ramona."*[6]

What followed this dramatic revelation, according to Callahan, was that Gonzales (Ramona) related to him her entire life story, all of it evidently every bit as good as the part Jackson had first told in the novel. Callahan, long interested in any possible Ramona offspring, now became most intrigued, not by Ramona's own story, but by what happened to Ramona's daughter Lolita. At this point, Callahan's foreword ends and his novel begins, though likely the fiction began much earlier in Callahan's tale.[7]

Robert E. Callahan was no one-trick-pony when it came to capitalizing on Ramona. In 1928 he announced ambitious plans for a "Ramona Village" theme park. To be located on West Washington Boulevard, "near Hollywood and the millionaire's colony of Beverly Hills," the Village, according to Callahan, would be assured "perpetual publicity" by the passing not of foot, trolley, or railroad traffic, but of twenty to thirty thousand automobiles each day. In addition to the flow of automobile traffic, Callahan figured that "visitors to our Ramona Center will become so absorbed in its beauty

A rendering of Callahan's ambitious plan for his Ramona Village. Pageant Files, Ramona Bowl Museum; reprinted by permission.

they will become walking talking machines of publicity."[8] Ever ambitious, Callahan planned to open the Village by New Year's Day 1929.[9]

Just as the Ramona Bowl natural amphitheater bolstered its authenticity as a *Ramona* landmark in part by pointing out connections between the San Jacinto Valley region and places described in the novel, Callahan made a rather extravagant claim for the site of the proposed Ramona Village. Writing in his promotional brochure, he claimed he had met an "aged Indian chief" named Don Okarche, who recalled that on the night Ramona and Alessandro fled the Rancho Moreno, heading for San Diego, Alessandro tied his horse to a post on this spot (in order to throw anyone who might be following the runaways off the track), before rejoining Ramona at a neighboring rancho. Callahan further proposed to preserve the post itself as an authentic Ramona landmark. Unlike the claims made surrounding the Ramona Pageant and *its* location, no reference whatsoever could be found in the novel for Callahan's claim, a fact that he himself left unexplained.[10]

Despite this apparent "oversight," Callahan, an advertising man by trade,[11] was confident of his project's success and reminded readers of his brochure:

> Remember, if you please, it has been forty years since Helen Hunt Jackson
> wrote this immortal story. It has been translated into foreign languages,
> is a classic in all libraries, has been read by eight million people, screened
> three times, 130 editions have been published, and it has never been re-
> duced in price.[12]

Issuing a reported $1 million in stock, Callahan incorporated his Ramona Village and began industriously to build on the three-and-a-half-acre Culver City site to which he had obtained a forty-nine-year lease. Typical of his ambitious claims, Callahan announced that the Village was "[t]o be the most interesting spot in California."[13] By June 1928 a "one-story class A" administration building was already in place on the site and Callahan had enlisted the services of architects Meyer and Holler, builders of the renowned Grauman's Chinese and Grauman's Egyptian theaters in Hollywood.[14]

Callahan's concept for the Village can be likened to a theme park, of which Ramona Village might have been the first. The entire complex was to be encompassed by a "9 ft. Mission wall," inside of which were to be found the Ramona Garden, the Ramona Theater, the Indian Village, the Indian Trading Post, the mission-style Spanish Café, a miniature reproduction of Death Valley, and the resplendent, bejeweled Ramona Tower.[15]

Much impressed by the commercial success of Ramona's Marriage Place, Callahan literally intended for his Ramona Garden to resemble the lavish garden at Ramona's Marriage Place, including "enticing nooks" and a "lucky well."[16] And, similar again to Ramona's Marriage Place, in the garden would also be found the Ramona Chapel, which was to be used as a "literary center and unique marriage place."[17]

The Ramona Theater, also on the Village grounds, was to be a "Class A theater to seat 2,000 people," and, according to the *Los Angeles Times,* promised "to be one of the finest amusement houses in Los Angeles."[18] The peculiar attraction of this theater was that it was intended for a repertory of only three plays: first (and foremost) an adaptation of *Ramona,* through which Callahan optimistically envisioned that there would be "thousands of hearts . . . touched by [the] pulsating drama." The two other performances would consist of *Cadman's Golden Trail,* written by Charles Wakefield Cadman, a partner in Callahan's enterprise, and *Heart of an Indian,* based on Callahan's own 1927 novel.[19]

Ramona Village, as Callahan conceived it, would mix entertainment with education and heritage: Indeed, Ramona Village letterhead proclaimed, "There is Only One [Ramona Village]," announced that the Village "will preserve the historical west," and declared that the Village would be "entertaining, historical and educational."[20] Blurring the distinction between the entertaining and educational aspects of the Village, Callahan featured elements from the novel *Ramona,* which, of course, were not strictly speaking part of the "historical west."

Dedicating Ramona Village to Native Americans, Callahan planned an Indian Village at the rear of the site. To be constructed to look like a Hopi Indian pueblo, the Indian Village, according to Callahan, was intended as "a home in which Indians will have opportunity and be encouraged to increase [their] work of arts and crafts."[21] There the visitor would be able to actually "see Indians making beads, hammering bracelets and weaving rugs."[22] The items could then be purchased at the on-site Indian Trading Post.

Nearby the Indian Village would be the Death Valley scene where Callahan promised "the tourist may see the desert in miniature, with its grotesque, gnarled shrubs and thorny cacti; also a pit inhabited by live Gila monsters, chuckawallas and other reptiles that inhabit the mysterious wastelands of the West." With these sorts of educational displays Callahan felt assured that his project would "receive the support of schools, churches, service clubs and women's clubs" thinking of it as an "ideal place for school children, Boy Scouts and Campfire Girls" to visit.[23]

Ramona Village would be a full-service attraction. For those who were hungry there was to be the Spanish Café, where one could not only obtain a "distinctive meal" but also, upon entering, "breathe the air of quaint old Spain."[24] The crowning glory of the project, though, was to be the Ramona Tower, which at nightfall would "burst into a flood of prismatic light" and illuminate the "artificial mountains, mesas, canyons and plains . . . [with] replicas of California's glorious sunrises and sunsets."[25]

In addition to visualizing his Ramona Village as a solid moneymaker Callahan had high, conservative ideals. He wrote in the brochure, "We have too much jazz and speed of modern life, too little of early music and the atmosphere so rich in romance and glory." He looked to the past, and in particular to the Spanish and Indian past of southern California, to provide lessons for the future, and, conflating fact and fiction, saw Ramona Village as a place that would "perpetuate the immortal story of 'Ramona' and portray the beauty of early California." The Village would be, according to Callahan, a "permanent institution where we can help preserve the interesting and authentic history of the American Indian."[26] Despite such ideals, however, Callahan's project met with opposition.

In July 1928, as publicity for the Village was mounting, Dr. Guy Bogart, mayor of the city of Beaumont, wrote to Charles Fletcher Lummis in an effort to launch a protest. The mayor had not been fooled by Callahan's reference to the fence-post scene, which had not occurred in the novel, referring to it in his letter to Lummis as an "absurd" claim. And though, through the Village, Callahan sought to reject the jazzy speed of modern life, Mayor Bogart found Callahan's Ramona Village a "jazz commercial version" of California's past that was an "outrage to the spirit of history" and should "not be permitted to flourish." Lummis had already expressed his disapproval of the project to Callahan some time before and now agreed with the mayor that Ramona Village, as proposed, would "undoubtedly degenerate into the worst kind of a Coney Island."[27]

Opposition to the Village came from more than just those concerned about its accuracy in regard to the "real" places in *Ramona* or its representation of California history. Callahan had secured the rights to a theatrical version of *Ramona*, which had long been in the hands of Virginia Calhoun. Calhoun had once toured the West with her production of the novel (and herself in the title role; see chapter 3) and was ever-reluctant to relinquish the rights she had acquired from Little, Brown and Company, *Ramona*'s publishers. In fact, the producers of the Ramona Pageant had paid her a royalty every year since the pageant opened.[28] How Callahan managed to obtain the rights is unclear, but what was immediately clear to the Ramona Pageant Association was that another stage presentation of *Ramona* in southern California would be a direct threat to their own continued success.[29]

Callahan thought differently of the matter, or at least, so he wrote in his letters to pageant executives. Stating that his intention was to produce the play *indoors* and in the *winter*, he argued that it would only add to the interest in Hemet's *al fresco* production given in the late spring. Hemet area residents and pageant officials were unconvinced, however, and incensed regional newspapers ran headlines such as "Would Steal Ramona Play," "Ramona Village Inquiry Ordered," and "Los Angeles Wants Ramona." Pageant officials even met with representatives of Little, Brown and Company in an effort to secure protection for their production.[30]

In the end, it was not the efforts of those interested in a different version of California history nor those interested in protecting their own Ramona market share that put a stop to Callahan's dream. Despite Callahan's plans to open the Village by 1 January 1929, by the end of 1928 references to the project disappeared from the *Los Angeles Times,* which had previously been closely monitoring events, and Callahan's correspondence with officials of the Ramona Pageant also mysteriously desisted. Then, in 1931, on an entirely new letterhead, that of the "Ramona Supper Club—A nonprofit organization to help preserve the traditions of the Romantic West" with an address at "Ramona Village Pueblos," Callahan wrote to Edward Poorman, president of the Ramona Pageant Association, "In times of depression it is those who are careful and cautious who usually achieve their goal, and . . . we have given up the idea of building an expensive theater."[31]

Thus, it seems that the changing financial climate of the late 1920s and early 1930s had brought about a change in Callahan's project. But he had not yet completely surrendered his dream, writing to Poorman that a concert hall for 1,000 called the Ramona "Fiesta" hall had been completed and that one of the Village buildings had been rented as a "Ramona Village Cafe."[32] Despite this progress, however, by 1934 a representative of Callahan's wrote to Poorman that Callahan was "no longer doing anything in connection with Ramona at the Village."[33] The deepening Depression, it seems, had hurt Callahan still further.

By the middle of the decade Callahan had reconceptualized the Village yet again—and again he relied on the link between automobile travel and tourism. Presumably he was still responsible for the remains of his original forty-nine-year lease on the property (which would not have run out until 1977) and any business was better than no business. New

Ramona Village never took shape as Callahan originally envisioned, but his dream saw at least partial fruition in the Mission Village tourist court. Postcard circa 1938.

brochures proclaimed "Mission Village" the "Most Unique Tourist Court in America" and, despite Callahan's own experiences with the property, "The Place Where You Have Good Luck." Callahan's new brochure claimed that he catered to "the Better Type Traveling Public" with features such as "Private Trailer Garden—Tile Showers—Rolled Gravel—Clean Grounds—Well Lighted—Fiesta Hall—Ping Pong—Billiards" and boasted that "numerous movie stars . . . consider the Village an unusual place of charm" including Bette Davis, Joan Crawford, and Henry Fonda. Not ashamed of his Ramona Village's reincarnation as a tourist court, the brochure stated that it was "[o]riginally conceived as an Indian Art Center— later developed as Mission Bungalows—Indian Pueblos—Teepee Homes and 'Fiesta' Hall for the comfort of westbound travelers."[34] Though clearly some of Callahan's plans had been scaled back, Mission Village's "quaint . . . 21 motor-in Pueblos" still catered to tourists seaking a "themed experience."[35]

Callahan had proclaimed that Ramona Village would be "the most entrancing place in California" and hoped that it would be "an enterprise to which future generations may look back with pride and joy,"[36] but despite his embracing of automobile tourism, the Great Depression devastated his first attempt. Transformed into Mission Village, Callahan's construction might have persevered, but the automobile itself proved his undoing.

In its incarnation as trailer park and tourist court Ramona Village might well have survived its lease, but in 1962 the construction of Interstate 10, the Santa Monica Freeway, forced the removal of the Village's remains. Still not willing to give up, Callahan moved some of the buildings to Canyon Country in the mountains northeast of Los Angeles, where he created an even more minor tourist attraction dubbed "Callahan's Old West."[37] When Callahan died in 1981 his widow donated the Village's original Ramona Chapel to the Santa Clarita Valley Historical Society, which moved it to its Heritage Square, where it still stands, the only remnant of Callahan's ambitious Ramona Village theme park.[38]

CONCLUSION
─────────

RAMONA AND SOCIAL MEMORY
IN SOUTHERN CALIFORNIA

> And so for a second time the [Ramona] jewels were passed
> on . . . into the keeping of that mysterious, certain, un-
> certain thing we call the future, and delude ourselves
> with the fancy that we can have much to do with its
> shaping.
> —*Ramona*, 358

So powerful was the affiliation with Ramona that, for decades around
the turn of the twentieth century, a story circulated claiming that the central California town of San Juan Bautista had *not* been chosen as the setting for the novel. Explaining this first in 1902, Rufus Steele lamented San
Juan's lost opportunity:

> San Juan missed the fate that was meant for it. It missed the glory of a
> world-wide reputation such as would have made a city of the town, a sub-
> urb of the hills, industrial hives of its beet fields. . . . It missed becoming
> the Mecca of money-spending tourists from over half the globe. It missed
> becoming the scene of the story of "Ramona."[1]

Ramona affiliation had become so powerful, with such strong potential
tourist revenue, that any claim for Ramona-relatedness, it seems, was worth
staking. Jackson's book, Steele pointed out, had attracted "countless thousands" to southern California. Drawing attention to the specific association of the Home of Ramona, Steele wrote:

> About the country of the Camulos ranch, where the scene of Ramona was
> laid, a sort of beckoning halo was fixed whose influence was more potent
> than all the advertising agencies which ever boomed the State and all the
> "special excursions" ever ran.[2]

San Juan Bautista, he claimed, had been Jackson's intended Home of Ramona, but when, planning to spend months there writing her novel and familiarizing herself with the town, she was unable to rent the house she desired, she departed and set those scenes elsewhere.

Steele, in his research, had relied for much of his information on interviews with three San Juan residents. His key informant had been a man named Mark Regan, a San Juan stage operator who claimed to have been Jackson's driver. By the time Regan spoke with the *Overland Monthly*'s correspondent in 1919, his story was beginning to lay more specific blame for San Juan's missed opportunity. He clearly asserted that Jackson's argument with the manager of the house she had sought to rent caused her to set the scenes of her novel elsewhere. The manager, Regan described, was a "woman whose brogue might without great difficulty, be attributed to a nativity in the Emerald Isle. She had been equally blessed with hair of a fiery hue, and temperament that is generally thought to accompany its possession."[3]

Years later, in 1938, Regan was still available for interviews, speaking this time with a reporter from the Automobile Club magazine *Touring Topics* and laying the blame all the more squarely at the caretaker's feet:

> [I]f it hadn't been for that red-headed fire-eating caretaker . . . San Juan
> Bautista would be famous today as the place where Ramona lived and
> loved. Now what is it? I'll tell you; it's a forgotten village that mighty few
> come to see. . . . Mister, that Ramona book would have boomed San Juan.
> I'd have gotten rich hauling sightseeing tourists. Now ordinarily I ain't
> a vengeful man, but I sure hope that [caretaker] gets all that's coming to
> her and no time off for good behavior in that hot place, or wherever it is
> she's gone.[4]

That Jackson was not in California seeking a place to write her novel, and that she did not even have in mind to write a novel while in California, was addressed neither by Steele, by the other reporters, nor, evidently by Regan himself.[5] *Ramona*, even through spurious claims, had become a powerful attraction.

Places associated with *Ramona*—like Rancho Camulos and Ramona's Marriage Place—became powerful and popular landmarks to visit, drawing thousands of visitors annually and even entering the list of canonical California tourist attractions. Seen in this light, San Juan's story may seem unsurprising, but it does demonstrate, perhaps even more powerfully than the "real" Ramona attractions, the importance of Ramona landmarks

CONCLUSION

and Ramona affiliation until well into the twentieth century. In fact, it is precisely because San Juan's claims were spurious that they so clearly show Ramona's importance. Indeed, as scholars of social memory James Fentress and Chris Wickham have pointed out, when studying social memory we should be blinded neither by truth nor by falsity, for here it may paradoxically be in false claims that the power of such tales can really be found.[6]

In the case of Ramona, claims, whether deemed valid or false, tied themselves directly to the novel, to its characters, plot, and landscapes. A host of other places, products, and businesses sought Ramona affiliation as well. Many wrote Ramona into southern California's landscape in new ways, as they inscribed Ramona references onto the landscape even though they could not be directly linked to the novel. Just as questionable claims to a *Ramona*-based location were thought beneficial and could be hotly contested, so too could it be with places named for the characters in the novel. In the mid-1880s, when developer J. De Barth Shorb subdivided his Alhambra Addition Tract (near Los Angeles), he renamed it after his daughter Ramona, from whom he claimed Helen Hunt Jackson had gotten the name (see chapter 7).[7] By 1886 the "romantic spell cast by *Ramona* . . . [had] cast a commercial spell over Shorb's town site" and the *Los Angeles Times* reported that "property around Ramona [was] jumping like an Irishman's flea."[8] At about the same time, however, residents of the little town of Nuevo in San Diego County were applying to officially change the name of their town and post office to Ramona in honor of the fictional heroine.[9] On hearing this news Shorb allegedly was outraged, firing off letters of protest to "almost everyone with political power except President Cleveland."[10] To railroad magnate Charles Crocker he wrote,

> Now this attempt at larceny I want to defeat and I would be under any obligations to you if you would telegraph Gov. Stanford and any other friends at Washington to see the post office officials and stop this outrage.
>
> I have a great deal of feeling in this matter as the name is a family name and certainly by prescription as well as priority belongs to me. My wife's mother bore this name and my daughter of 14 years also carries the name of Ramona. Mrs. Jackson obtained the name during a visit at my home. Do what you can immediately.[11]

To California Postmaster General William Freeman Vilas he wrote,

> The name of "Ramona" was given to a protected town site by myself long before the parties in San Diego thought of establishing their town.

The name of "Ramona" belongs in every right to myself and family, and Mrs. Jackson first obtained the name at my home. My wife's mother and my daughter carry the name which belongs to one of the oldest Spanish families in this State.

The Mayor of Los Angeles, Chairman of the Board of Supervisors and Chairman of our County Committee *signed* the protest which can be supplemented by a thousand names if found necessary to prevent the consummation of the very indecent attempt to steal the name of the town site.[12]

Shorb soon received assurance in the form of a letter from newly appointed assistant U.S. Postmaster General Adlai E. Stevenson: "I beg to state that the order changing the name of Nuevo Post Office, San Diego County, California to Ramona, has been rescinded. The name of Ramona has been disproved." The Ramona post office in San Diego County had been designated on 12 November 1886, only to be changed back, at Stevenson's order, to its previous name of Nuevo on 31 January 1887.[13]

The saga, however, did not end. Despite its postal designation as Nuevo, residents of the San Diego County town continued to refer to their town as "Ramona." Opportunity knocked in 1895 when Shorb's Ramona post office merged with that of his neighboring town of Alhambra. The Nuevo residents leaped at their chance and on 18 June 1895 Nuevo officially became Ramona, a town name it still carries over one hundred years later. Nor has their eager embracing of the name Ramona abated in the intervening century: officials of the town celebrated their centennial in 1986 at the anniversary of the first name change.[14]

Other developments sought affiliation with *Ramona* as well, like the southern California towns of Alessandro and Moreno, or the Ramona Tract and Ramona Park (tract).[15] Ramona affiliation was not only for the relatively prosperous: the Housing Authority of the City of Los Angeles named one of its first public housing projects, designed by architect Lloyd Wright, for the heroine.[16] Streets were named for her all across southern California, projecting Ramona's imagery onto the landscape in new ways.[17] Marked on maps, places and streets named for *Ramona* gained cartographic actuality—even when the places themselves were fictional, such as when tourist maps marked the Home of Ramona or Ramona's Grave.[18]

Even the Los Angeles freeway system had its connections with Ramona. In the 1950s, when still largely in its planning stages, an even more elaborate freeway network than the one now existing was envisioned. Nearly all of the freeways had names that were place- or direction-oriented, like the

Santa Monica, the Venice, and the Foothill. The two exceptions to this naming scheme were the freeways Ramona and Alessandro, and, as if in tribute
to the two lovers' fictional tragedy, on the landscape of Los Angeles these
two freeways never met. While some of the freeways in the early plans were
never built, the Ramona and the Alessandro both were, although today
their names have been changed to the San Bernardino and the Glendale
respectively.[19]

ON STAGE AND SCREEN

If Ramona left the printed page for the landscape and the outdoor amphitheater, she appeared also on the legitimate stage and the silver screen.
Such productions often emphasized not just their faithfulness to the
original text, but also their faithfulness to the landscapes accepted as
the novel's setting, especially Rancho Camulos.[20] Virginia Calhoun's five-
hour-long 1905 production of *Ramona* made numerous specific references
to the rancho, both in its script and in its program.[21] The unwieldy length
of the play, however, precluded those who had arrived at the premiere by
streetcar from staying until the end: many left early, at least ostensibly, to
catch the last train.[22] Despite Calhoun's ambitious plans to take her production on the road, something that would enable her to "carry the life
tide of this sun-kissed land to the people of less fortunate climes, where it
will riot through their veins," she was none too successful, reopening in
Los Angeles that September with a "carefully rewritten" script now "preg-
nant with dramatic climaxes."[23]

Calhoun's production was less successful than she might have hoped,
but one of her actors, Lawrence Griffith, who played Alessandro oppo-
site Calhoun's Ramona, went on to have a noteworthy film career. Now
known as D. W. Griffith, in his later years, his wife reported, he was possessed with an "urge to do 'Ramona' in a motion picture"—and so he
did.[24] Griffith's *Ramona*, the first screen adaptation of the novel, premiered
for Biograph in 1910 with Mary Pickford starring as Ramona. Like other
Griffith films (and like each Ramona film in its own way), his Ramona took
on epic proportions: forty-five scenes were photographed from twenty-
two different camera positions during the two days of location shooting.
Griffith's wife reminisced that it was "the most expensive picture put out
by any manufacturer up to that time" and that it was Griffith's "most artistic creation to date" for even "bells that were cast in old Spain rang silently
on the screen."[25]

Such location shooting at that time was unusual but, for Griffith, essential in order to lend his film credibility in its portrayal of the tale. Most of its scenes were filmed—very recognizably—at or near Rancho Camulos, and, a first in film history, the released print of *Ramona* gave special screen credit to the locale where the picture was filmed. Ramona-related landscapes were so recognizable and Rancho Camulos had become so important in symbolizing *Ramona* that the screen credit lent Griffith's picture credibility and authenticity.[26]

When later filmic Ramonas appeared, their links to the landscape would continue to be important: Clune's Studios' 1916 production was said to

Ramona was filmed at the Camulos chapel in Clune's Studios 1916 production (starring Adda Gleason as Ramona and Monroe Salisbury as Alessandro).

have been filmed "so far as possible on the very scenes that Mrs. Jackson endeared to millions of readers." In 1936, when Loretta Young and Don Ameche starred as Ramona and Alessandro in the first *Ramona* talkie, Technicolor technology brought the Warner Ranch near Temecula in San Diego County to the screen. As one reviewer noted, even after fifty years "this modern color version of the Helen Hunt Jackson novel has something of vital interest to theater goers" and filming at the locations (ostensibly) described in the novel was a critical part of that appeal.[27] Of course, as one reviewer of Griffith's film made clear, seeing Ramona-related locations on the screen served to further interest and encourage viewers to visit those locations as tourists, to "visit the scenes wherein lived the simple, patient Ramona, and the noble-hearted Alessandro."[28]

A VICTORY DEFERRED

By the time Griffith's film was released, Helen Hunt Jackson had been dead twenty-five years, having died convinced *Ramona* was a failure because it had, to her mind, failed to attract sufficient attention to her Indian cause. Written not to dramatize *historic* Indian mistreatment—of which there had been a great deal, whether by Spaniards, missionaries, Mexicans, or Californios[29] —but rather to call attention to what was, in the early 1880s, ongoing, contemporary mistreatment of Native Americans at the hands of Anglo-Americans, *Ramona* presented a past romanticized as Jackson deliberately contrasted the troubled present with a fictitious past, a life of repose in the shade of a veranda amid southern California's bloom and verdure.

When her book, despite its meticulously accurate details of American wrongdoing—details taken from Jackson's own research in California for the Commissioner of Indian Affairs—became beloved for its early scenes of a "simpler" life rather than its outcry, Jackson had died thinking her goals were unattained. The novel that immortalized Jackson had taken on a life of its own. Like petals tossed to the wind, or the inherited jewels in this chapter's epigraph that Ramona (in the novel) left for uncertain others, once it was published Jackson could no longer control her novel's fate. Left to that "uncertain thing we call the future" (358), *Ramona* immortalized Jackson, though not for what Jackson herself had desired. Her characters and the scenes she described lived on to become integral to social memory in southern California, integral to the way southern Californians thought about their past.

Some of Jackson's goals were, in fact, achieved. Organizations like the Women's National Indian Association, and the Indian Rights Association, among others, carried on the struggle Jackson had been so influential in and championed her cause. In 1891 the Act for the Relief of the Mission Indians in the State of California, the one based on recommendations Jackson made in her 1883 report with Abbot Kinney, was passed, thus providing care for the elderly and destitute, and setting aside over one hundred thousand acres of land on reservations that still exist in southern California today.[30]

So Jackson's Indian-reform efforts did go on to shape the future. But for most southern Californians and for most visitors to the region, Jackson's greatest impact was the one that she never imagined, setting in motion through her compelling work of regional fiction processes that would change the way southern California's landscape and southern California's past were interpreted. She set in motion a new social memory for the region, one that reached out, through the travels of tourists and the works of boosters, far beyond the boundaries of southern California.

An Unexpected Influence

Perhaps, though, Jackson herself might have seen some tiny glimmer of what was to come: Jackson died in San Francisco on 12 August 1885, but, in early July, newspapers reported that two "lady visitors" to the Monterey area, both "great admirers of Helen Jackson," had named a nearby lake "Lake Majella" in honor of the Indian name Alessandro gives to Ramona in the novel.[31] Thus the first of so many places, businesses, and products that would be associated with Jackson's work of fiction, was christened— even before Jackson's death—by tourists.

Surely Jackson never imagined the scope of what would later be called the Ramona myth or its powerful influence on the region's social memory. Jackson's friend, Charles Dudley Warner, the editor of *Harper's* magazine, wrote in 1887 that he was

> certain that she could have had no idea what the novel would be to the people of Southern California, or how it would identify her name with all that region, and make so many scenes in it places of pilgrimage and romantic interest.

But, imagining his late friend still to be observing events on Earth, Warner added,

I presume she [knows] that more than one Indian school in the Territo-
ries is called the Ramona School; that at least two villages in California
are contending for the priority of using the name Ramona; that all the
travellers and tourists . . . go about under her guidance, are pilgrims to
the shrines she has described, and eager searchers for the scenes she has
made famous in her novel.[32]

Indeed, in southern California between 1885 and the 1960s a tourist
could visit Ramona's home(s), her marriage place, her birthplace, and her
grave; take the Ramona Freeway to Ramona Boulevard; shop at the Ramona
Pharmacy, Ramona Jewelry, or the Ramona Beauty Shoppe; play with a
Ramona doll, or go to the arcade to play Ramona pinball; see *Ramona* on
the silver screen, on the stage, or in an outdoor amphitheater; listen to
"Ramona" at 78 or 45 rpm, with Paul Whiteman and Bix Beiderbeck or
the Four Tops; play "Ramona" on the piano or the ukulele; refresh with
Ramona drinking water, Ramona beer, Ramona brandy, or Ramona wine
tonic; eat Ramona brand lemons, tomatoes, or pineapples, and eat them
with Ramona cutlery (or a Ramona souvenir teaspoon) from a Ramona
bowl; have Ramona roof tiles on a home on Ramona Terrace, or in the
Ramona tract, or in the town of Ramona; cook like Ramona, dress like
Ramona, and even smell like Ramona.[33] Southern California had been
transformed into a region that was powerfully "Ramona conscious."[34]
Thousands of tourists and locals were engaging with the novel, seeking
out its scenes, and, in so doing, creating a new, Ramona-inspired social
memory for the region, one that was clearly having a distinct impact
upon the region's landscape, but one too, that tourists carried with them
when they left, spreading Ramona's influence beyond the boundaries
of southern California, as they bought and brought home Ramona souvenirs, mailed Ramona postcards, photographed themselves at Ramona
landmarks, included Ramona in their scrapbooks and photo albums, and
continued to engage with the novel even after they returned home.

In the fall of 1896 Sharlot Hall, a well-known author, and her friend
Mary Gray received invitations—each one decorated with a "spray of yel-
low mustard blossoms"—to their friend Laura Haines's home for a "Ramona luncheon." Curious what a Ramona luncheon was, Hall and Gray
recalled that "*Ramona* was that pretty Indian story by Helen Hunt Jackson" that had been set in southern California at the end of the Spanish/
Mexican period, so, full of anticipation, they waited for the appointed day.
That day dawned "fair and beautiful" and when the two friends arrived at

Though Ramona did not drink, her name and fictional image were used (even during Prohibition) to sell beer, brandy, and wine tonic. Circa 1925.

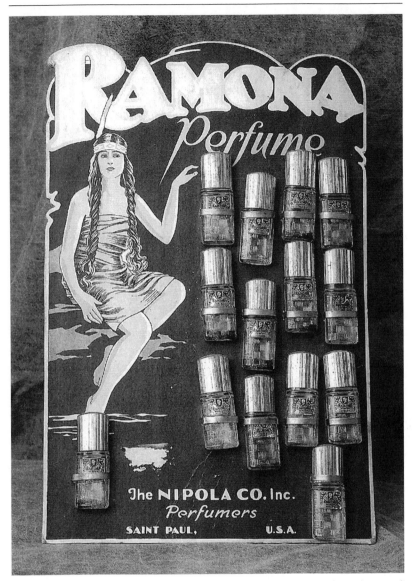

By the early twentieth century, Ramona's name and image had been used to sell a wide array of products. Perfume display circa 1937.

the Haines house they found it transformed as if in a scene from the novel, and its inhabitants (even the servants) transformed, too, into the novel's characters: The walls of the dining room had been lined with pale-gray cheesecloth to make them look like adobe, and the floors and window seats strewn with Indian blankets. Tall palms were "banked around the walls to simulate a *patio* or enclosed garden of old Spanish-American homes" and everywhere *ollas* (water vessels) stood filled with fragrant musk.

The young Laura Haines emerged as Ramona herself, wearing a "soft, dark skirt and a blouse of white linen, with an embroidered *reboss [sic]* thrown across her shoulders and a wonderful silver necklace and bracelets of Indian make." Her mother, Mrs. Haines, appeared as a "Spanish matron, with high comb of frost-like filigree silver and a mantilla lace falling softly over her shoulders," a "beautiful and stately" rendition of Ramona's stepmother, the Señora Moreno. Nor was the food any exception to the day's theme: the servants, similarly appropriately attired, appeared bearing "*frijole* croquettes," "*chile con carne,* served on crisp lettuce leaves," "sandwiches piled upon drawn-work squares in quaint baskets woven of reeds by the patient fingers of Pueblo women," and even "real olives served on tiny dishes of Indian pottery."

The Haineses had just returned from a trip to southern California, bringing with them "photographs and souvenirs of Ramona's land," which they now shared with their friends back home. The "Ramona luncheon" was a smashing success, leaving Sharlot Hall to recommend such entertainments to others, noting that even with "less faithful detail" they could still be "quaint," and leaving both Hall and Gray to "dream of . . . Ramona, romantic *patios,* stately *señoras,* and Spanish cookery."[35]

The occasion was not simply a luncheon, or just a sharing of photographs and mementos of the Haineses' vacation: while in southern California Laura Haines had gotten engaged, and her mother was using this luncheon as the occasion to introduce the young man, dressed as Ramona's husband, Alessandro, as her "son-to-be."

To a turn-of-the-century, white, upper- or middle-class audience like those gathered in the Haines dining room, these details all (except for some of the food) reminded quite precisely of the immensely popular novel. The *patio,* the musk, and even the mustard on the invitations all figure prominently in the novel's evocative early chapters, with one exception. In the novel Señora Moreno forbids her daughter to marry the Indian Alessandro, and when Ramona and Alessandro do marry, their lives are fraught with hardship that culminates in Alessandro's brutal murder. Not, it would seem, pleasant parallels for a cheerful engagement party.

But what is significant about the "Ramona luncheon," both for an understanding of the Ramona myth and for the understanding of social memory more broadly, is precisely the way that the Haineses acted out the story, and the way they got the story "wrong," for it was intentional. What the Haineses (and "Alessandro") had in fact done was to fold bits of the novel into their own lives: they had visited places the novel depicted, and had understood southern California, and southern California's past, at least partly through the story of the fictional Ramona. Now they took that story and made it meaningful in their own lives in the present, adapting the fictional characters, the fictional past, and their own (hopefully happier) ending, to meet their needs.

What this tale of the Ramona luncheon, first published as an article in *The Delineator* (a turn-of-the-century "journal of fashion, culture and fine art"), reveals is that the Haineses, like so many other tourists to southern California, actively took part in producing a new social memory for the region, and that they brought those ideas home with them. In their visit to southern California they were experiencing and remembering the region in part through the novel *Ramona* as they visited Ramona landmarks, and, now home, they not only decorated their home after scenes from the fictional region, they adapted the story to their own present—they were actively participating in the creation of social memory. Thus, while some have suggested that the Ramona myth represents a foolishly false past, one that was used to lure and dupe tourists—and in the process coax from them some of their cash—stories like this one suggest that something more significant (and perhaps less insidious) was also at play.[36]

REGIONAL FICTION AND LITERARY TOURISM

Works of regional fiction, like *Ramona*, so often read by tourists preparing to travel, offer powerful interpretations of landscape, character, and memory, in turn influencing the very real places the novels sought to fictionalize.[37] And *Ramona*, to be sure, is not the only work of fiction that has inspired tourists to visit its apparent real-life locales. Susanna Haswell Rowson's novel *Charlotte Temple*, first published in 1794, was the first best-selling novel in the new republic. Like *Ramona*, it inspired tourist pilgrimages to the scenes the writer described as readers journeyed to the cemetery where the heroine was said to be buried, and, upon a tombstone inscribed with the heroine's name, left their remembrances—"locks of hair, ashes of love letters, bouquets of flowers." Though no surviving records could document whose remains lay beneath the stone, a man who lived within view of the tombstone wrote that, despite the fact that Alexander Hamilton and other famous personages were buried in the same churchyard, it was Temple's grave that was "kept fresh by falling tears." And despite the lack of any verifiable historical basis linking the fictional Temple to factual details, various publications appeared attempting to link the novel, its scenes, and characters with actual events, places, and persons—readers, it seems, as one commentator noted, were not to be dissuaded by "any . . . arguments aimed at reducing fictional truth to mere fact." In fact, various editions of the novel were illustrated with pictures of "Charlotte Temple," like the 1860 edition that included a "detailed, full length 'Original Portrait.'"[38]

Neither is adult fiction the only genre to inspire such phenomena. The lead character in Lucy Maud Montgomery's 1908 children's novel *Anne of Green Gables* also took on a "life outside [of her] text."[39] The editor of a recent volume of criticism about the novel writes,

> I found myself repeatedly tripping over Anne while I was working on the novel. "Anne of Green Gables, never change. We love you just this way," sang my son as he walked in the door from school choir practice one day. Selections from the musical version of Anne's story, it seemed, were to be included on the spring concert program. My daughter was chosen to play Miss Stacy in her class's production of the same musical a year later. A visit to a local children's bookstore brought me home with an entry form for a contest; the first prize was a trip to "Green Gables." (That name has been given to the restored Cavendish house Montgomery identified as the prototype for the fictional house, although it is not the house in which she lived.) The calendar in my kitchen at the time was decorated with scenes from the Sullivan Productions films of Anne's story. A ballet about the girl from Green Gables is a standard Christmas presentation of the principal dance company in my city. Spin-offs both from the novel and the films seemed to be everywhere: I could have bought Anne of Green Gables dolls, cookbooks, address books, birthday books, diaries, coloring books, and a variety of abridged and rewritten versions of the novel.[40]

More recently, Robert James Waller's 1992 novel *The Bridges of Madison County* inspired a wave of tourism to the town of Winterset, Iowa. Couples flocked to the town, even to be married at the Roseman Bridge, a spot that figures prominently in the novel. The bridge became so popular a wedding site that a local entrepreneur could offer $325 wedding packages including a ceremony at the bridge, champagne, and a "wildflower bouquet like the one Kincaid gave Francesca." And, as with *Ramona*, it was not only tourists whom the novel compelled: Peggy Stanfield, a divorced former farmwife and mother of two grown children, placed a personal ad in the *Des Moines Register* that read "Francesca seeking Kincaid. If you understand this and are a nonsmoker, please call." Of the seven men who replied, one was Winterset resident and barn restorer Ray Raymond, who left Stanfield the voice mail message, "I'd like to meet you at dawn at the Roseman Bridge." They married seven months later, settled in Winterset, and opened a gift shop.[41]

Neither need a novel be current or new to be recalled in the landscape: "Roberts Country," a title linking Sackville, New Brunswick, Canada, to the works of nineteenth-century poet and "father of Canadian literature" Charles G. D. Roberts was not so dubbed until the late twentieth century. Whether current or not, fictional landscapes can clearly retain influence and significance, long after the work of fiction has been published, as visits (and guides) to Beatrix Potter's Hilltop Farm, Dickens's London, and Joyce's Dublin readily attest.[42]

Whether authors chose already famous places as the settings or subjects of their works, or whether it was the works themselves that made the places famous, the writing, as John Sears has noted about literary tourist attractions, "conferred value on the scenes depicted and helped shape the vision of [the] tourists who visited" such places.[43] Thus the visits of tourists to literary landscapes—whether self-motivated or encouraged by boosters or promotional materials—help to render imagined landscapes visible, as landscapes imagined in fiction become tangible and real.[44] Although visitors to such sites may remember the writers, scholars of literary tourism have shown that it is the fictional characters and worlds that evoke in the viewers the greatest emotion. Thus, despite the fact that the meanings of literary places are grounded in what is not factual, it is those very fictional elements that carry for visitors the most meaning.[45] The Ramona-related landscapes of southern California are no exception.

Neither is fiction the only mode to stimulate landscape-based tourism. Geographer Stephen Daniels has documented how, between 1880 and 1940, through the work of the landscape painter John Constable (1776–1837), a malleable, culturally constructed region known as Constable Country emerged in England. Daniels writes that

[Constable's] work is frequently reproduced and in a variety of ways: as posters, framed prints, tapestries, on greeting cards, calendars, table mats, tea trays and chocolate boxes. Constable's paintings are used as publicity images, to promote the virtues of nature and of nation; to advertise cheese, beer and breakfast cereal; to protest against oil drilling and against the deployment of nuclear missiles. . . . By the 1890s there were coach tours to Constable Country in the genuine Stour Valley organized by Thomas Cook and the Great Eastern Railway. . . . The places Constable painted have become as famous as the paintings themselves.[46]

And, though Constable's paintings have made his English landscapes recognizable, today we may be most familiar with this phenomenon when it is stimulated by film—such as when tourists seek to visit the scenes they saw on the silver screen. Such films as *Close Encounters of the Third Kind*, *Braveheart, Field of Dreams*, and the *Lord of the Rings* trilogy have stimulated dramatic increases in tourism to the locations where the movies were filmed—for *Close Encounters,* shot in part at Devil's Tower National Monument (already a tourist attraction before the film's release), that increase was 74 percent.[47] With the twenty-first-century rise of relatively affordable satellite-linked location tracking technology like handheld GPS (global positioning system) units, such films have spawned a new exactness of guidebook not known in Ramona's time. By 2002 fans of the filmed versions of J. R. R. Tolkien's *Lord of the Rings* trilogy, all three of which were filmed in New Zealand, had not only a location guidebook similar to George Wharton James's *Through Ramona's Country,* but now their full-color guide could direct tourists even to locations accessible only by helicopter, recommending a heli-tours outfit and providing, for each location (and even for the locations of former cast dressing rooms), precise map coordinates that could be located on tourists' own GPSs.[48]

As early as 1888 the *Southern California Tourists' Guide Book* had noted that many of *Ramona*'s readers, when visiting Rancho Camulos, became "somewhat smitten with its original romantic scenes." While some read *Ramona* in preparation for a southern California visit, others recommended reading it while in southern California. One writer pointed out that *Ramona*'s "local color, admirable descriptions and characterizations render it more fascinating when read in the scenes among which it is laid, than when read elsewhere." Whether readers read the novel before their visit or during, seeing the landscapes that appeared to have been described drew readers back into the text, something promotional materials encouraged. As the pamphlet "California's Old Mission Scenic Tour by Motor or Rail" advised, "the associations to be found in Ramona's Marriage Place bring one in closer touch and sympathy with [Jackson's] favorite character. An hour spent in this charming little spot is conducive of much enjoyment and rare education."[49]

Those who visited Ramona landmarks could "muse upon Ramona and her lover" and thus relive the novel in the landscape in which it was set, for, as one Camulos visitor wrote, "the story will seem like reality to us as we wander about."[50] As with those who shed their tears over Charlotte Temple's grave or were married at the Roseman bridge, visits to Ramona landmarks could convey powerful experiences to readers of the novel. At Camulos, for example, eager tourists

> picked the flowers and fruit, swarmed over the yard and gardens, took
> valuable articles for souvenirs, and invaded the dwelling uninvited. . . .
> [O]n one occasion, . . . in the room described in the novel as having been
> the sleeping apartment of Ramona a woman threw herself on the bed,
> exclaiming, "Now I can say I have laid on Ramona's bed!"[51]

In the case of *Ramona*, such experiences, such memories, can be traced not just to the novel's text, but also to particular constructions of southern California's past. Indeed, this is nothing unusual for works of literature: Beatrix Potter tourists visiting the British Lake District, for example, engage not just with the text of her fiction but also with particular cultural constructions of the countryside and English rural life, as well as a romanticized past.[52] Ramona tourists were no different, engaging with and helping to inscribe southern California's new social memory, one

Ramona tourists were not always mannerly. At Rancho Camulos, at least one invaded a bed-room exclaiming, "Now I can say I have laid on Ramona's bed!" Postcard circa 1906.

based on the idyllic and fictional Californio/mission past that the reader experienced through the text.

In the case of Ramona, such landscape manifestations—generally designed or built by locals but visited more often by tourists—can be, and were quite readily identified. But as interest in Ramona continued, the Ramona landmarks were expected to be preserved, and remain as much as possible as they were depicted in the novel. This was certainly what inspired Hazel Wood Waterman in her restoration of Ramona's Marriage Place as she sought not only to use historic materials, but also to incorporate even more elements from the novel into the restored building. But it extended beyond that as well. When Nachito del Valle installed a radio on the Camulos property in 1922, the *Ventura Post* was "aghast at this sacrilege": "now the quiet and quaint peace of the old ranch is permeated with the voices of operatic stars rather than the strum of guitars and mandolins of the Spanish lovers of *Ramona*."[53]

Ramona landmarks were expected to remain places, not just of fiction, but also of the past, apart from the growing modern cities around them. In 1894, one author elevated the potential threat to Ramona landmarks above that to other historic sites:

> [Once] the sustaining hands of the old padres were removed, the Indians sunk back easily into their indolent irresponsible life, and gradually vanished into the past. O, this crowded past! How soon will this historical landmark, Ramona's dwelling place, be a thing of the past too! Californians should see that this is not disturbed. . . . It would be a cold heart and an ignoble soul who would lend a hand to the destruction of Ramona's home. Of course, people must pour in. It is utterly impossible to keep such a land from being settled up, but this one spot should remain intact.[54]

If accepted at all, any modern intrusions at Ramona landmarks had to be justified. Years later (in 1943) at Rancho Guajome,

> The crooked tree trunks which were once used as plows, drawn by mules or oxen, or possibly by Indians themselves, have given way to a modern "Caterpillar" Diesel D 2 Tractor, with a Killefer chisel, and John Deere plow and combine. With this latest model "Caterpillar," Mr. Richardson [heir to the property] in a few hours can do the work that required days for the Indians with their crude equipment.
>
>   You say there isn't the glamour to plowing this ancient land with

modern equipment? Well, maybe not, but it's a lot more practical, and does not in the least detract from Guajome's position of being the link between the romantic past and the busy work a day present.[55]

But though those places directly connected to the novel held great interest as Ramona locales (at least so long as they "looked right"), other places sought affiliation with the novel, and with the new imagery of southern California's past as well. In part, these are the places named for Ramona—the businesses, streets, and towns, many of which still carry her name. But *Ramona* has been attributed an architectural legacy far beyond a few adobes, far greater than a few street names.

Before *Ramona*'s publication, the California missions nearly all lay in ruin, and, though by the 1870s they were already written about in the travel guides and intellectual magazines of the day as picturesque, decaying "piles," Anglo interest in the missions, especially outside of California, was just beginning. The missions, it was soon recognized, were the only sizable and concrete examples of California's claim to antiquity, of California's past. What helped elevate the missions themselves to mythic status was the writing of Helen Hunt Jackson, particularly the novel *Ramona*. With the novel's popularity, with the wealth of promotional materials related to the novel, and inspired by the novel's evocative imagery, local preservation-minded citizens launched efforts to save the missions, culminating in the Landmarks Club, which was able to preserve a half dozen of the original structures.[56]

At the same time that the original missions were being preserved, architects launched a style directly influenced by the heavy adobe walls, red-tiled roofs, tall bell towers, and arched and colonnaded walkways—Mission Revival. By the 1890s prominent public buildings in California—city halls, county courthouses, libraries, chic resort hotels, and Stanford University—as well as residences, first of prominent citizens like Harrison Gray Otis of the *Los Angeles Times*, and later homes, apartments, and even bungalow courts for those of more modest means, were all built in the trendy Mission Revival style.[57]

But the style did not remain in California. Significantly, it spread eastward, as both the Atchison, Topeka and Santa Fe and the Southern Pacific railroads adopted Mission Revival style for many of their stations across the country. No less significant, Mission Revival was the chosen style for the California pavilions at World's Fairs from 1893 until 1915. Further, as the style became recognized for not just architectural details but also for

The Ramona Hospital in San Bernardino employs a modernized Mission style in its tiled roof, arcade-style porch, and arcaded tower. Postcard circa 1910.

the "patient handicraft" and "loving sincerity" thought to be evocative of the missions themselves, other artisans affiliated themselves with the style. By the turn of the twentieth century those involved in the Arts and Crafts movement were affiliating themselves with the Mission style, too. Even the very design of Ramona landmarks left a lasting impact upon twentieth-century architectural styles. The noted architect Irving Gill, whose own roots lay in the Mission Revival style, wrote in 1916 of the "home of the future" that "Ramona's house, a landmark as familiar in the South as some of the Missions, was built around three sides of an open space. . . . In California we have liberally borrowed this home plan, for it is hard to devise a better, cozier, more convenient or practical scheme for a home."[58] Thus, Ramona's impact spread in the tangible landscape—both inside and outside—from coast to coast.

FICTION AND SOCIAL MEMORY

In the influential book *The Invention of Tradition* Eric Hobsbawm explains that many of the traditions we think most natural, most ancient, were in fact invented in the late nineteenth or early twentieth centuries. At a time when rapid social dislocations and technological changes caused the present to feel past-less, influential figures invented traditions to make the present feel grounded in the past.[59] In a region like southern California, transformed in the late nineteenth century by the American conquest, and then even more rapidly by railroads and the waves of incoming Anglo-American tourists and homeseekers, the image of powerful boosters inventing a new past for the region has been a compelling one. And so, for some sixty years, the story of the Ramona myth has been told.[60] What Hobsbawm and these interpreters of southern California's past overlook, as John Bodnar points out, is the role of individuals and "public discourse and exchange in the creation of traditions."[61] To suggest, then, that those tourists and homeseekers who visited Ramona attractions were merely naïve dupes lured by manipulative boosters to accept a patently phony fictional past is to overlook the complexities of the role of the past in the present, and to shortchange those many visitors who sought and found meaningful moments at Ramona-related landmarks.

In attempting to understand not the past per se, but the way the past is collectively remembered, the way the past is understood in the present, issues of fact and fiction take on new roles. Despite the fact that certain events can be said factually (and actually) to have taken place, that of itself is no guarantee that they will be remembered—at all or in that way—for social memory owes its allegiance to contemporary cultural meaning, not to factual fidelity. As scholars James Fentress and Chris Wickham point out, "The natural tendency of social memory is to suppress what is not meaningful or intuitively satisfying in the collective memories of the past, and interpolate or substitute what seems more appropriate."[62] With the waves of incoming upper- and middle-class white tourists and homeseekers, and with the eclipse of the preindustrial lifeways of both the Californios and the Mission Indians, those newly arrived accepted a version of the past not accurate in all its details, but nevertheless intelligible and comfortable to *them*.

That a work of fiction should serve this end may at first seem laughable, but it is, in fact, quite natural, for *stories* are common vehicles for social memories. Despite the fact that we may know a story to be fictional, we nevertheless often accept it as a version of reality, particularly when, as with *Ramona*, we also know that much in the story was based on fact. Further, certain works of fiction serve these purposes explicitly—recall that *Ramona* fit into the then-popular genre of regional fiction, one of whose primary principles was "the description of the surviving elements of a local past that [could] infuse the present with new meaning."[63]

It was the emergence at the same time of "gentry-class vacation practices"—touring the United States at first by rail and later by automobile—that created a literary audience for regional novels like *Ramona*. As Charles Miner Thompson, writing in the *Atlantic Monthly* just after the turn of the twentieth century, observed, "In the early [eighteen] seventies the summer boarder, so soon to develop into the summer cottager, was born, and with him a new audience for any writer who could describe the scenes in which he found so great a pleasure."[64] *Ramona*, though written as a social protest novel, was also made to order for the rush of tourists and homeseekers who poured into southern California beginning with the railroad-inspired "boom of the eighties." Soon seeking the places familiar from the novel, when automobile tourism allowed for individualized vacations and access to more remote sites, even the more difficult-to-reach Ramona landmarks (like Ramona's grave, located on a remote Indian reservation) became accessible and touristed.

In most cases, the very actions of tourists enshrined Ramona landmarks as tourist attractions: it was the tourists themselves, visiting Rancho Camulos in large numbers, who caused Reginaldo del Valle to request that a train station be built there. And it was the tourists themselves, carrying away souvenirs or carving their names in the walls of Ramona's Marriage Place, that demonstrated that the house could be a viable tourist attraction before it was renovated.[65]

Thus, the practices of tourists, some compelled independently by their own interest in the novel, others encouraged by the publications of boosters, literally helped shape southern California's landscape and, along with it, social memory in the region. As John Sears has pointed out, tourism, though often overlooked, has been important in the very creation of American culture, in defining places and regions.[66] As Ramona-related landmarks joined the canonical list of southern California tourist attractions, the Ramona-inspired version of the past was easily enfolded into social memory.

After all, as Marita Sturken has demonstrated, social memory is an "inventive social practice," integrating elements of fantasy and invention with memory and history. It does not "stand for the truth" but rather forms part of the "active, engaging practice of creating meaning." The trick, according to Lucy Lippard—and this applies particularly for understanding landscapes—is "to see how people weave stories into and out of places so as to construct identities," or, put slightly differently, how people weave stories into and out of places, and thereby engage the ongoing process of creating social memories—social memories upon which identities are based.[67]

As Sturken has explained,

> By recognizing that memory manifests itself in different and unexpected forms, that it integrates fantasy, invention, and reenactment, that it is a process of engaging with the past rather than a means to call it up, we will come to understand its role in enabling individuals to imbue the past with value in the present.[68]

The Ramona myth, more than an extravagant example of literary tourism, or a ridiculous case of tourists fooled by manipulative boosters, has permeated southern California's landscape and culture. To be sure, each year at performances of the Ramona Pageant, when pageant historian Phil Brigandi explains to eager questioners that *Ramona* was a work of fiction, and that, while some of the characters, places, and incidents are based on fact, they are, ultimately, still all fictional, some leave disappointed—still wishing to believe she was real. No doubt this has always been the case: some who visited Ramona landmarks or bought Ramona souvenirs believed the story to be true, like the woman whose picture was taken at Mission San Gabriel in 1894 who penned on the back of the photograph "Ramona once worshipped in this Mission." But debating whether or not these tourists were duped or manipulated by boosters desirous of profit or, for that matter, disputing which was the *real* Home of Ramona[69] or the *real* Real Ramona, cannot be the final point about the Ramona myth, about tourist sites more broadly, or about social memory in general.

In the study of social memory elements of fiction and fantasy take on new roles. Not to be disregarded as the detritus of history, the fictional and the fantastic—the symbolic—can instead be understood as just as important as the factual in narrating who we are and in making a place for our collective past in the present. The fact that American children grow up learning that George Washington chopped down his father's cherry tree, and upon being confronted replied, "I cannot tell a lie," is no less significant when we understand that that story is fictional.[70] Indeed, it is then perhaps more significant, more symbolic.

But at tourist sites in particular, the factual and the fictional often freely interpenetrate; neither necessarily has priority in the framing of a given site.[71] And this is not because tourists are unable to differentiate the real from the false, but because they (we) are eager to engage both the factual *and* the fictional as they (we) actively create meaning at given sites, linking in different ways the more public narratives to their (our) own personal lives and experiences.[72] As Mark Neumann has pointed out, observing contemporary tourists at the Grand Canyon, and it applies here to the tourists at Ramona sites in days gone by:

> [T]he scenes made famous through television[, fiction,] and film are points for observing and identifying a [place] traveled over by popular characters [that tourists] have known elsewhere. . . . Fictional events that carry significance precisely because they have been first known somewhere that is not [this place]. Recognizing them validates a knowledge [that tourists] already hold about the place they may be visiting for the first time, yet seeing again.[73]

At places like the Home of Ramona and Ramona's Marriage Place, as at the Grand Canyon described by Neumann, tourists actively combine "varying fragments of fantasy, film, literature, personal experience and manufactured views . . . [taking] products projected towards a mass audience and turn[ing] them toward their own horizons." And, at bottom, as geographer Katherine Hannaford has made clear, the point is not so much whether the image or the story is false or true, but rather to understand that these stories and images, once available, can become self-perpetuating—causing people to view their very real encounters with places through the fictional stories or images.[74]

While it is impossible to precisely determine the demographics of readership for a particular historical text, and therefore impossible to know exactly who was reading *Ramona* and, by extension, who was visiting Ramona landmarks, we can speculate that the novel had a mainly white, middle- and upper-class audience that was made up of more women than men.[75] To be sure, many of the tourists who engaged with the novel in southern California's landscape whom we have met in the course of this book were indeed women: Olive Percival, the "pilgrim" to Camulos who made her "Home of Ramona" album, full of photographs and pressed plants.[76] And Ruby Faye Dennis who dedicated two pages of her honeymoon album to Ramona's Marriage Place, describing the items she bought at the curio shop, but not revealing the wish she made at "Ramona's well."[77] Or Mrs. Haines and her daughter Laura, who recast the story of Ramona and Alessandro, along with some fanciful food, to announce to their friends Laura's engagement.

Not all were women, however. Many of those who promoted Ramona attractions were men—Edwards Roberts, who wrote the first article establishing a link between the novel and a southern California locale; Charles Fletcher Lummis, influential southern California (and southwestern) promoter whose *Home of Ramona* became the first book spun off from the novel; Tommy Getz, who operated Ramona's Marriage Place for more than twenty years; or even Robert Callahan, who tried unsuccessfully to build a Ramona Village. Nor can it be said that these men merely profited from the novel while the women readers were lured by their promotional materials. These men were not only participants in the construction of the Ramona-inspired social memory because they profited from it, they also each *lived it* in important ways—like Lummis, who was so engaged in the Ramona-inspired romanticized version of California's past that he dressed as a Californio and wished to marry into the Del Valle family.

While some might be tempted to argue that it was the "suggestible" Victorian (and later) women who were lured by Ramona landmarks, upon closer examination it is clear that the fictional images from *Ramona* exerted their influence upon men as well. For example, attorney William A. Alderson, who, together with Carlyle Channing Davis authored *The True Story of Ramona; Its Facts and Fictions, Inspiration and Purpose*, revealed in his book his own experiences at Rancho Camulos—experiences much like those of other tourists, whether male of female. Recounting his first visit there on 2 July 1913 (after Señora Ysabel Del Valle had died but well before the family sold the property), he found the house "just as Mrs. Jackson saw and described it." And he went on,

> The feelings which obsessed me were indescribably intense. I knew the name and life of every character mentioned in the "Ramona" story, and they lived again in the dreamy fancy that possessed me. . . . I stood on every spot of Camulos ranch mentioned in "Ramona." . . .
>
> [Sitting on the south] veranda [I] fancied I could see Alessandro as he played his violin to soothe the suffering Felipe, his music at all times sad and plaintive because of his love for Ramona. . . .
>
> I went to the little chapel, with its white walls, set in the orange grove. . . . There was the altar cloth, so deftly repaired by Ramona that the rent in it might not be noticed; but it did not escape the keen and observing eyes of Helen Hunt Jackson.
>
> What thoughts seized me! How vividly real seemed all that is in the "Ramona" story concerning this sacred place![78]

Alderson, along with so many other men and women before him and since, seamlessly blended the real details he saw at Rancho Camulos that day

No 104 Ramona Haunts. The Back Veranda. Ramona pages 7, 19.

The interior verandas of Rancho Camulos are identified on this circa 1910 postcard as a "Ramona Haunt," with page numbers from the novel indicating how this precise view could be appreciated.

with the fictional experiences of Ramona and Alessandro that he recalled from the text, and both became components of the remembered past. Describing at one point how "[t]he torn altar cloth is still in existence and use," adding that "[t]his particular piece was made from Señora del Valle's wedding gown," the altar cloth was, nevertheless, most evocative for him when it compelled him to recall its place in the novel rather than its place in the lives of the del Valles. Alderson, with so many others, understood southern California's landscape and southern California's past, in part, through the novel *Ramona*, enfolding elements from the text into the real landscapes they saw, and into their memories of the region.

In 1940, more than fifty years after the first tourists began visiting Ramona landmarks, artist Maude Gunthrop visited Ramona's Marriage Place. Basing her understanding of the novel's characters on regional fiction's tradition of portraying what were perceived to be threatened remnant cultures, but understanding Ramona's impacts upon the region in broad terms, she wrote,

> This is one of the places made famous by Helen Hunt Jackson's immortal story of Ramona—a book which has preserved for us as nothing else has done, the memory of a vanished race and a way of life unique in the history of the world. What matter that the characters of the story are

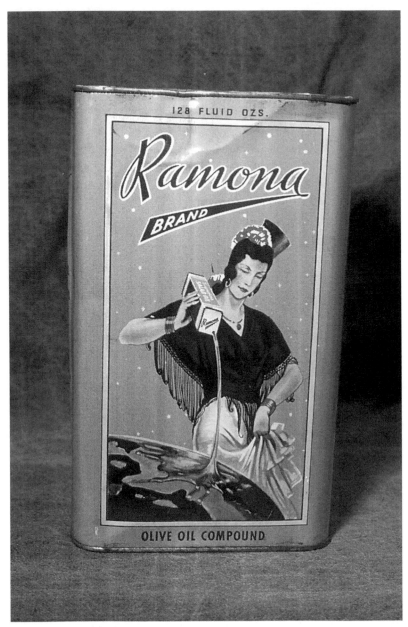

Ramona Brand Olive Oil, circa 1930.

largely fictional or that the places which claim the distinction of having played an intimate part in Ramona's life drama are legion? The pathetic Ramona and her Indian lover Alessandro live as truly in the hearts of the American people as do Sir Francis Drake or General Frémont and perhaps more vividly. Sentimental travelers have contentedly carried away, whether by their own prowess or the enterprise of the souvenir vendor, almost enough "fragments of Ramona's home" to build a hangar for a giant dirigible and will in all probability still be carrying them when the current dirigible is as obsolete as Fulton's steamboat. Any estimate of literary merit or historical accuracy is beside the point. This is immortality![79]

Indeed, Gunthrop was right—both about the dirigible and about Ramona. For many thousands of tourists and boosters in southern California, the fictional past represented in *Ramona* could be made meaningful in their present. In place, street, and business names; in the red-tiled roofs of mission-inspired architecture; in the annual performances of the Ramona Pageant; in the popular press; in history books, scrapbooks, and in the names of children now grown,[80] the golden glow cast over the region's past has not yet completely faded. The most important woman in the history and geography of southern California never lived, nor has she yet died, for Ramona lingers here still.

Acknowledgments

This work began as my first undergraduate term paper, followed me throughout my undergraduate career (revived in several more sophisticated papers), into graduate school (where it emerged as my master's thesis), and now, as part of my academic career and very much a part of my life, unfurls in book form. For me, and for several people who have helped me and known me most closely, this has quite literally long been a dream. Sadly, in a work whose incarnations have spanned more than fifteen years, some of those most important to the project have not lived to see its completion. My first gratitude is to them: to Mary F. Ward, former San Diego County historian; to James Davis, former UCLA Rare Books librarian; and to my mother, Femmy DeLyser, and my father, Hans Delyser. Like Helen Hunt Jackson, none reached "old age" and, also like Jackson, three of them died of cancer. Much of my life continues to follow their memories.

Many others closely involved with this project remain vibrantly among the living. Phil Brigandi, Ramona Pageant historian and Ramonaphile extraordinaire, began our long friendship by allowing me to examine, photocopy, and reproduce anything from his museum's collection and his own private collection. Later he patiently read and commented on my thesis, as well as this book's manuscript, and his exacting commitment to accuracy saved me from many of my own errors. Sharing Ramona with him as friends rather than rivals has enriched not only my research but also my life.

Many people at libraries and archives around southern California proved invaluable. David Zeidberg, director of the Huntington Library, as well as Dan Luckenbill, Lilace Hatayama, Simon Elliott, Jeff Rankin, Octavio Olvera, and others at the UCLA Library Department of Special Collections encouraged my passion for Ramona when I was an undergraduate student, then hired me as a staff member at UCLA Special Collections where that passion could flourish. Curiously, one of them once "discovered" a photograph showing me as the "Real Ramona"—but never did say where it came from. For their superb assistance I am grateful to Glen Creason, David Strother, and Bettye Ellison of the Los Angeles Public Library's Central Branch History Division, as well as to Richard Buchen and the other staff at the Southwest Museum's Braun Research Library, to Sally West and the other staff at the San Diego Historical Society, to Ranger Dick Miller and Ron Quinn at Old Town San Diego State Historic Park, to Kevin Hallaran at the Mission Inn Museum, to Vince Moses at the Riverside Municipal Museum, to the staff at the Seaver Center for Western History Research at the Los Angeles County Museum of Natural History, to the staff at the Huntington Library, and to Charles Johnson at the Ventura County Museum of History and Art. Shirley Rubel Lorenz, who grew up at Rancho Camulos, generously shared her stories and opened her family home to me, despite its then-recent devastation due to earthquake. Ramona Elizabeth ("Betty Ramona") (Brown) Patterson shared with me the story of her naming, and made me think differently about all the girls named for the novel's heroine.

From the day when Bruce Henstell suggested that I write that first term paper on the Ramona myth, he and many others have encouraged me in this research and writing and have read and contributed to drafts of this work. David Zeidberg taught that first undergraduate class; Michael Curry and Stephen Matthews later encouraged me and Ramona in their classes as well; Bob Bogdan inspired me with his postcard collection and the cultural importance of postcards; my M.A. and Ph.D. advisor Jim Duncan thought Ramona a great topic from the outset and provided guidance and valuable counsel; and Mark Monmonier held the vision for a book strongly enough to work with me through five drafts of a proposal. I knew I would find a good home on the Louisiana State University faculty when, during my interview, Bill Davidson, chair of the Department of Geography and Anthropology, burst out singing "Ramona." Many others have been important readers and supporters, including Bill Anders, Jill Brody, Richard Candida-Smith, Craig Colten, Denis Cosgrove, Arlene D'Avilla, Bill Deverell, Nancy Duncan, Tim Edensor, Mike Heffernan, Michael Martone, Eric Monkkonen, Steve Pile, Lydia Pulsipher, Helen Regis, Miles Richardson, Keith Sculle, Vicki Steele, and Karen Till.

Stan Hollwitz of the University of California Press met with me when I had just completed my master's thesis and even then believed I could turn this into a book. When someone else confounded our efforts, George Thompson and Randy Jones at the Center for American Places provided a welcoming home for the manuscript, and Carrie Mullen and Jason Weideman of the University of Minnesota Press had the vision and the ability to see this book to publication, with Therese Boyd offering insightful edits.

I am grateful to Kerry Lyle, who skillfully and patiently photographed items from my Ramona collection; to Rebecca Sheehan and Scott Brady, who helped with reference formatting; and to John Anderson, who created the index. This work was generously supported by a Syracuse University Fellowship, by an Ahmundson Short-Term Research Grant from the UCLA Library's Department of Special Collections, and by a grant of research leave for pretenure faculty from the Louisiana State University's College of Arts and Sciences.

The list is long: my gratitude is deep and sincere to each (and to those whose names are not mentioned but whose support has definitely been felt). Above all, I thank Paul Greenstein, for reading numerous drafts and always keeping me on track; for answering countless queries and always remaining patient; for pointing out new tidbits in obscure sources and always digging up more; for snaking the competition in several "critical" eBay auctions and always being willing to do it again; for living with Ramona and me for so many years. From our first kiss at "Ramona's Birthplace" he has been my partner—in Ramona and in all else besides.

Notes

Introduction

1. See, for example, James, *Through Ramona's Country.*

2. "Materials of Ramona" reports that Jackson knew of the christening of the lake; a clipping from 3 July 1885 in the same file reports of the naming of the lake near Monterey.

3. The first to leave a published account seems to have been Roberts, "Ramona's Home."

4. Callahan, *Daughter of Ramona,* viii; Callahan, *The Reason for a Ramona Village,* 12.

5. Foote, *Regional Fictions.*

6. Shaffer, *See America First.*

7. McWilliams, *Southern California;* Pitt, *Decline of the Californios;* Camarillo, *Chicanos in a Changing Society;* Almaguer, *Racial Fault Lines;* Haas, *Conquests and Historical Identities in California.*

8. See, for example, McWilliams, *Southern California;* Walker, *A Literary History of Southern California;* Dobie, "Introduction"; Davis, *City of Quartz;* Deverell, *Whitewashed Adobe.*

9. See Neumann, *On the Rim,* who discusses how tourists may visit the Grand Canyon for the first time while they are in fact seeing it "again" because its imagery is so ubiquitous.

10. See, for example, Connerton, *How Societies Remember;* Fentress and Wickham, *Social Memory;* Halbwachs, *The Collective Memory;* Irwin-Zarecjka, *Frames of Remembrance;* Kammen, *Mystic Chords of Memory;* Lipsitz, *Time Passages;* Middleton and Edwards, *Collective Remembering;* Nora, "Between Memory and History," 7–25; Sturken, *Tangled Memories;* Young, *The Texture of Memory;* and Zelizer, "Reading the Past Against the Grain," 204–39.

11. See Sturken, *Tangled Memories,* who describes memories of the *Challenger* explosion. Sturken further notes that this "particular mechanism of remembering, whereby we imagine our bodies in a spatial location, is also a means by which we situate our bodies in the nation" (26). Thus, social memory is importantly an *embodied* form of recollecting the past.

12. See Foote, *Shadowed Ground.*

13. Fentress and Wickham, *Social Memory,* xi, 59.

14. See Lears, *No Place of Grace;* and Monroy, *Thrown Among Strangers.*

15. Connerton, *How Societies Remember;* Fentress and Wickham, *Social Memory;* Sturken, *Tangled Memories.*

16. Marling, *George Washington Slept Here.* The story seems to first have appeared in Weems, *The Life of George Washington,* 16.

17. See Fentress and Wickham, *Social Memory,* particularly chapter 5 on the Mafia and Sicilian national identity.

18. Carey McWilliams coined the term *fantasy heritage* in his 1949 book *North from Mexico.* He also wrote critically of southern California's phony, Ramona-inspired past (and began a wave of such interpretations); see McWilliams, *Southern California.*

19. The quote is from Clough, *Ramona's Marriage Place.* For more on myth and the missions, see Pohlman, "California's Mission Myth," particularly the footnote on page 11. In geography, James and Nancy Duncan have utilized Roland Barthes's explanation of myth, writing that "myths occur when objects suitable for communication, landscapes included, become [in Barthes's words] 'appropriated by society'"; Duncan and Duncan, "Ideology and Bliss," 19.

20. See Lowenthal, *The Past Is a Foreign Country.*

21. See Mathes, *Helen Hunt Jackson and Her Indian Reform Legacy;* Mathes, *The Indian Reform Letters of Helen Hunt Jackson;* and Odell, *Helen Hunt Jackson. (H.H.).*

22. See Sandos, "Historic Preservation and Historical Facts," 168–85, 197–99, who more than one hundred years after *Ramona's* publication still insists on presenting evidence in an attempt to "prove" Camulos the undisputed home of the heroine.

23. See, for example, Cosgrove and Daniels, *The Iconography of Landscape;* DeLyser, "Authenticity on the Ground," 602–32; Duncan, *The City as Text;* Duncan and Duncan, "(Re)reading the Landscape," 117–26; Goss, "Once-upon-a-Time in the Commodity World," 45–75; Hanna, "Is It Roslyn or Is It Cicely?" 633–49; Lewis, "Axioms for Reading the Landscape," 11–32; Lowenthal, "Past Time, Present Place," 1–36; Mitchell, *The Lie of the Land;* Schein, "The Place of Landscape," 660–80.

24. Particularly in this case, as white, middle-class Americans since most of the visitors to Bodie are from that group. See DeLyser, "Authenticity on the Ground."

25. Lummis to Bogart, 29 July 1928, Lummis Papers.

1. A Determined Author and Her Novel

1. Rothman, *Living in the Shadow of Death,* 97; on her mother's opinions of her, see also Odell, *Helen Hunt Jackson.*

2. Jeanne C. Carr, "Recollections of Helen Hunt Jackson and Genesis of the Novel *Ramona*," n.d., 3, box 5, CA 44, Carr Papers.

3. Quoted in Powell, *California Classics,* 270.

4. Rothman, *Living in the Shadow of Death.*

5. Odell, *Helen Hunt Jackson,* 22.

6. Rothman, *Living in the Shadow of Death,* 90–91, 94.

7. Ibid., 95.

8. Phillips, *Helen Hunt Jackson.* Both Odell *(Helen Hunt Jackson)* and Phillips note, for example, that years later when living in Colorado Springs, Jackson was criticized for refusing to attend formal church services at all. Just the same, Jackson was not without religious beliefs.

9. Phillips, *Helen Hunt Jackson,* documents the profound influences of both of Jackson's parents on her writing.

10. Odell, *Helen Hunt Jackson;* Rothman, *Living in the Shadow of Death;* Phillips, *Helen Hunt Jackson.*

11. Phillips, *Helen Hunt Jackson.*

12. Rothman, *Living in the Shadow of Death,* notes Mrs. Fiske's attitudes toward abolitionism, women's suffrage, and female public speakers; Odell, *Helen Hunt Jackson,* traces those of Jackson.

13. Details about the life and death of Major Hunt, and the lives and deaths of their children, can be found in Odell, *Helen Hunt Jackson,* and in Banning, *Helen Hunt Jackson.*

14. Odell, *Helen Hunt Jackson,* includes a bibliography of Jackson's published writings; Phillips, *Helen Hunt Jackson,* also includes works of Jackson's not later collected and not mentioned by Odell.

15. Phillips, *Helen Hunt Jackson,* documents Jackson's relationship with Higginson more closely; it is clear from their surviving correspondence (both together and with others) that, though Higginson was married, the two had an ongoing and important intimate relationship.

16. Odell, *Helen Hunt Jackson,* details Jackson's travels as well as her commissions; Phillips, *Helen Hunt Jackson,* writes about them both in vivid detail; see also Powell, *California Classics.*

17. Phillips, *Helen Hunt Jackson;* Odell, *Helen Hunt Jackson.*

18. Phillips, *Helen Hunt Jackson,* 223. As Phillips documents, Jackson often wrote against the spread of "civilization."

19. Banning, *Helen Hunt Jackson,* 149.

20. Phillips, *Helen Hunt Jackson.*

21. Jackson's letter of 22 January 1885 is reprinted in Mathes, *Indian Reform Letters of Helen Hunt Jackson,* 341. Some, however, did listen: though Jackson was deeply disappointed with the book's sales, in 1881 Congress did approve reparations for the Poncas, also passing a bill allowing them to choose for themselves which reservation they would live on (Phillips, *Helen Hunt Jackson*).

22. Odell, *Helen Hunt Jackson*. Jackson visited California in the winter and spring of 1881–82, in the spring of 1883, and then for the last time in the winter, spring, and summer of 1884–85.

23. Phillips, *Helen Hunt Jackson*.

24. Estimates of the Mission Indian population vary: according to Odell (*Helen Hunt Jackson*, 184), the population had once numbered "over twenty thousand." Mathes sets the 1852 Mission Indian population at some 15,000 and notes that Jackson's own estimation of the population at the time of her 1872 visit was around 5,000. Mathes also cites a census of Indian villages (which Jackson also cites in her "Report") that lists the number of Mission Indians at just under 3,000. Mathes, "Helen Hunt Jackson," 65 and n. 14.

25. Jackson, "Echoes in the City of the Angels," 199.

26. Phillips, *Helen Hunt Jackson*.

27. *Californio* is the term used for those of Mexican or Spanish descent living in Alta (now American) California before the American conquest. Originally, during the Spanish (and later Mexican) colonial periods, the term helped to distinguish the *gente de razon* (people of reason; the colonizers) from the Native Americans in the region who were referred to as *sin razon* (without reason). Thus the term implied an elevated status and came eventually to imply people of "quality." Though many Californios were poor or working class, others were wealthy and commanded large estates, and they considered themselves in a class apart from those of the lower class, from those Mexicans who had intermarried with Indians, and those who came to California later. Though representing just a small minority of the Mexican population of California, these Californios were part of what became a landed aristocracy: some had been granted vast tracts of land by the king of Spain, many more by Mexican governors after Mexican independence, in large part through the seizure of former mission properties (Haas, *Conquests and Historical Identities in California*). Because of these landholdings (ranchos) they are also called *Rancheros*. Pitt, in *The Decline of the Californios*, notes that the term was in widespread use from the 1830s to the 1880s (although by his definition any person born in California of Spanish-speaking parents qualified). McWilliams, in *Southern California*, applies the term to the *gente de razon* (which he defines as "people of quality") and notes that as they began to lose their money and landed holdings the term fell into disuse, replaced by the term *Mexicans*. The term *Californio* came back into usage at least by the writing of McWilliams's book in 1946. Before then, those who wished to refer to these aristocratic citizens often used the term *Spanish*, and this included some Californios themselves, who actively proclaimed their own Spanish lineages (though that often bespoke an exaggeration). In the novel *Ramona*, written after the change in usage had begun, Jackson uses the term *Mexican*, not *Californio* (and she therefore leaves a less rigid distinction between the Mexican landed aristocrats and working-class Mexicans, although she does distinguish

the Señora Moreno as Spanish, and thus was herself aware of the distinction). I use *Californio* to describe the landed aristocracy of Mexican/Spanish descent because Jackson's romanticized portrayals of their lives (impressions she gathered in part directly from them) left such a lingering impression upon the region, and upon the white readers of Jackson's writings, that images of a romanticized life and lifestyle enjoyed by only a few came to eclipse the realities of the majority of southern California's Spanish-speaking population. See Almaguer, *Racial Fault Lines;* Camarillo, *Chicanos in a Changing Society;* Haas, *Conquests and Historical Identities in California;* McWilliams, *North from Mexico;* Monroy, *Thrown Among Strangers;* and Sánchez, *Telling Identities.*

28. Though some have confused this matter (a recent example is Sandos, "Historic Preservation and Historical Facts"), it was on this solo trip that Jackson made her first and only visit to Rancho Camulos in Ventura County, visiting there shortly before her 23 January arrival in Santa Barbara and only very briefly; her illustrator, Henry Sandham, did not arrive in California until April. Sandham did eventually draw illustrations of Rancho Camulos, but he cannot have visited there with Jackson, as the first leg of their trip together to the north of Los Angeles was conducted by ship, rather than along an overland route that could have taken them past the landlocked Camulos. Though Sandham's illustrations graced Jackson's articles for *The Century,* his work was also used, long after Jackson's death, to illustrate a two-volume edition of her novel *Ramona.* In his introduction to this edition, Sandham relates that it took him seventeen years to complete the illustrations for the novel. Most likely then, Sandham's visit to Camulos came after Jackson's novel *Ramona* was published, and after Jackson herself had died. Indeed, since Camulos had, by 1900, become irrevocably associated with the novel, it is likely that Sandham made his visit to Camulos specifically because of the rancho's postpublication link to the novel. By 1900 (unlike in 1884) references to the novel *Ramona* could scarcely be made without the inclusion of Camulos. Phil Brigandi (personal communication with author) further notes that, since many of Sandham's illustrations of Camulos feature *characters* from the novel, they could not have been made on this early trip. For details of Jackson's and Sandham's itineraries, see Mathes, *Indian Reform Letters;* Phillips, *Helen Hunt Jackson;* and Odell, *Helen Hunt Jackson.* Sandham's "Notes on Ramona Illustrations" appears in volume 1 of the Monterey edition of *Ramona.* For more on the association of Rancho Camulos with Jackson's novel, see chapter 2 below.

29. Kinney was a wealthy cigarette manufacturer who had settled in Sierra Madre, California, in the hope of curing his asthma. He met Jackson on her first visit to southern California while she was staying at the Kimball Mansion boarding house in Los Angeles and the two became fast friends, sharing a mutual concern for the Mission Indians. Not wishing to travel alone, Jackson had requested of Secretary Teller that Kinney be appointed her co-commissioner (Mathes, *Indian Reform Letters*). Kinney was so fond of the elder Jackson that he described his

wife, whom he married in 1884, as a "second Helen Hunt Jackson" (Kinney is quoted in Alexander, *Abbot Kinney's Venice-of-America*, 5). During the massive California land boom of the mid-1880s Kinney began a career as a real estate developer and became extremely influential in the development of the California beach towns of Santa Monica and Ocean Park. Kinney is now most known for his development there, in 1905, of Venice, complete with canals and gondoliers (ibid.).

30. Odell, *Helen Hunt Jackson;* Phillips, *Helen Hunt Jackson.*

31. Odell, *Helen Hunt Jackson;* Jackson, however, was not the most infallible of fieldworkers: on a visit to a Saboba Indian village she wore a "gray bonnet . . . upon which was the head of a large gray owl . . . the [Indian] bird of ill omen" and death. When local schoolteacher Mary Sheriff explained to her that it was the owl that was frightening the children of the village away, she decided not to wear it again (Mary Sheriff, quoted in Odell, *Helen Hunt Jackson,* 188–89).

32. Secretary Edward Teller in a letter to Jackson, quoted in Odell, *Helen Hunt Jackson,* 193; see also Phillips, *Helen Hunt Jackson,* 247.

33. Quoted in Odell, *Helen Hunt Jackson,* 200.

34. Philips, *Helen Hunt Jackson,* 245. See also Cook, *Conflict Between the California Indian and White Civilization;* Shipek, *Pushed into the Rocks;* and Gutiérrez, *When Jesus Came, the Corn Mothers Went Away.*

35. Phillips, *Helen Hunt Jackson,* 250; Mathes, *Indian Reform Letters,* 215–16. The "Report" was also published as an appendix to subsequent editions of Jackson's *A Century of Dishonor.*

36. Jackson to Thomas Bailey Aldrich, Los Angeles, 4 May 1883, quoted in Mathes, *Indian Reform Letters,* 258.

37. Jackson describes the experience in a letter to Higginson dated 5 February 1884 (in ibid., 313); see also Odell, *Helen Hunt Jackson,* and Phillips, *Helen Hunt Jackson.*

38. Phillips, *Helen Hunt Jackson,* 260.

39. Letter dated 8 November 1883, printed in James, *Through Ramona's Country,* 20.

40. Odell, *Helen Hunt Jackson;* Mathes, *Indian Reform Letters;* Phillips, *Helen Hunt Jackson.*

41. Quoted in Mathes, "Helen Hunt Jackson," 75.

42. The time is noteworthy because Jackson customarily did her serious writing only in the mornings (ibid.). This time she made an exception, writing to Thomas Bailey Aldrich, editor of the *Atlantic Monthly,* that it was "the first time in my whole life, that I ever wrote anything more than a letter, in the evening:—but I could not leave off within ten pages of the end" (quoted in Mathes, *Indian Reform Letters,* 318).

43. Ibid. In fact, Jackson herself insisted on simply Helen Jackson. Helen Hunt Jackson, a name she disliked, became established only after her death. See Phillips, *Helen Hunt Jackson.*

44. Letter dated 1 January 1884, quoted in Mathes, "Helen Hunt Jackson," 75.

45. Banning, *Helen Hunt Jackson,* 216.

46. Jackson to Warner, 2 October 1884, quoted in Mathes, *Indian Reform Letters,* 330.

47. Jackson had long complained of health problems, and never believed she would live a long life. See Phillips, *Helen Hunt Jackson.*

48. Ibid.

49. Jackson to Grover Cleveland, 8 August 1885, quoted in Mathes, *Indian Reform Letters,* 352.

50. About Jackson's death, see Odell, *Helen Hunt Jackson,* and Phillips, *Helen Hunt Jackson.* Jackson herself thought of *A Century of Dishonor* and *Ramona* as her only works of merit. Higginson and other literary contemporaries of hers thought it would be her poems that would leave lingering impressions. In fact, over one hundred years after her death, Jackson is remembered almost exclusively as the author of *Ramona,* albeit for reasons other than Jackson had intended (see Whitaker, *Helen Hunt Jackson,* and Phillips, *Helen Hunt Jackson*).

51. Helen Hunt Jackson, *Ramona: A Story* (New York: Signet Classic, 2002), 1. For the convenience of readers, all quotes from the novel are from this edition, still in print and currently the most recent, with introduction by Michael Dorris, and an afterword by Valerie Sherer Mathes. All page numbers appear in the text.

52. *North American Review* (1886), quoted in Dorris, "Introduction," v. See also Powell, *California Classics.*

53. Jackson, for all her attention to accurate detail elsewhere (she even wrote a California acquaintance to consult in the naming of one of Ramona's children), chose an Italian and not a Mexican name for her leading man: the Mexican version of the name is Alejandro. Kate Phillips, in her biography of Jackson, speculates that this may have been in order to assure that her white American audience who would be largely unfamiliar with Spanish pronunciation would speak the name correctly (*Helen Hunt Jackson,* 322 n. 91).

54. Carey McWilliams commented on *Ramona,* "The legendary quality of Mrs. Jackson's famous novel came about through the way in which she made elegant pre-Raphaelite characters out of Ramona and 'the half-breed Alessandro.' Such Indians were surely never seen upon this earth" (*Southern California,* 75).

55. Coolidge, "Introduction," in Jackson, *Ramona,* Monterey ed., xxi.

56. Letter dated 1 January 1884, quoted in Mathes, "Helen Hunt Jackson," 75.

57. Brodhead, *Cultures of Letters.*

58. Ibid., 150.

59. Ibid.

60. Odell, *Helen Hunt Jackson;* Mathes, *Indian Reform Letters;* Phillips, *Helen Hunt Jackson.*

61. On Jackson, Mathes, *Indian Reform Letters;* see also Brodhead, *Cultures of Letters,* 115–16, and Foote, *Regional Fictions.*

62. Brodhead, *Cultures of Letters*, 116.

63. As Kate Phillips documents, Jackson was also accustomed to using auto-biographical elements in her fiction, and *Ramona* shows this most strongly. Indeed, Ramona herself shares many of Jackson's own experiences: she is, for example, orphaned, widowed, and forced to wander. Phillips also traces the sources for many of the "real" people portrayed in the novel (Phillips, *Helen Hunt Jackson*). Further, Jackson clung so close to factual matters when it came to Native American issues that some passages in the novel appear almost exactly as they do in her "Report on the Conditions and Needs of the Mission Indians" co-authored with Abbot Kinney (Byers, "The Indian Matter of Helen Hunt Jackson's *Ramona*," 331–46).

64. Foote, *Regional Fictions*, 3; Brodhead, *Cultures of Letters*, 146.

65. Lears, *No Place of Grace*, 45.

66. Foote, *Regional Fictions*, 5.

67. Ibid., 16.

68. Jackson to Kinney, 20 February 1884, quoted in Mathes, *Indian Reform Letters*, 317.

69. Kate Phillips points out that *Ramona*'s ending is, in fact, not happy, for Ramona never recaptures the ecstasies of her early life with Alessandro. Further, she notes, Ramona and Felipe's departure for Mexico suggests California's impending demise. Phillips thus places *Ramona* not only as the first southern California novel, but also the first work in an important line of dystopic fiction about the region, a line including such works as Nathaniel West's *The Day of the Locust* (1939), John Steinbeck's *The Grapes of Wrath* (1939), and Evelyn Waugh's *The Loved One* (1948) (Phillips, *Helen Hunt Jackson*, 277).

70. Whitaker, *Helen Hunt Jackson*.

71. As is typical of regional fiction, Jackson's work was not written for the people she described (neither for the Indians nor the Californios in this case), but rather for an educated eastern (and midwestern) audience (see Brodhead, *Cultures of Letters*, 122).

72. Despite its prevalence, and despite the naturalistic way in which Jackson portrayed it, mustard is not native to California (see Sauer, "Historical Geography of the Western Frontier," 45).

73. She conveyed the same message in her other writings on the region. See Phillips, *Helen Hunt Jackson*.

74. Brodhead, *Cultures of Letters*.

75. Recall that Jackson sought to sugar the pill of Indian mistreatment by wrapping the Indian material in an engaging non-Indian introduction. See Mathes, *Indian Reform Letters*, 337.

76. See, for example, ibid., 41, 57, 175.

77. Through most of the novel Alessandro does not call Ramona by her name. At first he addresses her as Señorita Ramona or later as "my Señorita" (181).

When this offends Ramona he confides that he has given her an Indian name, Majel, meaning Wood Dove. This she accepts, only in a hispanicized version, "Majella" to make it feminine. For the rest of the novel Alessandro refers to Ramona as Majella, while Jackson, in the narration, still generally uses Ramona. For the sake of clarity, I have chosen to use only the name Ramona here.

78. Jackson to William Hayes Ward, 1 January 1884, in Mathes, *Indian Reform Letters*, 307.

79. See Mathes, *Indian Reform Letters;* O'Dell, *Helen Hunt Jackson;* and Phillips, *Helen Hunt Jackson.*

80. As Phillips in *Helen Hunt Jackson* makes clear, patient suffering and the strength that comes from it were characteristics that Jackson shared with her heroine.

81. Noriega, "Birth of the Southwest," 218.

82. Whitaker, *Helen Hunt Jackson*, 37.

83. Brodhead, *Cultures of Letters*, 120.

84. Nochlin, *The Politics of Vision*, 17.

85. Brodhead, *Cultures of Letters*, 121. Brodhead further makes the connection between regional fiction and early ethnography, claiming that regional writing was in fact a nineteenth-century form of ethnography. For all of Jackson's fieldwork, and for her desire to be true to factual details laced amid her fiction, she does rather appear as an ethnographer.

86. Foote, *Regional Fictions*, 16, 38.

87. Ibid., 183

88. Ibid., 5; and Brodhead, *Cultures of Letters.*

89. Noriega, "Birth of the Southwest," 214.

2. RAMONA'S PILGRIMS

1. MacCannell, *The Tourist;* Jakle, *The Tourist;* Urry, *The Tourist Gaze.*

2. Shaffer, *See America First.*

3. Ibid.

4. Ibid.

5. Ibid., 186; and Meinig, "Symbolic Landscapes," 164; Cosgrove, *Social Formation and Symbolic Landscape.*

6. Charles Fletcher Lummis, *The Old Missions* (1888), and "Missions" (*Drake's Magazine*, 1889, 193), quoted in Weitze, *California's Mission Revival*, 15. Shaffer, *See America First*, 190, 193.

7. Shaffer, *See America First*, 199, 194, 198.

8. Sears, *Sacred Places*, 5; Shaffer, *See America First*, 4.

9. Broadhead, *Cultures of Letters*, 125, 151; Foote, *Regional Fictions.*

10. Carr, *Los Angeles*, 128; Allen, *Ramona's Homeland.*

11. Sears, *Sacred Places*, 4.

12. Rice, Bullough, and Orsi, *The Elusive Eden*; Pitt, *Decline of the Californios*.

13. Meinig, *The Shaping of America*.

14. McWilliams, *Southern California*, 50; Meinig, *The Shaping of America*; Rice, Bullough, and Orsi, *Elusive Eden*; Cleland, *Cattle on a Thousand Hills*.

15. Pitt, *Decline of the Californios*, 249; McWilliams, *Southern California*.

16. Mayo, *Los Angeles*, 72; Dumke, *Boom of the Eighties*; Rice, Bullough, and Orsi, *Elusive Eden*; Meinig, *The Shaping of America*.

17. Meinig, *The Shaping of America*; Mayo, *Los Angeles*, 74, 77–78.

18. Dumke, *Boom of the Eighties*.

19. Ibid., 42.

20. Quoted in McWilliams, *Southern California*, 120.

21. Pitt, *Decline of the Californios*, 275.

22. A much smaller number of grants were made to those not in the upper class, and a few were made to California Indians as well; these generally were also smaller grants (see Haas, *Conquests and Historical Identities*).

23. Rice, Bullough, and Orsi, *Elusive Eden*; Pitt, *Decline of the Californios*; Haas, *Conquests and Historical Identities*.

24. Californios maintained what Lisbeth Haas describes as an "oral residual culture" where, though writing was present and influential, literacy was not essential and many operations and transactions still continued without it, following oral traditions; see Haas, *Conquests and Historical Identities*, 115, 116–17.

25. Rice, Bullough, and Orsi, *Elusive Eden*; Pitt, *Decline of the Californios*; see also Robinson, *Ranchos Become Cities* and *Land in California*.

26. Haas, *Conquests and Historical Identities*; Pitt, *Decline of the Californios*; Rice, Bullough, and Orsi, *Elusive Eden*; see also Camarillo, *Chicanos in a Changing Society*.

27. Camarillo, *Chicanos in a Changing Society*; Pitt, *Decline of the Californios*; Haas, *Conquests and Historical Identities*.

28. Phillips, *Helen Hunt Jackson*; Brodhead, *Cultures of Letters*; Foote, *Regional Fictions*.

29. Pitt, *Decline of the Californios*; Odell, *Helen Hunt Jackson*; Phillips, *A Literary Life*.

30. "'Ramona' and the Old Coronel House," 3; Phillips, *A Literary Life*; Pitt, *Decline of the Californios*; Cullimore, "The House of Don Antonio Coronel," 3, 19; James, *Through Ramona's Country*; Coronel Papers.

31. Padillo, *My History Not Yours*; Haas, *Conquests and Historical Identities*; Phillips, *A Literary Life*, 242; see also Jackson in *Ramona*, and "Echoes in the City of the Angels."

32. Jackson, "Echoes in the City of the Angels," 205.

33. Ibid., 200–201.

34. See Nochlin, *Politics of Vision*.

35. Pitt, *Decline of the Californios;* Camarillo, *Chicanos in a Changing Society;* Haas, *Conquest and Historical Identities;* Dumke, *Boom of the Eighties,* 276.

36. Pitt, *Decline of the Californios,* 274; Camarillo, *Chicanos in a Changing Society;* Haas, *Conquest and Historical Identities;* Phillips, *A Literary Life.*

37. Pitt, *Decline of the Californios,* 284; Mayo, *Los Angeles,* 89.

38. Eric Hobsbawm and Terrence Ranger, in their influential book, *The Invention of Tradition,* have suggested that the nineteenth century was a particularly important time for the invention of traditions, like those associated with *Ramona.*

39. Dumke, *Boom of the Eighties,* 36.

40. Ward, "Time and Place," 53–74; Nordhoff, *California for Health, Pleasure, and Residence;* see also Meinig, *The Shaping of America.*

41. Zimmerman, "Paradise Promoted," 22–33; Shaffer, *See America First.*

42. McWilliams, *Southern California;* Zimmerman, "Paradise Promoted"; Starr, *Inventing the Dream,* 76.

43. Gottlieb and Wolt, *Thinking Big,* 17.

44. Dumke, *Boom of the Eighties; Los Angeles Times,* 16 November 1886; McWilliams, *Southern California;* Gottlieb and Wolt, *Thinking Big,* 24.

45. *La Fiesta de Los Angeles. Official Program for 1895; La Fiesta de Los Angeles. Programme;* Starr, *Inventing the Dream.*

46. Weitze, *California's Mission Revival,* 65.

47. Named by Otis the "Outpost," the building no longer stands, but the nearby street, Outpost Drive, still exists in the Hollywood Hills above Franklin Avenue near La Brea.

48. *La Fiesta de Los Angeles. Official Program for 1895; California: The Empire Beautiful;* Gordon, *Charles F. Lummis.*

49. Gordon, *Charles F. Lummis;* Fiske and Lummis, *Charles F. Lummis;* Gottlieb and Wolt, *Thinking Big;* Starr, *Inventing the Dream,* 85.

50. Quoted in Thompson, *American Character,* 185–86.

51. Bingham, *Charles F. Lummis.*

52. Thompson, *American Character.*

53. Starr, *Inventing the Dream;* Smith, *This Land Was Ours.*

54. Meinig, *The Shaping of America,* 57; McWilliams, *Southern California;* Rice, Bullough, and Orsi, *Elusive Eden;* and Starr, *Inventing the Dream.*

55. Pomeroy, *In Search of the Golden West;* Shaffer, *See America First.*

56. Sears, *Sacred Places.* Jakle, *The Tourist,* notes the increase in leisure time.

57. Jakle, *The Tourist;* Pomeroy, *In Search of the Golden West;* Smith, *This Land Was Ours,* describes the Camulos rail stop.

58. Jakle, *The Tourist;* Pomeroy, *In Search of the Golden West.*

59. Hugo A. Taussig, *Retracing the Pioneers from West to East in an Automobile* (San Francisco: the author, 1910), quoted in Jakle, *The Tourist,* 108.

60. Jakle, *The Tourist.*

61. Ibid., 113.

62. Ibid., 103

63. Shaffer, *See America First.*

64. Jakle, *The Tourist,* 117, 121.

65. Ibid., 122; Pomeroy, *In Search of the Golden West.*

66. Jakle, *The Tourist,* 169; Pomeroy, *In Search of the Golden West.*

67. Jakle, *The Tourist,* 225; Shaffer, *See America First,* 161; Pomeroy, *In Search of the Golden West.*

68. Shaffer, *See America First.*

69. W. D. Rishel, "What Transcontinental Touring Really Means," *American Motorist* (May 1913), quoted in Shaffer, *See America First,* 148.

70. Weitze, *California's Mission Revival,* 14; Wood, *The Tourist's California,* 286–87.

71. Shaffer, *See America First.*

72. Jakle, *The Tourist.*

73. Expositions and Fairs Collection; Rydell, *All the World's a Fair;* Weitze, *California's Mission Revival.*

74. *The "Monarch" Souvenir of Sunset City and Sunset Scenes;* the Ramona's Cottage reference appears in portfolio 4.

75. Pageants, mostly outdoor ones, were held in towns and cities all across the United States. See Glassberg, *American Historical Pageantry.* Pomeroy, *In Search of the Golden West;* Jakle, *The Tourist;* Callahan, *The Reason for a Ramona Village.*

76. Jakle, *The Tourist.*

77. See Stewart, *On Longing;* Taft, *Photography and the American Scene.*

78. Shaffer, *See America First;* Israels, "Twelve Million Dollars a Year for Memories," 91–95.

79. The quote is from Israels, "Twelve Million Dollars a Year for Memories," 91; the Ramona souvenirs are from the collection of Phil Brigandi, Tustin, Calif. (hereafter Brigandi collection), and the author's collection.

80. Shaffer, *See America First;* Dotterer and Cranz, "The Picture Postcard," 44–50.

81. This is not always the case, however: Malek Alloula used French colonial postcards of Algeria to write his own "exorcism" from the colonial gaze in *The Colonial Harem,* 5.

82. Dotterer and Cranz, "The Picture Postcard," 44.

83. Taft, *Photography and the American Scene;* Shaffer, *See America First.*

84. Advertisement for Brewster photographs in *Southern California Tourists' Guide Book.*

85. Shaffer, *See America First;* Jakle, *The Tourist.*

86. See Shaffer, *See America First.*

87. Saunders, *Under the Sky in California,* 103. Subsequent page numbers appear in the text.

88. Honeymoon Scrapbook of Ruby Faye Dennis, author's collection.

89. Shaffer, *See America First*, 264, 265.

3. RANCHO CAMULOS

1. Smith, *This Land Was Ours*.

2. It was not unusual, by the 1870s and into the 1880s, for Californio house-holds to be headed by a woman—in the 1870s they headed some 25 percent of all Californio households (Haas, *Conquests and Historical Identities*). Griswold del Castillo, "The del Valle Family and the Fantasy Heritage"; Smith, *This Land Was Ours*.

3. Smith, *This Land Was Ours*, 252; Pitt, *The Decline of the Californios*, 253.

4. Smith, *This Land Was Ours*.

5. Griswold del Castillo, "The del Valle Family," 5.

6. The Native Sons is a fraternal organization, made up of Californios and Anglos alike, whose purpose is the "perpetuation of the romantic and patriotic past" (Peter Thomas Conmy, *The Origins and Purposes of the Native Sons and Daughters of the Golden West*, 10, quoted in Griswold del Castillo, "The del Valle Family," 8–9). The Ramona Parlor is still extant.

7. Griswold del Castillo, "The del Valle Family"; Smith, *This Land Was Ours*.

8. James, *Through Ramona's Country*, 109. For presentations and discussions of the arguments favoring both ranchos as the Home of Ramona, the list of sources is lengthy indeed, but see also, for example, Davis, "*Ramona*"; Davis and Alderson, *The True Story of "Ramona"*; and Vroman and Barnes, *The Genesis of the Story of Ramona*.

9. See, for example, Lummis, *Home of Ramona*; Vroman and Barnes, *The Genesis of the Story of Ramona*; Vroman Photographs.

10. Edwards Roberts, "Ramona's Home" (in 1887 edition of *Ramona*), 6.

11. Of course, since *Ramona* was never intended to be a strictly documentary work, neither Guajome nor Camulos fits Jackson's descriptions perfectly, a fact that advocates of either rancho were likely to ignore whenever it suited them. For example, though the altar cloth and the crosses on the hill matched Camulos, the home of the Morenos in the novel had an arched veranda, which Camulos did not. The Rancho Moreno further is described with a tiled roof, while Camulos had wooden shingles. See Brigandi, "The Rancho and the Romance," 5.

12. Roberts, "Ramona's Home," 1, 6–7.

13. Ibid., 7.

14. Roberts, *Santa Barbara and Around There*, 144.

15. Roberts, "Ramona's Home," 2–3.

16. Ibid.

17. Smith, *This Land Was Ours*; Griswold del Castillo, "The del Valle Family."

18. H. W. Patton, *Los Angeles Express,* 22 December 1920, quoted in Smith, *This Land Was Ours,* 210.

19. Pitt, *Decline of the Californios;* Smith, *This Land Was Ours;* Fiske and Lummis, *Charles F. Lummis.* Lummis was a member of the del Valle inner circle at this time and Smith puts him almost positively in attendance at Ulpiano's party. When marriage plans were broken off, Susana Carmen herself was heartbroken and did not marry until 1906 when she was thirty-five. Tragically, though it seemed she at last found happiness, she died in childbirth less than a year after her marriage (see Smith, *This Land Was Ours*). The star-crossed romance between Lummis and Susana Carmen del Valle (the daughter of Ygnacio's illegitimate son) suggests some parallels with Ramona and Alessandro, but it is not known whether the lovers involved saw it in this light.

20. Smith, *This Land Was Ours,* 239–40.

21. Lummis, *Home of Ramona,* n.p.

22. Ibid.

23. Ibid.

24. Smith, *This Land Was Ours.* A train schedule can be found in the del Valle family papers at the Huntington library.

25. Roberts, *Santa Barbara,* 146–47; "Camulos. The Real Home of Helen Hunt Jackson's 'Ramona.'"

26. Warner, "Camulos: Charles Dudley Warner on 'Ramona's' Home."

27. C. F. Crocker to R. F. del Valle, in del Valle Papers; Smith, *This Land Was Ours.* Photographs of the station house can be found at the Ventura County Museum of History and Art.

28. "Home of Ramona," *Los Angeles Times,* 7 June 1897

29. *Southern California Tourists' Guide Book,* n.p. Brewster's photo set included photographs of Del Valle family members enacting scenes from the novel. Copies can be found at the Ventura County Museum of History and Art.

30. Griswold del Castillo, "The del Valle Family," 9.

31. HM 43935, del Valle Papers. This letter is printed in its entirety; minor errors of spelling and punctuation have been altered toward modern grammatical Spanish. The letter is dated 1 October 1888.

32. "Autumn Days in Ventura," 562.

33. *In Semi-Tropical California,* 8; see also Wiseman, "Hacienda de Ramona."

34. The description of the Southern Pacific stop can be found in an undated Southern Pacific brochure in the James Marshal Miller Collection.

35. Wiseman, "Hacienda de Ramona," 114.

36. Vroman and Barnes, *Ramona,* n.p.

37. "Unmannerly Tourists."

38. "Noted Woman Passes Over," 16.

39. By J. Jones with music by L. F. Gottschalk; cited in U.S. Library of Congress, *Dramatic Compositions Copyrighted in the United States.*

40. The newspaper description of the set is an unidentified clipping, n.d., Pageant Files, Ramona Bowl Museum.

41. Original program at Sherman Foundation Library, Corona Del Mar, Calif.; photocopy of program in the Brigandi collection. James, *Through Ramona's Country,* identifies Griffith as Alessandro.

42. Niver and Bergsten, eds., *D. W. Griffith.*

43. *Souvenir Program, A Cinema Theatrical Entertainment of Ramona* (N.P.: Clune's Studios, 1915), available in the Ramona Collection at the UCLA Research Library, in the Brigandi collection, and in the author's collection.

44. "'Ramona' Is Picture of Plaintive Romance," 3.

45. Warner, "Warner's Scene of Mass for 'Ramona' Film," describes the set for the 1936 version.

46. Pageant Files, Ramona Bowl Museum.

47. Wiley-Kleemann, *Ramona's Spanish-Mexican Cookery.*

48. "Ramona's Home Closed," 19.

49. Home of Ramona Brand citrus labels are in the del Valle family papers, at Rancho Camulos, and in the Brigandi collection and the author's collection. Home of Ramona Brand raisins are mentioned in the register of the collection at the Seaver Center (the item itself is unavailable). Examples of the del Valle's Home of Ramona letterhead can be found in the correspondence files of Charles Fletcher Lummis, Lummis Papers. Both the citrus and wine labels were reproduced in vol. 42, nos. 3–4, of the *Ventura County Historical Society Quarterly* (1998).

50. Smith, *This Land Was Ours,* 197.

51. Mrs. Armitage S. C. Forbes, prominent Los Angeles clubwoman, spearheaded the movement to "restore" the "Kings Highway," which was based on the false notion (still widely believed: perhaps most notably by historian Kevin Starr; see Starr, *Inventing the Dream,* 11) that the original missions had been located one day's walk apart. In fact, since the original missions were founded over a period of fifty-four years it is unlikely that one single road ever connected them all. Furthermore, the distance between the missions varied widely, from as little as twelve miles to as much as seventy (clearly too far even for a stalwart sandaled padre to walk in a day). Nevertheless, Mrs. Forbes succeeded in her mission and the restored route was marked on many maps. Interestingly, in addition to passing all of the missions, the imagined route also passed Ramona's Marriage Place and both Homes of Ramona. At numerous points along the way the route was marked by replicas of mission bells, hung on posts shaped like shepherd's staves. It should be noted, also, that Mrs. Forbes's husband was the only bell manufacturer west of the Mississippi. The company also produced novelty and souvenir

items, in particular miniature replicas of the El Camino Real bell markers; see Pohlmann, "California's Mission Myth"; Smith, *This Land Was Ours;* and Roads to Romance maps (*Road Map to the Roads to Romance,* 1946 and 1952) among others; see also Kropp, "All Our Yesterdays."

52. Mission Play stock certificates, issued to members of the del Valle family are in the Reginaldo Francisco del Valle Papers. See also Deverell, *Whitewashed Adobe.*

53. "Farewell Fete Given at Ranch."

54. Smith, *This Land Was Ours,* 242.

55. Lummis's comment on the sale of the rancho is quoted in his correspondence, Lummis to Norton, 25 May 1924, ms. no. 1.1.3331B, Lummis Papers.

56. Shirley Rubel Lorenz, personal communication with author, 1994.

57. Camulos Ranch Landmark Application, author's collection.

58. Sandos, "Historic Preservation and Historical Facts," 168–85, 197–99. Unfortunately, Sandos's new evidence is unreliable, but, even more unfortunate, the argument itself is unfruitful: Jackson's is a work of fiction, and thus there can be no "real" Home of Ramona.

59. Wiseman, "Hacienda de Ramona," 112, 121.

60. Olive Percival's "Home of Ramona" can be found in Percival Papers.

61. Mrs. C. B. Jones's copy of the novel is in the author's collection.

4. A CLOSE SECOND

1. [Bohan], "Rancho Guajome," 585.

2. Haas, *Conquests and Historical Identities;* Engstrand and Ward, "Rancho Guajome," 250–83.

3. In fact, in the nineteenth century, particularly before the boom of the 1880s, it was not at all uncommon for entrepreneurial Anglos to marry the daughters of prominent Californios. These men generally took on some Hispanic customs and hispanicized their names. Thus, Benjamin Wilson became Don Benito, Abel Stearns became Don Abel, Stephen Foster became Don Estevan, William Wolfskill became Don Guillermo, and Cave Johnson Couts became Don Cuevas. These men became influential in the region before the boom of the 1880s: "two dozen of them owned one-third of Southern California's developed land in estates as large as 60,000 acres." Since the early Anglo-American settlers often came as single men to what was perceived by those in the United States as a frontier area, it is not surprising that they sought spouses among the local population and since many were aggressively upwardly mobile neither is it surprising that they chose their wives from among the local elite. (Pitt, *The Decline of the Californios;* the quote is from page 124; Haas, *Conquests and Historical Identities.*)

4. The Bandini family home was across the street from the Estudillo House, which would later become known as Ramona's Marriage Place. The Bandinis and

the Estudillos were close not only by proximity: Arcadia and Ysidora Bandini's father, Juan, had married Maria Dolores Estudillo in 1822 (Engstrand and Ward, "Ranch Guajome").

5. Engstrand and Scharf, "Rancho Guajome," 3. They question the accuracy of this family legend, but provide details of the actual wedding. According to Guajome historian Mary F. Ward, this account of the meeting between Couts and Bandini is purely fictitious and was propagated, along with a number of other myths about the Couts and Bandini families, by descendant Arcadia Scott Brennan (personal communication).

6. After the secularization of the missions it was not unusual for the Native American population formerly tied to the missions to work for those granted mission property after the Mexican conquest. At least three such indentured servants worked for the Coutses as house servants (Monroy, *Thrown Among Strangers*). Further, it is likely that these laborers used the same techniques as the Native Americans who built Mission San Luis Rey (from where Couts's crew hailed) (Engstrand and Ward, "Rancho Guajome," 19).

7. Engstrand and Scharf, "Rancho Guajome."

8. Couts to Thomas J. Henley, 7 July 1856, quoted in Engstrand and Ward, "Rancho Guajome," 19.

9. Engstrand and Scharf, "Rancho Guajome."

10. Stanford, *San Diego's L.L.B. Legal Lore and the Bar*, quoted in Engstrand and Ward, "Rancho Guajome," 278 n. 27.

11. See Monroy, *Thrown Among Strangers*; Gutiérrez, *When Jesus Came, the Corn Mothers Went Away*; Shipek, *Pushed Into the Rocks*.

12. Engstrand and Ward, "An Architectural Legacy."

13. Engstrand and Scharf, "Rancho Guajome," 5.

14. Engstrand and Ward, "Rancho Guajome"; the quote is from a National Survey of Historic Sites and Buildings report of 1967 and is cited on p. 259. Guajome's architectural historians, Engstrand and Ward, note, "The features of Rancho Guajome incorporated from an American Colonial tradition included a finished fireplace, milled doors and windows of American sash design, continuous house-barn-sheds, and a south orientation to protect from cold winter winds" (260).

15. Engstrand and Scharf, "Rancho Guajome," 7.

16. Ibid.; Mary F. Ward, personal communication.

17. Engstrand and Scharf, "Rancho Guajome," 8.

18. Odell, *Helen Hunt Jackson*, 181. Couts asserted that Jackson remained at Guajome for a period as long as three weeks, but his assertion cannot be true: Jackson's schedule scarcely left time for such a long visit, and her daybooks show her moving constantly in this period. Further, Jackson biographer Kate Phillips has actually questioned whether Jackson visited Guajome at all (*Helen Hunt Jackson*, 320 n. 53).

19. Odell, *Helen Hunt Jackson*, 181.

20. Authors who claim that Jackson was in California explicitly to gather material for a novel include "The Home of Ramona" *Los Angeles Times*, 7 June 1897; Vroman and Barnes, *The Genesis of the Story of Ramona;* Sandos, "Historic Preservation and Historical Facts," 168–85, 197–99. This list includes also Couts Jr. himself who was interviewed by Virginia Kassler in 1932. He showed Kassler the room Jackson had used "when she was writing Ramona" (Kassler manuscript, Richardson correspondence, Guajome files, San Diego County Historian's Office. A published version of Kassler's article appeared in the *Butterfield Express* for December 1963).

21. Vroman and Barnes, *The Genesis of the Story of Ramona,* n.p.

22. Kate Phillips, in *Helen Hunt Jackson,* points out that it actually can not be demonstrated that Jackson ever visited Guajome, only that she was near there (320 n. 53). See Odell, *Helen Hunt Jackson;* Brigandi, "The Rancho and the Romance," 5–40; Allen, *Ramona's Homeland.* Odell refutes Vroman and Barnes's claims.

23. For Guajome's similarities to the Moreno house in the novel, see, for example, Vroman and Barnes, *The Genesis of the Story of Ramona;* James, *Through Ramona's Country.*

24. Allen, *Ramona's Homeland,* n.p. Romer makes a similar claim for Guajome in her "*Ramona* Trails in Southern California."

25. The *Times* article appeared on 7 June 1897. The confusion in spelling here comes from the pronunciation of the Luiseño Indian word *Guajome,* meaning "frog pond." Ramona scholar George Wharton James (*Through Ramona's Country,* 98) notes that there are numerous springs in the area and that at one "many frogs 'do congregate.'" Descendants of the Couts family pronounce the name, not in the Spanish way, but in what is said to be the Native American pronunciation, "wah-HO-mah" (Romer, "*Ramona* Trails"; and personal communication, Mary Ward, San Diego County historian).

26. [Bohan,] "Rancho Guajome," 592, 585.

27. The reissued Santa Fe pamphlet, "Rancho Guajome: The Real Home of Ramona," is undated, but ca. 1895. A copy exists in the Brigandi collection.

28. Undated Santa Fe Railroad pamphlet, "Rancho Guajome: the Real Home of Ramona," in the Brigandi collection; the quotes are from the inside cover and page 6. Oddly enough, it is not known who A. McWhirter was, or in fact what the nature of his claim to the Guajome property was. San Diego County historian Mary Ward suggested that he may have been a lien holder of either Cave Jr. or William B. Couts's but, nevertheless, she has found no extant records containing McWhirter's name (personal communication).

29. W. B. Couts's undated pamphlet can be found in W. B. Couts correspondence, Lummis Papers.

30. Though they are far more rare than the very common postcards of Camulos, postcards identifying Guajome as Home of Ramona can be found in the Postcard Collection at the UCLA Research Library, the Brigandi collection, and the author's collection. Photographs of Guajome as the Home of Ramona include Vroman photographs, Seaver Center for Western History Research, Los Angeles County Museum of Natural History, in a series entitled "Ramona's Haunts."

31. Allen, *Ramona's Homeland*, n.p.

32. Del Rio [Lummis], "The California Classic," 4–10.

33. Vroman and Barnes, *The Genesis of the Story of Ramona*, n.p.

34. Davis and Alderson, *The True Story of "Ramona,"* 92.

35. James, *Through Ramona's Country*, 94, 97.

36. Ibid., 98.

37. Ibid.

38. Ibid.

39. William Deverell, Department of History, California Institute of Technology, personal communication.

40. Vroman and Barnes, *The Genesis of the Story of Ramona*, n.p.

41. Chase, *California Coast Trails*, quoted in Engstrand and Scharf, "Rancho Guajome," 10.

42. Quoted in Engstrand and Ward, "Rancho Guajome," 270.

43. Engstrand and Scharf, "Rancho Guajome," 10.

44. Engstrand and Ward, "Rancho Guajome," 273.

45. Poorman to Couts, 7 April 1928, Historical Files, Ramona Bowl Museum.

46. Engstrand and Ward, "Rancho Guajome," discuss Kyne's novel and Hearst's film. Phil Brigandi points out that the scenes apparently filmed at Camulos may in fact have been filmed at a set built to resemble Camulos (personal communication). Either way, the resemblance to Camulos was purposeful and remains unmistakable.

47. The real estate agent is quoted in the column of Frank Rhoads, *San Diego Union*, 20 October 1966.

48. Engstrand and Scharf, "Rancho Guajome."

49. James, *Through Ramona's Country*, 94–95.

50. Ibid., 95. Of course it is unlikely that Jackson could have imagined the reader response to her novel, and, though she herself was a very private person, preferring not to have her life discussed in the media and ordering her personal papers destroyed upon her death, it is not therefore necessary that she sought to maintain such privacy for her fictional characters. On Jackson's private life see Phillips, *Helen Hunt Jackson*.

51. Saunders, *Under the Sky in California*, 127.

52. Ibid., 129–30.

5. Ramona's Marriage Place

1. "Old Town San Diego's Suburb That Has Existed a Century."

2. In the novel, Ramona's name is entered as Majella Phaeel. Ramona had already taken the name Majella from Alessandro, and the Señora Moreno had told her that her father's name was Phail. In the novel, Ramona mispronounces her own last name (having never seen it written) and thus it is entered incorrectly into Father Gaspara's marriage record (see *Ramona*, 236).

3. Father A. D. Ubach of San Diego, who was very certain that he was the model for Father Gaspara, was fond of telling visitors and the press that no Catholic priest would have married a couple anywhere but in the church (see, for example, "Father Ubach Gives the Real Facts of Ramona's Marriage Place").

4. Works identifying the Estudillo adobe as the marriage place of Ramona include Vroman and Barnes, *The Genesis of the Story of Ramona;* James, *Through Ramona's Country;* Allen, *Ramona's Homeland.*

5. Thus, the Estudillo house was the only Ramona-identified adobe to actually have been built under Spanish or Mexican rule, rather than under the American regime, as both Camulos and Guajome were. Details of the construction of the house can be found in the Estudillo Files.

6. Before then it had been mentioned in Roberts, "Ramona's Home" (later reprinted in many editions of the novel) as well as in the *New York Post,* 19 June 1886.

7. "Old Town San Diego's Suburb That Has Existed a Century."

8. Ibid.

9. Estudillo, quoted in a letter to H. W. Waterman, 30 July 1909, in Waterman Papers.

10. Larkin column.

11. "The Day at Coronado."

12. Titus's purchase is documented in the article "Historic Mansion to Be Restored to Condition"; his transfer of the property to the company is recorded in the Estudillo Files. Salvador Estudillo himself stated that he sold the property in 1905 (letter to H. W. Waterman, 30 July 1909, Waterman Papers) but title searches conducted by California State Park employees indicate that the sale was actually finalized on 4 January 1906 (Estudillo Files).

13. Adams, *The Man John D. Spreckles,* 185, 192. See Jakle, *The Tourist;* and Shaffer, *See America First.*

14. "Historic Mansion to Be Restored to Condition."

15. Waterman's connections to the company and to Spreckles are described in an interview with Waldo Dean Waterman by Mary F. Ward, 25 February 1970, Historic Site Files, San Diego County Historian's Office.

16. Her research on adobes is described in Thornton, *Daring to Dream,* 65. Of course, the Estudillo adobe was originally built in the Spanish, not the Mexican, period.

17. Waterman's own quote about the restoration is from her "Specifications for Restoration of Typical Spanish California Dwelling Popularly Known as 'Marriage Place of Ramona,' Old Town, San Diego" (hereafter "Specifications for Restoration"), 6, Waterman Papers.

18. Ibid.

19. Ibid., 6, 13.

20. Waterman, "The Restoration of a Landmark," 11; Waterman, "Specifications for Restoration," 7, 9. Waterman's original drawings and the typescript for "Restoration of a Landmark" are in the Waterman Papers.

21. Waterman, "Specifications for Restoration," 7.

22. Waterman, "Restoration of a Landmark," 1–2.

23. Ibid., 3, 10; the italicized portion of her quote is from *Ramona*, 232, emphasis and quotation in original. Her drawings, including the details mentioned, are in the Waterman papers, San Diego Historical Society.

24. Authors who rely heavily on her 1935 document (typescript among her papers at the San Diego Historical Society) include her biographer; see Thornton, *Daring to Dream*.

25. Quotes from *Ramona* can be found on pp. 9 and 11 of "Restoration of a Landmark."

26. Waterman, "Restoration of a Landmark," 12.

27. Again, in the novel, these are features of the Rancho Moreno that Waterman sought to incorporate into Ramona's Marriage Place. Her quote is from pp. 10–11.

28. Mr. Spreckle's pleasure is expressed in a letter from W. Clayton to Waterman, 7 March 1910, in Waterman Papers.

29. The date of the building's opening, and the lease and sale (for the nominal fee of $10) of the property to Getz are recorded in the Estudillo Files.

30. Details about Getz can be found in La Suen, "Ramona's Marriage Place," 369; Miller, *Harbor of the Sun*, 225–26; "City Feels Keen Loss in Passing of Tommy Getz."

31. Glover, "In Ramona's Footsteps," 406–10. Signs on San Diego trolleys actually read "Ramona's Home"; this kind of confusion about Ramona landmarks, whether deliberate or not, was common.

32. James, *Through Ramona's Country*, 59.

33. The Ramona's Marriage Place pamphlet at the San Diego Historical Society, in "Info box 56," is one given away on a train, for example.

34. Thomas P. Getz's poem appeared in his undated pamphlet, "The Story of Ramona's Marriage Place," 1. A copy of this widely available pamphlet is in the California Ephemera Collection at the UCLA Research Library, the Brigandi collection, and the author's collection.

35. "Marriage Place of Ramona Spot Famed in History" describes the sign, as does Thomas P. Getz's pamphlet, "The Story of Ramona's Marriage Place," 11.

36. Getz's postcard offerings are listed at the back of his "Ramona's Marriage Place" pamphlet; his simulated cancellation stamp appears on many of the postcards that were sold there.

37. Getz, "Ramona's Marriage Place," 8. Information about Getz's souvenirs and their popularity is from ibid. Descriptions of the souvenir items sold by Getz are found in this pamphlet; some of the items themselves are in the Brigandi collection, the author's collection, and at the Ramona Bowl Museum.

38. Miller, "Harbor of the Sun," 227; Getz, "Ramona's Marriage Place," 10; "Marriage Place of Ramona Spot Famed in History."

39. "Looking Back in Our Files," 2 May 1967.

40. Lloyd, *The Birthplace of California*, n.p.

41. Miller, "Harbor of the Sun," 229.

42. Callahan, *Daughter of Ramona*, 6.

43. "Tommy Getz Vacationing in Arizona"; "City Feels Keen Loss in Passing of Tommy Getz."

44. Author's collection.

45. Details of the property's purchase records can be found in the Estudillo Files.

46. Old Town San Diego State Historic Park brochure, 1977, author's collection.

47. La Casa de Estudillo brochure, 1977, author's collection.

48. Clough, *Ramona's Marriage Place*.

49. Album in the author's collection.

6. Ramona's Birthplace

1. Though later Reid moved elsewhere, when he first married his Native American wife they lived near Mission San Gabriel, in a house he built as a wedding gift for his wife. On Reid see Dakin, *A Scotch Paisano in Old Los Angeles;* and Rasmussen, "Their Story Inspired *Ramona*." The quote is from James, *Through Ramona's Country*, 116.

2. James, *Through Ramona's Country*, mentions the rail and trolley connections.

3. Ibid.

4. Author's collection.

5. Postcard Collection, UCLA Research Library, and author's collection.

6. Bartlett and Bartlett, *Los Angeles in Seven Days*, 239.

7. A copy of Calhoun's program is in the Sherman Foundation Library, Corona del Mar, California.

8. Southern California Writers' Project, U.S. WPA, *Los Angeles*, 324.

7. "REAL" RAMONAS

1. The search in fact involved every character (and place) mentioned in the novel, though more attention was focused on Ramona than any other. See, for example, Vroman and Barnes, *The Genesis of the Story of Ramona*; Hufford, *The Real Ramona of Helen Hunt Jackson's Famous Novel*; Davis, "Ramona," 575–96; James, *Through Ramona's Country*; Allen, *Ramona's Homeland*; and Davis and Alderson, *The True Story of "Ramona."* Interest, both scholarly and otherwise, still exists, and contemporary explanations of the backgrounds of the characters can be found in Brigandi and Robinson, "The Killing of Juan Diego," 1–24.

2. James, *Through Ramona's Country*, 63.

3. Coolidge, introduction to *Ramona*, xx–xxi.

4. See, for example, James, *Through Ramona's Country*.

5. Davis and Alderson, *The True Story of "Ramona,"* 48; "Ethel R. Shorb," 362.

6. Sherwood, *Days of Vintage, Years of Vision*, 99. Sherwood's book is interesting particularly because of such spurious claims relating to Ramona for it shows that, even one hundred years after the novel's publication, such claims were still considered important enough to warrant publication.

7. James, *Through Ramona's Country*; Dakin, *A Scotch Paisano in Old Los Angeles*; Rasmussen, "Their Story Inspired *Ramona*."

8. Descriptions of the supposed real-life Ramona jewels and the lives of Blanca Yndart and Guadalupe Ridley can be found in Davis, "Ramona"; James, *Through Ramona's Country*; Davis and Alderson, *The True Story of Ramona*.

9. James, *Through Ramona's Country*, 64.

10. "Home of Ramona," *Los Angeles Times*, 7 June 1897.

11. Hufford, *The Real Ramona*, 39. Hufford's book is full of discrepancies. For example, he claims that Jackson wrote the bulk of the book in California (not New York City). Others are more subtle—while on page 3 Hufford claims that *Ramona* was written at a faster pace than Jackson's other works, later in the book he details how it was written over the course of four years (27–33).

12. Ibid., 7 (his italics), 45–47, 53.

13. The del Valle servant, mentioned in chapter 2 above, who sold photographs of herself was not widely heralded as a Real Ramona, although she clearly did earn some amount of money from some association with the novel.

14. Lubo herself, as a Cahuilla, was not what most had in mind when considering "Mission Indians," for the Cahuilla were never fully missionized and so cannot properly be numbered among California's Mission Indians, whom Helen Hunt Jackson had sought to help in writing *Ramona*. Nevertheless, by the time Jackson would have visited them, they had adopted many of the cultural traits and technologies of their colonizers (Spanish, Mexican, American) and would have appeared to outside observers much like "true" Mission Indians. Lubo was referred to as the "Cahuilla Ramona" but it never seems to have been an issue

that if she was a Cahuilla, then she was not a Mission Indian (Phil Brigandi, personal communication; see McWilliams, *Southern California,* on Cahuillas as nonmissionized Indians; see, for example, James, *Through Ramona's Country,* who uses the term *Cahuilla Ramona*).

15. James, *Through Ramona's Country;* "Materials of Ramona."

16. Jackson's report was published in 1883 and later as an appendix to *A Century of Dishonor.*

17. Jackson to Aldrich, 1 December 1884, quoted in Valerie Sherer Mathes, *Helen Hunt Jackson and Her Indian Reform Legacy,* 81.

18. Details of Lubo's life are presented in Brigandi and Robinson, "The Killing of Juan Diego."

19. "Ramona Makes Baskets to Sell to Tourists."

20. "Tales of the Hills," 3.

21. "Ramona Is Living." The same article appears as [James,] "The True Story about Ramona."

22. Quoted in Houston, *San Pedro City Dream,* 37.

23. Carr, "Ramona on Native Health."

24. Postcards of Lubo can be found in the California Postcard Collection, UCLA Research Library, the Brigandi collection, and the author's collection.

25. "Ramona Has Photo Taken."

26. "'Ramona' Will Be Exhibit at Fair."

27. "Hemet's Display Much Admired."

28. Powell, "Ramona's Real Story"; Pope, "(W)Here Lies Ramona."

29. It may seem unlikely that Farrar sought to publicize a pageant that, in 1922, had not happened yet, but Farrar was also president of the Chamber of Commerce at this time and so was involved in the planning for the pageant, which by mid-1922 was already well underway (Phil Brigandi, personal communication). Farrar's typescript autobiography is in the Irwin E. Farrar Papers.

30. "Monuments Planned for Indian Dead."

31. The Deagan Tower Chimes are promoted in Neuses to Poorman, letter dated 8 April 1931, 1 September 1931, and other correspondence "grave stones," Pageant Files, Ramona Bowl Museum.

32. "Hundreds to See Grave of Ramona"; Poorman to Newman Manufacturing Company, 19 May 1931, Pageant Files, Ramona Bowl Museum.

33. "Grave of Indian Martyr Marked in Sunday Rites."

34. "Tribe Says Tourists Won't Be Allowed to Visit Ramona's Grave This Year"; Morrison, "'Ramona' Tradition Since 1923."

35. Hopkins to Chamber of Commerce, 17 March 1927, Pageant Files, Ramona Pageant Museum.

36. Poorman to Hopkins, 19 March 1927, Pageant Files, Ramona Bowl Museum.

37. Powell, "Ramona's Real Story."

38. "Story of Ramona Told by Condino Hopkins of Banning."

39. "'Ramona' Last Living Child of Novel Heroine Dies."

8. THE STAGING OF A NOVEL

1. Brigandi, *Garnet Holme;* Cheney, "Study of the Sociological Impact of Helen Hunt Jackson"; the quote is from Cheney's interview with Mrs. Irene Baumer, 91.

2. "Ramona Production Will Be Annual Event."

3. See Glassberg, *American Historical Pageantry,* on the era of pageantry

4. Brigandi, *Garnet Holme,* 43; Phil Brigandi, personal communication.

5. Raynor, "How the Ramona Pageant Idea Was Conceived," pt. 3. Details of the early set can be found in the Ramona Pageant programs, 1923 and 1924, collection of the Ramona Bowl Museum.

6. Raynor, "How the Ramona Pageant Idea Was Conceived," pt. 2; Farrar, "Biography," in Farrar Papers.

7. The "Latest Touring Car" clipping (dated 23 March 1924, but further unidentified) can be found in the scrapbooks of the Pageant Files, Ramona Bowl Museum. Raynor, "How the Ramona Pageant Idea Was Conceived," pt. 2.

8. "Hemet's Display Much Admired"; Raynor, "How the Ramona Pageant Idea Was Conceived," pt. 2; "Romance Follows Trail of Ox Cart Trio Through City."

9. "Romance Follows Trail of Ox Cart Trio Through City."

10. Ibid.

11. "Ox Team Big Hit Over Southland."

12. Homer King to Lee Shippey, 24 April 1930, Pageant Files, Ramona Bowl Museum. Information about King from Phil Brigandi, personal communication.

13. Carr, *Los Angeles;* Harry Carr to Homer King, 2 April 1934, Pageant Files, Ramona Bowl Museum.

14. Poorman to Chandler, 28 May 1930, Pageant Files, Ramona Bowl Museum.

15. Hofmann to Secretaries [1936], Pageant Files, Ramona Bowl Museum.

16. Myers to Hemet–San Jacinto Chamber of Commerce, 5 April 1927, Pageant Files, Ramona Bowl Museum.

17. Thomas to Manager, Ramona Pageant, 30 November 1932, and other correspondence with All Year Club, Pageant Files, Ramona Bowl Museum.

18. Pageant correspondence with the Automobile Club of Southern California. Pageant Files, Ramona Bowl Museum.

19. Rathbun to Beall, 9 April 1926, Pageant Files, Ramona Bowl Museum.

20. Correspondence with Motor Transit Company and Pacific Electric Railway Company, Pageant Files, Ramona Bowl Museum.

21. *The Arrowhead Magazine,* undated clipping [1932], Pamphlet File 14, Literature Department, Los Angeles Public Library.

22. Undated clipping [1932], Pamphlet File 11, Literature Department, Los Angeles Public Library.

23. Ramona Pageant brochure, 1925, Ramona Bowl Museum.

24. "Early Romance to Be Revived."

25. Unidentified and undated [1924] clipping, Pageant Files, Ramona Bowl Museum.

26. Finch, "She Saw Alessandro Killed," 5.

27. Poorman to Kramer, 23 March 1928, Pageant Files, Ramona Bowl Museum.

28. Welch to Rathburn, 13 December 1926, Pageant Files, Ramona Bowl Museum.

29. Brigandi, *Garnet Holme,* 44; Pageant Files, Ramona Bowl Museum.

30. Pageant Files, Ramona Bowl Museum.

31. Brigandi, *Garnet Holme.* The region is proclaimed as a mecca in correspondence with Motor Transit Company, Pageant Files, Ramona Bowl Museum, as well as in the *Arrowhead Magazine* article.

32. Phil Brigandi, personal communication; Cheney, "Examination of the Sociological Impact of Helen Hunt Jackson."

33. Fish, "Romance Meets Reality in Hemet," 18.

34. "La Jolla Miss [Raquel Tejada Welch] Wins Role of Ramona in Hemet Play."

35. Shirley, "Welcome Changes in Ramona Pageant."

36. 1994 pageant brochure, author's collection.

9. RAMONA VILLAGE, FROM CONEY ISLAND TO TRAILER PARK

1. Callahan, *The Reason for a Ramona Village,* 2.

2. Later, a young woman who became Callahan's wife played the "second feminine lead" in a motion-picture version of *Daughter of Ramona,* which Callahan himself wrote and coproduced ("Indian Expert Reveals Marriage of 21 Months").

3. Callahan, *Daughter of Ramona,* vii.

4. Ibid., ix.

5. Ibid., ix–x.

6. Ibid., xii–xiii (emphasis added).

7. Ibid.

8. Callahan, *Reason for a Ramona Village,* 8, 11.

9. "Indian Village to Rise at Once."

10. Callahan, *Reason for a Ramona Village,* 4–5. Callahan writes that he believed the story told him by Don Okarche, or at least that Okarche "must have known characters similar to those in the book" (4).

11. Sculle, "Viewing the Roadside through Robert Callahan's Westerns."

12. Callahan, *Reason for a Ramona Village,* 12.

13. Callahan, *Daughter of Ramona;* Callahan to Poorman, 21 April 1931, Callahan correspondence, Ramona Bowl Museum files.

14. "Indian Village to Rise at Once"; "Chapel Will Grace Project."

15. Anonymous brochure, "Mission Village Tourist Court," in "Hotels, taverns, etc.," California Ephemera Collection, UCLA Research Library; "Indian Village to Rise at Once"; Callahan, *Reason for a Ramona Village.*

16. Callahan, *Reason for a Ramona Village,* 8.

17. "Chapel Will Grace Project."

18. "Indian Village to Rise at Once"; "Ramona Building Completed."

19. Callahan, *Reason for a Ramona Village,* 9.

20. Callahan to Ramona Pageant Association, 11 March 1928, Historical Files, Ramona Bowl Museum.

21. "Indian Village to Rise at Once."

22. Callahan, *Reason for a Ramona Village,* 9.

23. Ibid., 10–11.

24. Ibid., 8–9.

25. "Ramona Building Completed."

26. Callahan, *Reason for a Ramona Village,* 11–12.

27. Bogart to Lummis, 24 July 1928, and Lummis to Bogart, 29 July 1928, Lummis Papers. Because of the poor state of his health at the time Lummis wrote that he would be unable to campaign further against the Village. Indeed, Charles Fletcher Lummis died of a brain tumor at his home, El Alisal, on the night of 25 November 1928 (Fiske and Lummis, *Charles F. Lummis*).

28. Brigandi, *Garnet Holme.*

29. A letter written by an assistant of Callahan's to the Hemet Chamber of Commerce mentions negotiations with Alice Calhoun (whose relation to Virginia Calhoun is unknown, perhaps just a mistaken first name), but throws no further light on the matter; Cole to President, Chamber of Commerce, 27 March 1928, Callahan folder, Historical Files, Ramona Bowl Museum.

30. Clippings in Ramona Pageant scrapbooks, Ramona Bowl Museum.

31. Callahan to Poorman, 6 March 1931, Callahan file, Historical Files, Ramona Bowl Museum.

32. Callahan to Poorman, 6 March 1931 and 30 March 1931, in ibid.

33. Cook to Poorman, 16 April 1934, in ibid.

34. Callahan's plans are described in an anonymous brochure, "Mission Village," ca. 1938, in "Hotels, taverns, etc.," California Ephemera Collection, UCLA Research Library.

35. "Originality, Enterprise, Good Taste," 5–6, 26, 28, the quote is from p. 5, quoted in Sculle, "Viewing the Roadside," 100.

36. Callahan, *Reason for a Ramona Village,* cover, 12.

37. Advertisement for Callahan's Old West.

38. "Reverent Restoration." The chapel still stands at Heritage Square, part of William S. Hart Regional County Park. See http://www.scvhistory.com/scvhistory/sg022701.htm.

CONCLUSION

1. Steele, "The Town That Missed Its Chance to Become Famous."
2. Ibid.
3. Treleaven, "Why Ramona Was Not Written at San Juan," 491.
4. Watson, "And Ramona Left San Juan," 26–27.
5. Phillips, *Helen Hunt Jackson;* Mathes, *Indian Reform Letters of Helen Hunt Jackson;* Odell, *Helen Hunt Jackson.*
6. Fentress and Wickham, *Social Memory.*
7. Shorb's story, as related by family biographer Midge Sherwood in an unreferenced work, is likely as full of hyperbole as stage driver Regan's or theme-park developer Callahan's. Just the same, in the study of social memory, issues of truth and falsehood take on new meanings, for such exaggerated tales about the past as these reveal not just their (likely) spurious nature, but also the power of such stories in the popular imagination. Sherwood's work, therefore, takes on new interest, as a testimonial to Ramona's power, even in the late twentieth century. See Fentress and Wickham, *Social Memory;* and Sherwood, *Days of Vintage Years of Vision.*
8. Sherwood, *Days of Vintage, Years of Vision,* 254; *Los Angeles Times,* 28 July 1886, quoted in Sherwood, *Days of Vintage, Years of Vision,* 254. The "Irishman's flea" quote is from the *Los Angeles Times,* 3 February 1887.
9. LeMenager, *Ramona and Round About.*
10. Sherwood, *Days of Vintage, Years of Vision,* 253.
11. Quoted in ibid.
12. Quoted in ibid., 252 (emphasis in original).
13. Quoted in ibid., 253; Frickstad, *A Century of California Post Offices.*
14. Sherwood, *Days of Vintage, Years of Vision;* LeMenager, *Ramona and Round About.*
15. For Alessandro, Gunther, *Riverside County, California, Place Names,* 11; Moreno still exists, now as Moreno Valley, see any current southern California map; for the Ramona tract, see "New Map of the City of San Diego" (San Diego: Jacobs and Rock, n.d.), Pamphlet Maps Collection, UCLA Research Library; for Ramona Park see an advertisement in the *Los Angeles Times,* 22 December 1907.
16. "Ramona Village," later called "Ramona Gardens," still stands in East Los Angeles. A sketch of the project is featured on the masthead of *Public Housing and Slum Clearance News* 1, no. 1 (1939), Box 12, Wright Papers.
17. See Yeoh, "Street Names in Colonial Singapore," 313–22. Today many streets still carry the name of the heroine (including Ramona Avenue, Boulevard, Court,

Drive, Parkway, Place, Road, and Street), her spouse (Alessandro Avenue and Place, and, following the common misspelling, Allesandro Street and Way) and even places in the novel (Camulos Place and Street).

18. For the Home of Ramona, see, for example, maps by the Southern Pacific (James Marshal Miller Collection; Southern Pacific Railroad Company Collection, UCLA Research Library); for Ramona's Grave, see, for example "Roads to Romance" maps (Los Angeles Public Library and UCLA Research Library).

19. Los Angeles City Planning Commission, *Accomplishments*.

20. U.S. Library of Congress, *Dramatic Compositions*, indicates that the first dramatization was in 1885. Others followed rapidly: in 1887, '88, '89, '97, 1904, '05, '15, and '40. Most were set in five acts, but some were adapted for the stage in three, four, or even six acts.

21. Original program at Sherman Foundation Library, Corona Del Mar, Calif.; photocopy of program in the Brigandi collection; James, *Through Ramona's Country*, mentions the length of the production. See chapter 3 above for discussion of the script's references to Camulos.

22. James, *Through Ramona's Country*, 353–56, reprints a lengthy review from the *Los Angeles Times*.

23. "California's Great Drama"; unidentified clipping, 18 September 1905, Pageant Files, Ramona Bowl Museum; "'Ramona' Billed for the Burbank."

24. Arvidson, *When Movies Were Young*, 169.

25. Niver and Bergsten, eds., *D. W. Griffith*; Arvidson, *When Movies Were Young*, 169–70.

26. Niver and Bersten, eds., *D. W. Griffith*.

27. "'Ramona' Beautiful California Panorama"; McCarthy, "'Ramona' Filmed on Story Site in Color," 16. Ramona was also filmed in 1927 (and released in 1928) starring Dolores Del Rio, and in 1946 in a Spanish-language version. See DeLyser, "Ramona Memories: Constructing the Landscape in California Through a Fictional Text"; and Hershfield, *The Invention of Dolores Del Rio*.

28. *Motion Picture World* review of "Ramona," 28 May 1910, quoted in Noriega, "Birth of the Southwest," 203–26; the quote is from p. 219.

29. See, for example, Phillips, *Chiefs and Challengers*; Cook, *Conflict Between the California Indian and White Civilization*; Monroy, *Thrown Among Strangers*; Haas, *Conquests and Historical Identities*.

30. See Mathes, *Helen Hunt Jackson and Her Indian Reform Legacy*.

31. "Lake Majella. How It Was Formed and How It Was Christened," 3 July 1885, unidentified newspaper clipping in Jackson, comp., "Clippings about Helen Hunt Jackson"; also "H.H.," 13 August 1888, *The Transcript*, in ibid.

32. Warner, "'H.H.' in Southern California," 237.

33. Author's collection of Ramona-related ephemera and realia.

34. See McWilliams, *Southern California*; the quote is from p. 73.

35. Hall, "A 'Ramona' Luncheon," 506–7.

36. See, for example, McWilliams, *Southern California Country*; Starr, *Inventing the Dream*; Davis, *City of Quartz*.

37. See Brodhead, *Cultures of Letters*. Allen, *Ramona's Homeland*, notes that tourists read *Ramona* in preparation for a visit; and Carr, *Los Angeles*, writes that he and his family were among those tourists.

38. Davidson, "Introduction," xiii, xiv, xxix; quote from cemetery observer is from "H.S.B.," letter to the *New York Evening Post*, 12 September 1903, quoted on xiv.

39. Reimer, "Introduction," 1.

40. Ibid., 2. I am indebted to Michael Martone of the Creative Writing Program at University of Alabama, Tuscaloosa, for leading me to the texts on *Charlotte Temple* and *Anne of Green Gables*.

41. Levitt et al., "Meryl's Passion," 76.

42. McCabe, "Contesting Home," 231–45; the quote from p. 237 is attributed to local researcher and tourism promoter Charles Scobie; Luftig, "Literary Tourism and Dublin's Joyce," 141–54; Pemberton, *Dickens's London;* Squire, "Valuing Countryside," 5–10.

43. Sears, *Sacred Places*, 5.

44. See McCabe, "Contesting Home."

45. Herbert, "Literary Places, Tourism, and the Heritage Experience," 312–33; Pocock, "Haworth," 135–42.

46. Daniels "The Making of Constable Country," 9, 12.

47. Edensor, "National Identity and the Politics of Memory," 175–94; Edensor, *National Identity, Popular Culture and Everyday Life;* Mandel, *Is This Heaven?;* Riley, Baker, and Van Doren, "Movie Induced Tourism," 919–35; Brodie, *The Lord of the Rings Location Guidebook*.

48. Brodie, *Lord of the Rings Location Guidebook*.

49. *Southern California Tourists' Guide Book*, n.p.; Hanson, *The American Italy*, 141; Davis, *California's Old Mission Scenic Tour*, n.p.

50. Glover, "In Ramona's Footsteps," 406. Roberts, *Santa Barbara and Around There;* the quote is from p. 143.

51. Davis and Alderson, *The True Story of "Ramona*," 107.

52. Squire, "Valuing Countryside."

53. Undated editorial quoted in Smith, *This Land Was Ours*, 239.

54. [Bohan], "Rancho Guajome," 590.

55. "Guajome Link to Our Vanishing Yesterdays," 3.

56. Weitze, *California's Mission Revival*, 7–9. John Ogden Pohlman, "California's Mission Myth"; Thompson, *American Character*. Though not as widely read, Jackson's *Century* articles also raised awareness of and interest in the missions.

57. Weitze, *California's Mission Revival*.

58. Ibid., 115; Gill, "The Home of the Future," 85, quoted in ibid., 136.

59. Hobsbawm and Ranger, *The Invention of Tradition;* Hobsbawm, "Introduction."

60. See, for example, Davis, *City of Quartz;* McWilliams, *Southern California;* and Starr, *Inventing the Dream.*

61. Bodnar, *Remaking America,* 257 n. 8.

62. Fentress and Wickham, *Social Memory,* 58–59.

63. Ibid., 50; Foote, *Regional Fictions,* 183.

64. Charles Miner Thompson, "The Art of Miss Jewett," *Atlantic Monthly* 94 (1904), reprinted in *Appreciation of Sarah Orne Jewett: Twenty-nine Interpretive Essays,* ed. Richard Cary (Waterville, Maine: Colby College Press, 1973), 41, quoted in Brodhead, *Cultures of Letters,* 145.

65. See DeLyser, "Ramona Memories: Fiction, Tourist Practices, and the Place of the Past in Southern California," 886–908.

66. Sears, *Sacred Places.*

67. Sturken, *Tangled Memories,* 259; Lucy Lippard, quoted in Mitchell, "Lure of the Local," 76.

68. Sturken, *Tangled Memories,* 259.

69. Astonishingly, arguments in this vein continue to this day: Sandos, "Historic Preservation and Historical Facts," 168–85, 197–99.

70. Marling, *George Washington Slept Here.*

71. Rojek, "Indexing, Dragging and the Social Construction of Tourist Sights."

72. DeLyser, "Authenticity on the Ground," 602–32

73. Neumann, *On the Rim,* 173.

74. Ibid., 178, 186; Hannaford, "Culture Versus Commerce," 290.

75. Brodhead, *Cultures of Letters;* Foote, *Regional Fictions.*

76. Box 13, Collection 119, Percival Papers.

77. Author's collection.

78. Davis and Alderson, *The True Story of "Ramona,"* 197–214.

79. Gunthrop, *With a Sketch Book Along the Old Mission Trail,* 26.

80. See DeLyser, "Ramona Memories: Fiction, Tourist Practices, and Placing the Past in Southern California," 886–908, for an account of one woman named for the heroine.

BIBLIOGRAPHY

EDITIONS OF RAMONA

Jackson, Helen Hunt (H.H. [pseud.]). "Ramona: A Story." *The Christian Union,* 15 May to 6 November 1884.

———. *Ramona: A Story.* Boston: Roberts Brothers, 1884.

———. London: Macmillan and Company, 1884.

———. Boston: Roberts Brothers; San Francisco: Samuel Carson and Co., 1885, 1887.

———. With appendix, "Ramona's Home: A Visit to the Camulos Ranch, and to the Scenes Described by 'H.H.'" by Edwards Roberts. Boston: Roberts Brothers, 1887.

———. Boston: Little, Brown, 1899.

———. London: S. Low, Marston & Co., pre-1900.

———. Monterey Edition. Illustrations by Henry Sandham, Introduction by Susan Coolidge [Sarah Woolsey], and "Notes on Ramona Illustrations" by Henry Sandham. 2 vols. Boston: Little, Brown, 1900.

———. Monterey Edition de Luxe. Illustrations in color by Henry Sandham, Introduction by Susan Coolidge [Sarah Woolsey], and "Notes on Ramona Illustrations" by Henry Sandham. 2 vols. Boston: Little, Brown, 1900.

———. Pasadena Edition. Illustrations by Henry Sandham, Introduction by Susan Coolidge [Sarah Woolsey], and "Notes on Ramona Illustrations" by Henry Sandham. Boston: Little, Brown, 1907.

———. London: Sampson Low & Co., 1911.

———. New York: Grosset and Dunlap, 1912.

———. Tourists Edition. Introduction by A. C. Vroman, illustrations from original photographs by A. C. Vroman and decorative headings from drawings by Henry Sandham. Boston: Little, Brown, 1913.

———. Introduction by Shirley B. Jevons. London: Sampson Low & Co., 1914.

———. Introduction by A. C. Vroman and decorative headings from drawings by Henry Sandham. Illustrated by Jean Woolman Kirkbride with original watercolor photographs. Boston: Little, Brown, 1916.

———. Illustrations by Henry Sandham. Boston: Little, Brown, 1928.

————. Gift edition. Illustrations by Herbert M. Stoops. Boston: Little, Brown, 1932.

————. New York: Junior Literary Guild, 1932.

————. New York: Grosset and Dunlap, 1935.

————. Introduction by May Lamberton Becker, illustrations by N. C. Wyeth. Boston: Little, Brown. 1939.

————. New York: Triangle Books, 1941.

————. Edited by Art Type. New York: Books Inc., 1944.

————. Adapted by Olive Eckerson. New York: Globe Book Company, 1952.

————. Limited Editions Club Edition. Introduction by J. Frank Dobie, illustrations by Everett Gee Jackson. Los Angeles: Plantin Press for the Limited Editions Club, 1959.

————. New York: Avon Books, 1970.

————. Abridged by Nora Kramer. New York: Scholastic Book Services, 1973.

————. New York: Lighthouse Press, 1976.

————. New York: Pinnacle Books, 1981

————. Introduction by Michael Dorris. New York: Signet Classic, 1988.

————. *Ramona. The Heart and Conscience of Early California.* Read by Boots Martin. Abridged. Auburn, Calif.: Audio Editions, 1995.

————. Read by Flo Gibson. Washington, D.C.: Audio Book Contractors, ca. 1990.

————. Introduction by Michael Dorris, Afterword by Valerie Sherer Mathes. New York: Signet Classic, 2002.

————. *The Annotated Ramona.* Introduction and notes by Antoinette May. San Carlos, Calif.: Wide World Publishing/Tetra, 1989.

INTERVIEWS

Lorenz, Shirley Ruble. Interview by author. Camulos Ranch, Ventura County, California, March 1995.

Ward, Mary F. San Diego County Historian. Interview by author. San Diego, March 1995.

MANUSCRIPTS AND OTHER COLLECTIONS;
UNPUBLISHED MATERIALS

California Ephemera Collection. Department of Special Collections, University Research Library, University of California, Los Angeles.

California Postcard Collection. Department of Special Collections, University Research Library, University of California, Los Angeles.

Carr, Jeanne C. Papers. Huntington Library, San Marino, California.

Cheney, James A. "An Examination of the Sociological Impact of Helen Hunt Jackson on the San Jacinto Valley." Master's thesis, La Verne College, La Verne, California, 1973.

Citrus Label Collection. Department of Special Collections, University Research Library, University of California, Los Angeles.

Coronel, Antonio F. Papers. Seaver Center for Western History Research, Museum of Natural History, Los Angeles.

del Valle, Reginaldo Francisco. Papers. Huntington Library, San Marino, California.

del Valle family. Papers. Seaver Center for Western History Research, Museum of Natural History, Los Angeles.

DeLyser, Dydia. "Ramona Memories: Constructing the Landscape in California through a Fictional Text." Master's thesis, Department of Geography, Syracuse University, Syracuse, N.Y., 1996.

Dennerlein, Gerald E. "The History of the Ramonaland: The Economic and Social Development of San Jacinto, California." Master's thesis, Department of History, University of Southern California, Los Angeles, 1940.

Estudillo Files. Old Town State Historic Park. California Department of Parks and Recreation, San Diego Coast District Headquarters, San Diego, California.

Expositions and Fairs Collection. Department of Special Collections, University Research Library, University of California, Los Angeles.

Farrar, Irwin E. Papers. Department of Special Collections, University Research Library, University of California, Los Angeles.

———. "Riverside County Water Pioneer." Oral History, 1974. Department of Special Collections, University Research Library, University of California, Los Angeles.

Freud, Ralph. "A Career in Professional and University Theater." Oral History, 1969. Department of Special Collections, University Research Library, University of California, Los Angeles.

Hamilton [Adams], Peggy. Papers. Department of Special Collections, University Research Library, University of California, Los Angeles.

Historic Site Files, Descendant Files, Photograph Files. San Diego County Historian's Office, San Diego.

Historical Collection. Mission Inn Museum, Riverside, California.

Historical Files. Ramona Bowl Museum, Hemet, California.

Historical Files. San Diego County Department of Parks and Recreation, San Diego.

Hutchings, Frank Miller. Papers of the Frank Miller Family. Riverside Municipal Museum, Riverside, California.

Jackson, Opal, comp. "Clippings about Helen Hunt Jackson." California Scrapbook 68. Huntington Library, San Marino, California.

James, George Wharton. Papers. Braun Research Library, Southwest Museum, Los Angeles.

Los Angeles Chamber of Commerce Photograph Collection. Los Angeles Public Library, Los Angeles.

Los Angeles Daily News. Records, 1923–1958. Clippings file. Department of Special Collections, University Research Library, University of California, Los Angeles.

Los Angeles Herald Photo Morgue. Los Angeles Public Library, Los Angeles.

Lummis, Charles Fletcher. Papers. Braun Research Library, Southwest Museum, Los Angeles.

McLaughlin, Robert M. "A Descriptive Study of the Interrelationships Between the City of Hemet and the Ramona Pageant," Master's thesis, University of California, Los Angeles, 1972.

Miller, Dick. Collection of Postcards and Paper Ephemera, relating to Casa de Estudillo. "Ramona's Marriage Place." Old Town San Diego, California.

Miller, James Marshal, Collection. Department of Special Collections, University Research Library, University of California, Los Angeles.

Miscellaneous Manuscripts Collection. Department of Special Collections, University Research Library, University of California, Los Angeles.

Oversize Picture Collection. Department of Special Collections, University Research Library, University of California, Los Angeles.

Pamphlet File. Literature Department, Los Angeles Public Library, Los Angeles.

Pamphlet Maps Collection. Department of Special Collections, University Research Library, University of California, Los Angeles.

Percival, Olive. Papers. Department of Special Collections, University Research Library, University of California, Los Angeles.

Photograph Album Collection. Department of Special Collections, University Research Library, University of California, Los Angeles.

Photographer's Collection. Department of Special Collections, University Research Library, University of California, Los Angeles.

Picture Collection. Department of Special Collections, University Research Library, University of California, Los Angeles.

Pohlman, John Ogden. "California's Mission Myth." Ph.D. diss., Department of History, University of California, Los Angeles, 1974.

Postcard Collection. Department of Special Collections, University Research Library, University of California, Los Angeles.

Produce Label Collection. Seaver Center for Western History Research, Museum of Natural History, Los Angeles.

Pullen, William A. "The Ramona Pageant: A Historical and Analytical Study." Ph.D. diss., University of Southern California, 1973.

Ramona Collection. Department of Special Collections, University Research Library, University of California, Los Angeles.

Real Estate Business Scrap Book. Department of Special Collections, University Research Library, University of California, Los Angeles.

San Buenaventura Research Associates. National Register of Historic Places Application, Rancho Camulos. Santa Paula, California, 1995.

San Diego Historical Society, San Diego.

Security Pacific National Bank Historic Photograph Collection. Los Angeles Public Library.

Sheet Music Collection. Department of Special Collections, University Research Library, University of California, Los Angeles.

Southern Pacific Railroad Company Collection. Department of Special Collections, University Research Library, University of California, Los Angeles.

Vroman, Adam Clark. Photographs. Seaver Center for Western History Research, Museum of Natural History, Los Angeles.

Waterman Papers. San Diego Historical Society, San Diego.

Wright, Lloyd. Papers. Department of Special Collections, University Research Library, University of California, Los Angeles.

PUBLISHED MATERIALS SPECIFICALLY RELATED TO RAMONA

"Actress Dolores Del Rio Dead at 78." *Orange County Register,* 12 April 1983.

Adams, H. Austin. *The Man John D. Spreckles.* San Diego: Press of Frye and Smith, 1924.

Allen, Margaret V. *Ramona's Homeland.* Chula Vista, Calif.: Denrich Press, 1914.

Anderson, Roger. "Was Ramona Real?" *San Diego Reader* 17, no. 38 (September 1988): 1, 18, 20–21, 23–24.

"Anna Lehr Great Hit in Ramona." *Los Angeles Express,* 24 February 1916.

"Artists for Ramona." *Los Angeles Times,* 14 October 1928, sec. 3, p. 16.

Arvidson, Linda [Mrs. D. W. Griffith]. *When Movies Were Young.* 1925. Reprint. New York: Benjamin Bloom, 1968.

"The Author of Ramona Dead." *San Diego Union,* 13 August 1885.

"Autumn Days in Ventura." *Overland Monthly* (December 1889): 561–64.

Banning, Evelyn I. *Helen Hunt Jackson.* New York: Vanguard Press, 1973.

———. "Helen Hunt Jackson in San Diego." *Journal of San Diego History* 24, no. 4 (Fall 1978): 457–67.

Barker, Frances T. "Camulos, a Ranch of Romance." *Sunset Magazine* (December 1925): 65–66.

Bartlett, Laner, and Virginia S. Bartlett. *Los Angeles in Seven Days.* New York: Robert McBride and Company, 1932.

Battle, Don. "The Man Who Killed Alessandro." *Westways* 54, no. 2 (February 1962): 14.

Bednersh, Wayne. *Collectible Souvenir Spoons.* Paducah, Ky.: Collectorbooks, 1998.

Bicknell, Ralph G. "An Interrupted Wheeling." *Land of Sunshine* (March 1900): 228–35.

Biermann, Emil. "Ramona: Musical Gems from Clunes Cinema-Theatrical Production of Helen Hunt Jackson's Story of California and the Mission Indians." Pamphlet. Los Angeles: Lloyd Brown, 1916.

"Big Chief Thunder Cloud." *Los Angeles Record,* 15 September 1933.

"Bison Bluffs Bulldogs." *Los Angeles Times,* 26 March 1929, sec. 2, p. 5.

[Bohan, Elizabeth Baker.] "Rancho Guajome: The Real Home of Ramona." *Rural Californian* (November 1894): 585–92.

Bonestall, Cate C. "Home of Ramona Is Sold." *Los Angeles Times,* 10 August 1924.

"Bridegroom Is Ramona's Son." *Los Angeles Times,* 8 March 1907.

Brigandi, Phil. *Garnet Holme: California's Pageant Master.* Hemet, Calif.: Ramona Pageant Association, 1991.

———. "The Rancho and the Romance. Rancho Camulos: *The Home of Ramona.*" *Ventura County Historical Society Quarterly* 42, nos. 3–4 (1998): 5–40.

———, comp. *The Ramona Pageant: A Pictorial History, 1923–1998.* Hemet, Calif.: The Hemet News, 1997.

———, ed. *Looking Back . . . on the Ramona Pageant.* Orange, Calif.: Wrangler Press, 1985.

Brigandi, Phil, and John W. Robinson. "The Killing of Juan Diego: From Murder to Mythology." *Journal of San Diego History* 40, no. 1–2 (1995): 1–24.

Brown, John, Jr., and James Boyd. *History of San Bernardino and Riverside Counties.* Chicago: Lewis Publishing, 1922.

Byers, John R. "The Indian Matter of Helen Hunt Jackson's *Ramona*: From Fact to Fiction." *American Indian Quarterly* 2 (Winter 1975–76): 331–46.

Cairns, Ruth Cronyn. "As I Knew H.H.—Personal Memories of the Author of Ramona." *Los Angeles Times Sunday Magazine,* 11 October 1931.

California: The Empire Beautiful. San Francisco: Mrs. J .J. Owen, 1899.

"California Epic on Film." *Los Angeles Times,* 30 January 1916.

California for Health, Pleasure and Profit: Why You Should Go There. San Francisco: The Passenger Department of the Southern Pacific Co., 1894.

"California's Great Drama." *Los Angeles Times,* 26 February 1905.

"California's Stately Hall of Fame. Helen Maria Fiske Hunt Jackson." *Los Angeles Times,* 8 December 1940.

Callahan, Robert E. *Daughter of Ramona.* New York: Gaines Publishing, 1930.

———. *The Reason for a Ramona Village.* Los Angeles: Robert E. Callahan, 1928.

Callahan's Old West, 13660 Sierra Highway. Advertisement. *Van Nuys News and Green Sheet,* 9 July 1971.

"Camulos: The Real Home of Helen Hunt Jackson's 'Ramona.'" *Los Angeles Times,* 13 January 1887.

Capelle, Owen. "A Field for Fiction." *Land of Sunshine* (August 1894): 49–51.

Carleton, Robert L. "Blacks in San Diego County: A Social Profile, 1850–1880." *Journal of San Diego History* 21, no. 4 (1975): 7–20.

Carr, Harry. *Los Angeles: City of Dreams.* New York: D. Appleton-Century, 1935.

———. "'Ramona' on Native Health." *Los Angeles Times,* 1 April 1906.

———. *The West Is Still Wild.* Boston: Houghton-Mifflin, 1932.

Caughey, John, and Laree Caughey. *Los Angeles: Biography of a City.* Berkeley: University of California Press, 1976.

"Chapel Will Grace Project." *Los Angeles Times,* 18 November 1928.

Chase, J. Smeaton. *California Coast Trails: A Horseback Ride from Mexico to Oregon.* Boston: Houghton Mifflin, 1913.

"City Feels Keen Loss in Passing of Tommy Getz." *San Diego Union,* 2 August 1934.

"Clever Work of an Artist." *San Diego Union,* 8 February 1891.

Clough, Edwin H. *Ramona's Marriage Place: The House of Estudillo.* Chula Vista, Calif.: Denrich Press, [1910].

"Club Plans Memorial for Author. Pageant with Old Forest as Setting Tribute to Helen Hunt Jackson." *Los Angeles Times,* 4 May 1922.

Clune's Studios. *Clune's Production of Ramona, Adapted from Helen Hunt Jackson's Story of Early California and the Mission Indians: A Cinema-Theatrical Entertainment.* Los Angeles: Clune's Studios, 1915.

"Clune's 'Ramona' to Be at Hemet Theater." *Hemet News,* 19 May 1916.

Connor, E. Palmer. *The Romance of the Ranchos.* Los Angeles: Title Insurance and Trust Company, ca. 1928.

"Contract Is Let for Tommy Getz Memorial Bench." *San Diego Union,* 12 June 1935.

"Convent Building Will Be Only a Memory." *Los Angeles Times,* San Gabriel Valley edition, 24 August 1986.

Corey, W. A. "Author of *Ramona* in Los Angeles." *Los Angeles Times,* 28 March 1897.

Crowther, Mrs. Henry Christian. *High Lights: The Friday Morning Club, Los Angeles, California, April 1891–1938.* Los Angeles: The Friday Morning Club, n.d.

Cullimore, Clarence. "The House of Don Antonio Coronel." *Los Angeles Times Home Magazine,* 7 March 1943, 3, 19.

Custer, Elizabeth B. "Ramona's Land." *Boston Evening Transcript,* 14 May 1887.

Davis, Carlyle C. "*Ramona*: The Ideal and the Real." *Out West* 19, no. 6 (1903): 575–96.

Davis, Carlyle Channing, and William A. Alderson. *The True Story of "Ramona," Its Facts and Fictions, Inspiration and Purpose.* New York: Dodge Publishing, 1914.

Davis, Mike. *City of Quartz: Excavating the Future in Los Angeles.* London: Verso, 1990.

Davis, Nolan. *California's Old Mission Scenic Tour: By Motor or Rail.* Los Angeles: Los Angeles Chamber of Commerce, 1916.

"The Day at Coronado." *San Diego Union,* 23 May 1899.

Del Rio, Juan [Charles Fletcher Lummis]. "The California Classic." *Land of Sunshine* (1901): 4–10.

DeLyser, Dydia. "Ramona Memories: Fiction, Tourist Practices, and the Place of the Past in Southern California." *Annals of the Association of American Geographers* 93, no. 4 (December 2003): 886–908.

———. "Through Ramona's Country: A Work of Fiction and the Landscape of Southern California." *Ventura County Historical Society Quarterly* 42, nos. 3 and 4 (1998): 49–64.

"Demolition Sale." *Los Angeles Times,* San Gabriel Valley ed., 17 December 1987.

"Descendants of Bandinis Aid in N.D.G.W. [Native Daughters of the Golden West] Casa Marking." *San Diego Union,* 28 March 1946.

Deverell, William. *Whitewashed Adobe: The Rise of Los Angeles and the Remaking of Its Mexican Past.* Berkeley: University of California Press, 2004.

"Director Henry King, Discoverer of Stars, Dies." *Los Angeles Times,* 1 July 1982.

"Donald Duck in Old California!" Donald Duck Four Color no. 358. Walt Disney Productions, May 1951.

Eames, Ninetta. "Autumn Days in Ventura." *Overland Monthly,* 14, no. 84 (December 1889): 561–580.

"Early Romance to Be Revived: Helen Hunt Jackson's Novel Will be Re-enacted." *Los Angeles Times,* 25 May 1924.

"Elks Plan Elaborate Services and Monument to Tommy Getz." *San Diego Union,* 2 December 1934.

"Elks to Place Getz Memorial in Early Spring." *San Diego Union,* 16 January 1935.

Enderlein, Ella H. "Camulos and Ramona." *Sunset Magazine,* May 1903, 44–47.

Engstrand, Iris Wilson, and Thomas L. Scharf. "Rancho Guajome: A California Legacy Preserved." *Journal of San Diego History* (Winter 1974): 1–14.

Engstrand, Iris W., and Mary F. Ward. "Rancho Guajome: An Architectural Legacy Preserved." *Journal of San Diego History* (Fall 1995): 250–83.

"Estudillo House Center of Attraction." *San Diego Union,* 22 October 1910.

"Ethel R. Shorb: In Memoriam." *California Historical Society Quarterly* 38, no. 4 (September 1959): 361–62.

"Extol Memory of Hero-Padre." *Los Angeles Times,* 23 May 1913.

"Farewell Fete Given at Ranch: Del Valle Hosts at Final Bull's Head Feast." *Los Angeles Times,* 11 August 1924.

"Father Ubach Gives the Real Facts of Ramona's Marriage Place." *San Diego Union,* 25 June 1905.

Finch, R. M. "She Saw Alessandro Killed." *Los Angeles Times Sunday Magazine,* 19 April 1931.

Fish, Peter. "Romance Meets Reality in Hemet." *Sunset Magazine,* April 1995, 18.

"Fox Closes Adaptation of 'Ramona.'" *Los Angeles Times,* 14 August 1927.

"Freeway Was Final Insult to Indian Scholar's Dream." *Los Angeles Times,* 19 January 1981, sec. 1, p. 20.

Frickstad, Walter. *A Century of California Post Offices.* Oakland, Calif.: Philatelic Research Society, ca. 1957.

"Friends Boost for Memorial to Tommy Getz." *San Diego Union,* 10 October 1934.

"Fund for Getz Memorial Grows; Rhoads Contribute, Praises Move." *San Diego Union,* 12 October 1934.

Gale, Zona. *Frank Miller of Mission Inn.* New York: D. Appleton-Century, 1938.

"Garbage Scow [Ramona]: Yacht That Once Caught Eye Now Only Turns Nose." *Los Angeles Times,* 26 January 1970.

García Riera, Emilio. *Historia Documental del Cine Mexicano,* vol. 3, *1945–1948.* Mexico City: Ediciones Era, 1971.

Garrison, Myrtle. *Romance and History of California Ranchos.* Illustrations by William Johnson Goodacre. San Francisco: Harr Wagner Publishing, 1935.

[Getz, Thomas P.] "The Story of Ramona's Marriage Place, Old Town, San Diego, Calif." North San Diego: T. P. Getz or Ramona's Marriage Place [various editions, ca. 1914–56].

"Getz Memorial Is Dedicated by Rep M'Groarty." *San Diego Union,* 12 October 1935.

Gilbert, Helen. "Ramona's Country Today." *Desert Magazine,* May 1964, 11–12.

Gilbert, L. Wolfe, and Mabel Wayne. "Ramona. Waltz Song." Sheet Music. New York: Leo Feist, Inc., 1927.

Gill, Irving J. "The Home of the Future." *Architect and Engineer* (May 1916): 85.

Glover, A. K. "In Ramona's Footsteps." *Overland Monthly,* (October 1910): 406–10.

Good Roads in Southern California. Los Angeles: Los Angeles Chamber of Commerce for the members of Automobile Clubs of the United States, ca. 1914.

Goodman, Roland A., ed. *Plot Outlines of 100 Famous Novels.* New York: The Home Library, 1942.

Gover, M. E. *Sketches in the Country of Mrs. H. H. Jackson's "Ramona."* N.p., 1891.

Graham, Frank. "Chapel Is Real Ramona's Marriage Place." *San Diego Union,* 1 August 1937.

"Granddaughter of Ramona to Appear in Hemet Pageant." *Los Angeles Illustrated Daily News,* 12 April 1925.

"Grave Marking Plan Announced." *Hemet News,* 22 October 1937.

"Grave of Indian Martyr Marked in Sunday Rites." *Hemet News,* 21 August 1956.

Gregory, Lillian D. *Kingdom of the Sun in a Camera—Trip from Needles to the Sea.* Oro Grande, Calif.: Mesa Land, Lillian D. Gregory, ca. 1915.

Griswold del Castillo, Richard. "The del Valle Family and the Fantasy Heritage." *California History* 59 (1980): 3–15.

"Guadalupe Ridley: The Real Ramona." *Hollywood Daily Citizen,* 1 August 1931.

"Guajome: Link to Our Vanishing Yesterdays." *Southern California Rancher,* December 1943, 3.

Gulliver, Lucile. "Ramona's Country." *Book News Monthly* (August 1909).

Gunther, Jane Davies. *Riverside County, California, Place Names: Their Origins and Their Stories.* Riverside: Rubidoux Printing Co., 1984.

Gunthrop, Maude Robson. *With a Sketch Book Along the Old Mission Trail.* Caldwell, Idaho: Caxton Printers, 1946.

Hamblen, Abigail Ann. "Ramona: A Story of Passion." *Western Review* 8 (1971): 21–25.

Hampton, Ruth Haisley. "'El Pueblo' in the Days of H.H." *Touring Topics* (March 1931): 32–56.

Hanson, John Wesley. *The American Italy: The Scenic Wonderland of Perfect Climate, Golden Sunshine, Ever-Blooming Flowers and Always-Ripening Fruits.* Chicago: W. B. Conkey Co., 1896.

Hawthorne, Hildegarde. *Romantic Cities of California.* New York: D. Appleton-Century, 1939.

"Hemet's Display Much Admired." *Hemet News,* 14 October 1921.

Henderson, Robert M. *D.W. Griffith: His Life and Work.* New York: Oxford University Press, 1972.

Hershfield, Joanne. *The Invention of Dolores Del Rio.* Minneapolis: University of Minnesota Press, 2000.

Hill, Lawrence L. *La Reina: Los Angeles in Three Centuries. A Volume Commemorating the Fortieth Anniversary of the Founding of the Security Trust and Savings Bank of Los Angeles, February 11, 1889.* Los Angeles: Security Trust and Savings Bank, 1929.

"Historic Incidents in the Lives of Alessandro and Ramona." *Hemet News,* 5 April 1923.

"Historic Mansion to Be Restored to Condition." *San Diego Union,* 10 October 1907.

"Historic Picture of Ramona Shown by Owner." *Hemet News,* 2 May 1957.

Holder, Charles Frederick. *All About Pasadena and Its Vicinity: Its Climate, Missions, Trails and Cañons, Fruits, Flowers, and Game.* Boston: Less and Shepard, 1889.

"The Home of Ramona." *Los Angeles Times,* 7 June 1897.

"The Home of Ramona." *Christian Science Monitor,* 15 April 1910, 13.

Hoover, Mildred Brooke, H. E. Rensch, and E. G. Rensch. *Historic Spots in California.* Stanford, Calif.: Stanford University Press, 1932.

"How Ramona Was Written." *Atlantic Monthly* 86 (November 1900): 712–14.

Hufford, D. A. *The Real Ramona of Helen Hunt Jackson's Famous Novel*, 4th ed. Los Angeles: D. A. Hufford and Co., 1900.

"Hundreds to See Grave of Ramona." *Hemet News,* 17 April 1931.

"Hundreds to See Grave of Ramona." *Santa Ana Register,* 17 April 1931.

In Semi-Tropical California. N.p.: Southern Pacific Co., 1893.

"Indian Expert Reveals Marriage of 21 Months." *Los Angeles Times,* 18 November 1951.

"Indian Village to Rise at Once." *Los Angeles Times,* 10 June 1928.

Jackson, Helen Hunt. *A Century of Dishonor.* New York: Harper Brothers, 1882. 2d ed., Boston: Roberts Brothers, 1885.

———. "Echoes in the City of the Angels." *Century Magazine* 27 (December 1883): 194–209.

———. *Glimpses of California and the Missions.* Boston: Roberts Brothers, 1886; Little, Brown, 1919.

———. "Mountain Life: The New Hampshire Town of Bethlehem—Where It Is, What It Is, and All about It." *New York Evening Post,* 18 October 1865.

———. "Report on the Condition and Needs of the Mission Indians." Appendix in Jackson, *A Century of Dishonor,* 2d ed. Boston: Roberts Brothers, 1885.

James, George Wharton. *California Romantic and Beautiful: A History of Its Old Missions and of Its Indians; a Survey of Its Climate, Topography, Deserts, Mountains, Rivers, Valleys, Islands and Coast Line; a Description of Its Recreations and Festivals.* Boston: The Page Company, 1914.

———. *Picturesque Southern California.* Pasadena, Calif.: George Wharton James, 1898.

———. *Ramona, Western Empire.* N.d., 49–50. On file in Collection 200, James, G. W., Department of Special Collections, University Research Library, University of California, Los Angeles.

———. *Through Ramona's Country.* Boston: Little, Brown, 1908.

———. *Travelers' Handbook to Southern California.* Pasadena, Calif.: George Wharton James, 1905.

[James, George Wharton.] "The True Story about Ramona." *Riverside Morning Enterprise,* 8 July 1899.

Johnson, H. Cyril. *Scenic Guide to Southern California.* Susanville, Calif.: Scenic Guides, 1946.

Kassler, Virginia. Article about Ramona. *Butterfield Express,* December 1963.

Keeler, Charles A. *Southern California. Illustrated with Drawings from Nature and from Photographs by Louise M. Keeler.* Los Angeles: Passenger Department, Santa Fe, 1902.

Kessler, D. E. "The Restoration of Ramona's Marriage Place." *Pacific Monthly* (June 1910).

Kobrin, Jerry. "Dolores Del Rio Recalled as a 'Beautiful Person.'" *Orange County Register,* 13 April 1983.

La Fiesta de Los Angeles. Official Program for 1895. Los Angeles: Union Photo-engraving Co., 1895.

La Fiesta de Los Angeles. Programme. Los Angeles: Kingsley-Barnes and Neuner Co., 1895.

"La Jolla Miss [Raquel Tejada (Welch)] Wins Role of Ramona in Hemet Play." *Los Angeles Evening Herald,* 16 February 1959.

Lamb, Blaine P. "Silent Film Making in San Diego, 1898–1912." *Journal of San Diego History* 22, no. 4 (Fall 1976): 38–47.

Larkin, Polly. Column. *New Era,* Arbuckle, Calif., 1 April 1898.

La Suen. "Ramona's Marriage Place." *West Coast Magazine,* August 1910, 363–72.

Leadabrand, Russ. "Let's Explore a Byway: Along the Santa Clara River." *Westways* (June 1966): 21–23.

"Lee Shippey Says: Ramona's Story Charming but Untrue." *Los Angeles Times,* 7 July 1959.

LeMenager, Charles R. *Ramona and Round About: A History of San Diego's Little Known Back Country.* Ramona, Calif.: Eagle Peak Publishing, 1989.

"Life of 'Ramona' to Be Filmed at Warner Springs." *San Diego Union,* 18 April 1936.

Lindley, Walter, and J. P. Widney. *California of the South.* New York: D. Appleton and Co., 1888.

"The Little Lace Peddler. She Comes Out of H.H.'s Stories to Make a Collection." *San Diego Union,* 7 February 1891.

Lloyd, Mary. *The Birthplace of California: Old San Diego—Founded 1769.* San Diego: Neyenesch Printers, 1950.

"Looking Back in Our Files." *Los Angeles Herald Examiner,* 2 May 1967.

Los Angeles City Planning Commission. *Accomplishments.* Los Angeles: City Planning Commission, 1950, 1951, 1952.

Los Angeles General Directory Publishers, Inc. *Los Angeles City Directory.* Los Angeles: Los Angeles General Directory Publishers, Inc., 1899.

Luchetti, Cathy. *Home on the Range: A Culinary History of the American West.* New York: Villard Books, 1993.

Luis-Brown, David. "'White Slaves' and the 'Arrogant Mestiza': Reconfiguring Whiteness in *The Squatter and the Don* and *Ramona.*" *American Literature* 69, no. 4 (December 1997): 813–39.

Lummis, Charles Fletcher. *Home of Ramona.* Los Angeles: C. F. Lummis and Co., 1888.

"Marriage Place of Ramona Spot Famed in History." *San Diego Union,* 1 January 1917.

"Materials of Ramona: Real Scenes Invested with Composite Characters." *The Transcript,* n.d.

Mathes, Valerie Sherer. "Helen Hunt Jackson: Official Agent to the California Mission Indians." *Southern California Quarterly* 63 (Spring 1981): 63–82.

———. *Helen Hunt Jackson and Her Indian Reform Legacy.* Austin: University of Texas Press, 1990.

———. *The Indian Reform Letters of Helen Hunt Jackson, 1879–1885.* Norman: University of Oklahoma Press, 1998.

Maxwell, Ernest. "Justifiable Homicide California-Style." *Desert* (September 1980): 18–20.

May, Antoinette. *The Annotated Ramona.* San Carlos, Calif.: Wide World Publishing/ Tetra, 1989.

———. *Helen Hunt Jackson: A Lonely Voice of Conscience.* San Francisco: Chronicle Books, 1987.

May, Cliff. *Western Ranch Houses.* Menlo Park, Calif.: Lane Books, 1958.

Mayo, Morrow. *Los Angeles.* New York: Knopf, 1932.

McCarthy, Gus. "'Ramona' Filmed on Story Site in Color." *Motion Picture Herald,* 4 July 1936.

McClung, William Alexander. *Landscapes of Desire: Anglo Mythologies of Los Angeles.* Berkeley: University of California Press, 2000.

McGroarty, John S. "The Value of Property and Sentiment in the Real Estate Business." *West Coast Magazine* 12 (December 1912): 299–301.

McKinney, Dwight, ed. *Daily Doings and Guide.* Los Angeles: Federations of State Societies and Travelarians, 1932.

McWilliams, Carey. *Southern California: An Island on the Land.* New York: Duell, Sloane and Pearce, 1946; 2d ed., Salt Lake City, Utah: Peregrine Smith, 1973.

Miller, Max. *Harbor of the Sun: The Story of the Port of San Diego.* New York: Doubleday, Doran, 1940.

"Modern 'Ramonas' Meet at Hemet. Dolores Del Rio Greets Dorise Schukow and Minstrels." *Los Angeles Times,* 24 March 1928.

"Monarch" Souvenir of Sunset City and Sunset Scenes, Being Views of California Midwinter Fair and Famous Scenes in the Golden State. A Series of Pictures Taken by I.W. Taber, Official Photographer of the Midwinter Fair. N.p. 1894, 15 portfolios.

Monroy, Douglas. "Ramona, I Love You." *California History* (2003): 134–53, 171.

"Monuments Planned for Indian Dead: Graves of Ramona and Her Sweetheart to Be Marked." *Los Angeles Times,* 8 April 1931.

"More than 200 Indians at Impressive Services as Grave of Ramona in Cahuilla Cemetery Marked with Stone Monument." *Beaumont Gazette,* 21 April 1938.

Morrison, Patt. "'Ramona' Tradition Since 1923: Desert Drama Outlives Its Critics, Changing Times." *Los Angeles Times,* 2 May 1983.

Moylan, Michelle. "Materiality as Performance: The Forming of Helen Hunt Jackson's *Ramona*." In *Reading Books: Essays on the Material Text and Literature in America,* ed. Moylan and Lane Stiles, 223–47. Amherst: University of Massachusetts Press, 1996.

———. "Reading the Indians: The Ramona Myth in American Culture." *Prospects* 18 (1993): 153–86.

Myers, Virginia. *Ramona's Daughter.* New York: Pinnacle Books, 1981.

Nadeau, Remi. *City-Makers.* 1948; Corona del Mar, Calif.: Trans-Anglo Books, 1977.

———. *Los Angeles: From Mission to Modern City.* New York: Longmans, Green, 1960.

Neuhaus, Eugene. *The San Diego Garden Fair: Personal Impressions of the Architecture, Sculpture, Horticulture, Color Scheme and Other Aspects of the Panama California International Exposition.* San Francisco: Paul Elder and Company, 1916.

Nevins, Allan. "Helen Hunt Jackson—Sentimentalist vs. Realist." *American Scholar* 10 (Summer 1941): 269–85.

"New Light on 'Ramona': Two Women Bore Name of Famed Heroine." *Hemet News,* 20 May 1927.

Newcomb, Rexford. "Architecture of the Spanish Renaissance in California, Part XXII: The Estudillo House at Old Town, San Diego." *Western Architect* (November 1921): 119–23.

Niver, Kemp R., and Bebe Bergsten, eds. *D. W. Griffith, His Biograph Films in Perspective.* [Los Angeles]: Niver, 1974.

Noriega, Chon A. "Birth of the Southwest: Social Protest, Tourism, and D.W. Griffith's *Ramona*." In *The Birth of Whiteness: Race and the Emergence of U.S. Cinema,* ed. Daniel Bernardi, 203–26. New Brunswick, N.J.: Rutgers University Press, 1996.

Northrup, William M., and Newton W. Thompson, eds. *History of Alhambra.* Alhambra, Calif.: A. H. Cawston, 1936.

"Nuevo Is Now Ramona." *San Diego Union,* 8 July 1895.

O'Neal, Lulu R. *The History of Ramona, California and Environs.* Ramona, Calif.: Ballena Press, 1975.

Oandasan, William. "Ramona: Reflected Through Indigenous Eyes." *California Historical Courier* (February/March 1986): 7.

Odell, Ruth. *Helen Hunt Jackson (H.H.)* New York: D. Appleton–Century, 1939.

"Old Convent Enlarged." *Los Angeles Times,* 21 August 1910.

"Old Town San Diego's Suburb That Has Existed a Century: The Marriage Place of 'Ramona.'" *San Diego Union,* 28 August 1887.

"Orders of Restoration Granted." *Los Angeles Times,* 6 November 1919.

"Originality, Enterprise, Good Taste, and Lots of Effort and Money Make Mission Village." *Tourist Court Journal* 3 (December 1938): 5–6, 26.

"Ox Cart Here To Advertise Fete." *Santa Ana Register,* 14 March 1924.

"Ox Team Big Hit Over Southland." *Hemet News,* 23 March 1924.

Patterson, Tom. "As Anniversary Nears, Jackson's Romantic *Ramona* Studied." *Riverside Press-Enterprise,* 17 December 1984.

———. "'Real' Ramona Defies Conclusive Identification, But Many Have Tried." *Riverside Press-Enterprise,* 6 October 1985.

Patton, H. W. "Reminiscences of Ramona." *Los Angeles Times,* 12 February 1919.

Phillips, Kate. *Helen Hunt Jackson: A Literary Life.* Berkeley: University of California Press, 2003.

"Plan Monument for Ramona Grave." *Los Angeles Herald,* 8 April 1931.

Poingdestre, John Edmund. *Souvenir Hotel Ramona, San Luis Obispo, Cal.* San Francisco: N.p., ca. 1890.

Poole, Robert H. *Souvenir Program of Ramona: A Cinema Theatrical Entertainment.* Los Angeles: Clune's Productions, 1916.

Pope, Marie. "(W)Here Lies Ramona." *Western Woman* 9, no. 4 (1937): 46–47.

Powell, Garey. "Ramona's Real Story." *Los Angeles Times,* 1 October 1922.

Powell, Lawrence Clark. *California Classics: The Creative Literature of the Golden State.* Los Angeles: Ward Ritchie Press, 1971.

———. "California Classics Reread: Ramona." *Westways* 60, no. 7 (July 1968): 13–15, 55.

"Ramona." *San Diego Union,* 18 March 1887.

"*Ramona:* Charles Dudley Warner's Estimate of the Book." *Los Angeles Times,* 16 March 1887.

"Ramona: New Townsite Six Miles East on the S.P.R.R." *Los Angeles Times,* 15 January 1887.

"Ramona: The Greatest Attraction Yet Offered in the Way of Desirable Real Estate Investment." *Los Angeles Times,* 16 November 1886.

"'Ramona' and the Old Coronel House." *Los Angeles Saturday Post: Fruit, Forest and Farm,* 15 April 1905.

"'Ramona' Beautiful California Panorama." *Hemet News,* 2 June 1916.

"'Ramona' Billed for the Burbank." *Los Angeles Times,* 11 September 1905.

"Ramona Building Completed: Other Village Units to Be Rushed." *Los Angeles Times,* 8 July 1928.

"Ramona Has Photo Taken." *San Jacinto Register,* 23 January 1908.

"Ramona Honored at Unveiling of Monument on Reservation." *Los Angeles Times,* 10 April 1938.

"Ramona Is Living." *Riverside Morning Enterprise,* 9 July 1899, 6.

"'Ramona' Is Picture of Plaintive Romance; Stars Dolores Del Rio." *Los Angeles Times,* 26 February 1928, 3.

"'Ramona' Last Living Child of Novel Heroine Dies." *Los Angeles Evening Herald,* 1 October 1951.

"Ramona Loses 'Place' in Old Town." *San Diego Union,* 2 December 1968.

"Ramona Makes Baskets to Sell to Tourists." *Hemet News,* 25 April 1913.

"Ramona Ox Team Is Exhibited in City." *Corona Independent,* 13 March 1924.

"Ramona Pageant Rail Tour." *Los Angeles Herald Examiner,* 19 April 1964.

"Ramona Production Will Be Annual Event. Would Take Place of Annual Street Fair and Carnival." *San Jacinto Register,* 14 November 1913.

"Ramona Roof Tile." N. Clark and Sons advertisement. *California Arts and Architecture* (January 1931): 59.

"Ramona Squabble Just Now Timely." *Riverside Morning Enterprise,* 29 April 1931.

"Ramona Tent Village." *San Diego Union,* 27 June 1905.

"Ramona Village Housing Project to Contain 610 Units." *Southwest Builder and Contractor* 94, no. 13 (29 September 1939): 12–13.

"'Ramona' Will Be Exhibit at Fair: Noted Character of Helen Hunt Jackson to Occupy Hemet Booth Next Week." *Hemet News,* 7 October 1921.

"'Ramona' Wins Praise from National Board." *Hemet News,* 26 May 1916.

"Ramona's Grandson Starts Drive for Recreation Center." *Hemet News,* 10 November 1960.

"Ramona's Home Closed." *Touring Topics* (November 1920): 19.

"Ramona's Marriage Place Attraction Recalls Early Days." *Los Angeles Herald Examiner,* 22 March 1960.

"Ramona's Only Son Reveals Truth about His Mother." *San Jacinto Valley Register,* 7 May 1971.

"Ramona's Son Marries in Riverside." *Hemet News,* 30 May 1913.

"Rancho Guajome: The Real Home of Ramona." Santa Fe Railroad Pamphlet. ca. 1895. Collection of Phil Brigandi. Tustin, Calif.

Rasmussen, Cecilia. "L.A. Scene. The City Then and Now." *Los Angeles Times,* 17 January 1994.

———. "Their Story Inspired *Ramona.*" *Los Angeles Times,* 5 December 1999.

Raynor, Burdette. "How the Ramona Pageant Idea Was Conceived," part 1. *Hemet News.* Part 1, 4 April 1930; part 2, 11 April 1930; part 3, 18 April 1930.

Reed, Myrna C. "The Romantic Spirit of California." *Overland Monthly* 61 (1913): 595–600.

"Reverent Restoration. Tiny Ramona Chapel, Steeped in History, Gets a Face Lift in Newhall." *Los Angeles Times,* Valley Edition, 4 September 1989.

Rey, Felix. "A Tribute to Mission Style." *Architect and Engineer* (October 1924): 77.

Rhoads, Frank. Column. *San Diego Union,* 20 October 1966.

Rice, Richard B., William A. Bullough, and Richard J. Orsi. *The Elusive Eden: A New History of California.* New York: Knopf, 1988.

"Rich, Poor Unite in Tearful Tribute to Tommy Getz." *San Diego Union,* 4 August 1934.

Rieder, M. *Southern California.* Los Angeles: M. Rieder, 1906.

Road Map to the Roads to Romance, Southern California's Sunshine Empire. 1946, 1952. On file in the Department of Special Collections, University Research Library, University of California, Los Angeles.

Roberts, Edwards. "Ramona's Home: A Visit to Camulos Ranch, and to Scenes Described by 'H.H.'" *San Francisco Chronicle,* 9 May 1886.

———. "The Home of 'Ramona.' Scenes and Characters of Mrs. Jackson's Novel— the Journey from Santa Paula—The Ranch and Its Occupants—A Study in Identification." *New York Evening Post,* 19 June 1886.

———. *Santa Barbara and Around There.* Boston: Roberts Brothers, 1887.

Roberts, Gray, and Raymond Thorpe. "The Tragedy of Ramona." *True West* 12, no. 1 (October 1964): 39, 48–50.

Robinson, John W., and Bruce D. Risher. *The San Jacintos: The Mountain Country from Banning to Borrego Valley.* Arcadia, Calif.: Big Santa Anita Historical Society, 1993.

Robinson, W. W. *Panorama. A Picture History of Southern California.* Los Angeles: Title Insurance and Trust Company, 1953.

"Romance Follows Trail of Ox Cart Trio Through City." *Fullerton News,* 19 March 1924.

Romer, Margaret. "*Ramona* Trails in Southern California." *National Motorist* (April 1927): 10.

Ross, Nathanial. "Ramona-Affection Bites." *Song Sheet* (April 1994): 3–8.

"Sam Temple No More." *San Diego Union,* 25 August 1898.

San Diego Federal Writers' Project, U.S. Work Projects Administration. *San Diego: A California City.* San Diego: Neyenesch Printers Inc., 1937.

Sandos, James A. "Historic Preservation and Historical Facts: Helen Hunt Jackson, Rancho Camulos and Ramona." *California History* (Fall 1998): 168–85, 197–99.

Sarber, Mary A. *Charles F. Lummis: A Bibliography.* Tucson: University of Arizona Graduate Library School, 1977.

Saunders, Charles Francis. *The Story of Carmelita: Its Associations and its Trees.* Pasadena: A.C. Vroman, Inc., 1928.

———. *Under the Sky in California.* New York: McBride, Nas, and Co., 1913.

Scheick, William J. *The Half-Blood: A Cultural Symbol in 19th-Century American Fiction.* Lexington: University Press of Kentucky, 1979.

Schickel, Richard. *D.W. Griffith: An American Life.* New York: Simon and Schuster, 1984.

Sculle, Keith A. "Architecture and *Ramona:* An Influential Synergy." *Lamar Journal of the Humanities* 27, no. 1 (Spring 2003): 19–32.

———. "The Power of Myth in *Ramona* and Ramona's Marriage Place." *Mid-Atlantic Almanac* 12 (2003): 95–108.

———. "Viewing the Roadside through Robert Callahan's Westerns." *Mid-Atlantic Almanac* 9 (2000): 93–106.

Security Trust and Savings Bank. *El Pueblo: Los Angeles Before the Railroads.* Los Angeles: Equitable Branch, Security Trust and Savings Bank, 1928.

Sherwood, Midge. *Days of Vintage, Years of Vision.* Vol. 2. San Marino, Calif.: Orizaba Publications, 1987.

Shirley, Don. "Welcome Changes in Ramona Pageant." *Los Angeles Times,* 29 April 1995.

Smith, Wallace E. *This Land Was Ours: The Del Valles and Rancho Camulos.* Ventura, Calif.: Ventura County Historical Society, 1977.

"Son of Indian Maid Demands Percentage of Pageant Receipts." *Glendora Press,* 15 April 1927.

Southern California Tourist's Guide Book, 1888–9, 3d ed. *Embracing an Accurate Description of Cities, Towns Population, Climate, Products, Fertility of Soil, Places of Resort, and Objects of Interest, Etc., Etc., of Los Angeles, San Bernardino, San Diego, Ventura, and Santa Barbara Counties, and also a Condensed Guide to San Francisco.* Los Angeles: George E. Place and Co., 1888.

Southern California Writers' Project, U.S. Work Projects Administration. *Los Angeles: A Guide to the City and Its Environs.* New York: Hastings House, 1941.

Southern Pacific Lines. *Wayside Notes. Sunset Route.* N.p.: Southern Pacific Co., 1930.

Southwest Museum, Casa De Adobe. *Casa De Adobe Handbook.* 14th ed. Los Angeles: Southwest Museum, 1954.

"Special Bus Line to 'Ramona' Play." *Los Angeles Daily News,* 13 April 1948.

"Special Busses for Ramona Play." *Los Angeles Daily News,* 15 April 1952.

Stanford, Leland Ghent. *San Diego's LL.B., Legal Lore and the Bar: A History of Law and Justice in San Diego County.* San Diego: San Diego County Bar Association, Law Library Justice Foundation, 1968.

Starr, Kevin. *Inventing the Dream: California Through the Progressive Era.* New York: Oxford University Press, 1985.

Steele, Rufus M. "The Town that Missed Its Chance to Become Famous. True Tales of Old San Juan, II." *San Francisco Chronicle,* 2 November 1902.

Stellman, Louis J. "The Man Who Inspired 'Ramona.'" *Overland Monthly* (September 1907): 23–35.

Stevens, Errol Wayne. "Helen Hunt Jackson's *Ramona:* Social Problem Novel as Tourist Guide." *California History* 77 (Fall 1998): 158–67.

Stoddard, John L. *John L. Stoddard's Lectures: Complete in Ten Volumes.* Boston: Balch Brothers, 1898.

"Stone Ready for Ramona's Grave." *Beaumont Gazette,* 7 April 1938.

"The Story of Ramona's Marriage Place," North San Diego: T. P. Getz, ca. 1914.

"Story of Ramona Told by Condino Hopkins of Banning." *San Jacinto Register,* 8 May 1941.

Taber Photographic Co. *Ramona.* San Francisco: Taber Photographic Co., ca. 1890. On file in the Huntington Library, San Marino, Calif.

"Tales of the Hills: Romance and Reality of Life in the Mountains." *San Diego Union*, 31 July 1898, 3.

"Third Train to Ramona Scheduled." *Los Angeles Herald Examiner*, 7 April 1964.

Thomas, Brainerd. "California Singing Through the Play of Ramona." *California Southland*, ca. 1905, 7–8.

Thompson, David. "Ramona's Marriage Place." *California Magazine*, May 1952.

Thompson, Mark. *American Character: The Curious Life of Charles Fletcher Lummis and the Rediscovery of the Southwest*. New York: Arcade Publishing, 2001.

Thornton, Sally Bullard. *Daring to Dream: The Life of Hazel Wood Waterman*. San Diego: San Diego Historical Society, 1987.

Throwing Muses. *The Real Ramona*. Sound Recording. New York: Sire Records, 1991.

"Tommy Getz Vacationing in Arizona." *San Diego Union*, 8 April 1932.

"Towns Go Festive as Curtain for 'Ramona' Rises." *Los Angeles Daily News*, 17 April 1948.

Treleaven, Owen Clarke. "Why Ramona Was Not Written at San Juan." *Overland Monthly* (June 1919): 490–91.

"Tribe Says Tourists Won't Be Allowed to Visit Ramona's Grave This Year." *Riverside Press-Enterprise*, 18 April 1973.

"The True Story about Ramona: Jackson's Heroine Living at Cahuilla." *Riverside Press and Horticulturalist*, 13 July 1899.

"Unity Club. Basis of Fact in the Story of 'Ramona' Discussed." *San Diego Union*, 30 July 1887.

"Unmannerly Tourists. The Home of Ramona Closed to Visitors Because of Their Rudeness and Thievery." *Ventura Weekly Democrat*, 28 February 1896.

U.S. Department of the Interior, National Parks Service. National Survey of Historic Sites and Buildings, Statement of Significance. 9 February 1967.

U.S. Library of Congress. Copyright Office. *Dramatic Compositions Copyrighted in the United States, 1870–1916*. Washington, D.C.: U.S. Government Printing Office, 1918.

Ventura Free Press. No title; announcement that many "pilgrims" visit Camulos. 19 August 1887.

"Vice Squad Cracks Huge Bookie Setup." *Los Angeles Daily News*, 27 March 1951.

Vickery, Joyce C. "Contradictory Realities: Helen Hunt Jackson's California." *California Historical Courier* (February/March 1986): 6.

"Visits to Picturesque Scenes in the Romance of Ramona." *Los Angeles Times*, 1 January 1906.

"Vistas of the Past." *Los Angeles Times*, 18 April 1926.

Vroman, A. C., and T. F. Barnes. *The Genesis of the Story of Ramona: Why the Book Was Written, Explanatory Text of Points of Interest Mentioned in the Story*. Los Angeles: Press of Kingsley-Barnes Neuner Co., 1899. Cover title for *Ramona:*

Illustrated with an Explanatory Text and Thirty Illustrations from Original Photographs. Los Angeles: Press of Kingsley-Barnes Neuner Co., 1899.

Walker, Franklin. *A Literary History of Southern California.* Berkeley: University of California Press, 1950.

Wardrop, Daneen. "The Jouissant Politics of Helen Hunt Jackson's *Ramona*: The Ground That Is 'Mother's Lap.'" In *Speaking the Other Self: American Women Writers,* ed. Jeanne Reesman, 27–38. Athens: University of Georgia Press, 1997.

Warner, Charles Dudley. "Camulos: Charles Dudley Warner on 'Ramona's' Home." *Los Angeles Times,* 24 May 1887.

———. *Fashions in Literature and Other Literary and Social Essays and Addresses.* New York: Dodd, Mead, 1932.

———. "'H.H.' in Southern California." *The Critic* (14 May 1887): 237–38.

———. "Warner's Scene of Mass for 'Ramona' Film." *San Diego Union,* 22 May 1936.

Warren, Althea. "The 'Ramona' Tradition." *Saturday Review of Literature,* 30 December 1943.

Warren, Forest. "True Vow Club Visits Landmark. Golden Wedding Couples Wish for Happiness at Old Town Well." *San Diego Union,* 17 May 1938.

"Water for Temecula." *San Diego Union,* 6 February 1891.

Watson, Douglas S. "And Ramona Left San Juan." *Westways* (January 1938): 26–27.

Weiss, Marguerite [Getz]. "Old Town: It Was a Ghoulish Thing." *San Diego Union,* 28 October 1962.

Weitze, Karen J. *California's Mission Revival.* Los Angeles: Hennessey and Ingalls, 1984.

Wey, Auguste [Anna Picher]. "Side-Lights on *Ramona.*" *Land of Sunshine* (June 1895): 17–21.

"What Next? Shows Them How." *Los Angeles Times,* 6 January 1917.

"When Helen Hunt Jackson Sought Data for *Ramona.*" *Hemet News,* 16 May 1913.

"Where 'Ramona' Was Written, Near Highland Park." *Highland Park Herald,* 17 March 1906.

Whitaker, Rosemary. *Helen Hunt Jackson.* Boise, Idaho: Boise State University, 1987.

White, Clare. "Native Genius." *San Diego Magazine,* December 1984, 208–19.

Wiley-Kleemann, Pauline. *Ramona's Spanish-Mexican Cookery.* Los Angeles: Pauline Wiley-Kleeman, 1929.

Williamson, Mrs. M. Burton. "Mission Indians on the San Jacinto Reservation." *Annual Publications of the Historical Society of Southern California,* 1907–8.

Wiseman, Eleanor F. "Hacienda de Ramona." *Overland Monthly* (February 1899): 113–21.

Wolcott, Margorie T. "The House Near the Frog Pond." *Touring Topics* (December 1928): 40–54.

Wood, Ruth Kedzie. *The Tourist's California.* New York: Dodd, Mead, 1915.

GENERAL SOURCES

Alexander, Carolyn Elayne. *Abbot Kinney's Venice-of-America,* vol. 1, *The Golden Years: 1905–1920.* Los Angeles: Los Angeles Westside Genealogical Society, 1991.

Alloula, Malek. *The Colonial Harem.* Minneapolis: University of Minnesota Press, 1986.

Almaguer, Tomás. *Racial Fault Lines: The Historical Origins of White Supremacy in California.* Berkeley: University of California Press, 1990.

Bingham, Edwin R. *Charles F. Lummis: Editor of the Southwest.* San Marino, Calif.: The Huntington Library, 1955.

Bodnar, John. *Remaking America. Public Memory, Commemoration, and Patriotism in the Twentieth Century.* Princeton, N.J.: Princeton University Press, 1992.

Brodhead, Richard. *Cultures of Letters: Scenes of Reading and Writing in Nineteenth-Century America.* Chicago: University of Chicago Press, 1994.

Brodie, Ian. *The Lord of the Rings Location Guidebook.* Rev. ed. Aukland, New Zealand: HarperCollins, 2002.

Camarillo, Albert. *Chicanos in a Changing Society: From Mexican Pueblos to American Barrios in Santa Barbara and Southern California, 1848–1930.* Cambridge: Harvard University Press, 1979.

Cleland, Robert Glass. *The Cattle on a Thousand Hills: Southern California, 1850–1880,* 2nd ed. San Marino, Calif.: Huntington Library, 1951.

Connerton, Paul. *How Societies Remember.* Cambridge: Cambridge University Press, 1989.

Cook, Sherburne F. *The Conflict Between the California Indian and White Civilization.* Berkeley: University of California Press, 1979.

Cosgrove, Denis E. *Social Formation and Symbolic Landscape.* London: Croom Helm, 1984; Madison: University of Wisconsin Press, 1998.

Cosgrove, Denis, and Stephen Daniels. *The Iconography of Landscape: Essays on the Symbolic Representation, Design, and Use of Past Environments.* Cambridge: Cambridge University Press, 1988.

Dakin, Susanna Bryant. *A Scotch Paisano in Old Los Angeles: Hugo Reid's Life in California, 1832–1852; Derived from His Correspondence.* 1939; Berkeley: University of California Press, 1978.

Daniels, Stephen. "The Making of Constable Country, 1880–1940." *Landscape Research* 16, no. 2 (1979): 9–18.

Davidson, Cathy N. Introduction to *Charlotte Temple* by Susanna Haswell Rowson. New York: Oxford University Press, 1986.

DeLyser, Dydia. "Authenticity on the Ground: Engaging the Past in a California Ghost Town." *Annals of the Association of American Geographers* 89, no. 4 (December 1999): 602–32.

Dotterer, Steven, and Galen Cranz. "The Picture Postcard: Its Development and

Role in American Urbanization." *Journal of American Culture* 5, no. 1 (Spring 1982): 44–50.

Dumke, Glenn S. *The Boom of the Eighties in Southern California.* San Marino, Calif.: Huntington Library, 1944.

Duncan, James S. *The City as Text: The Politics of Landscape Interpretation in the Kandyan Kingdom.* Cambridge: Cambridge University Press, 1990.

Duncan, James S., and Nancy G. Duncan. "Ideology and Bliss: Roland Barthes and the Secret Histories of Landscape." In *Writing Worlds: Discourse, Text and Metaphor in the Representation of Landscape,* ed. Trevor J. Barnes and James S. Duncan. London: Routledge, 1992.

———. "(Re)reading the Landscape." *Environment and Planning D: Society and Space* 6 (1988): 117–26.

Edensor, Tim. *National Identity, Popular Culture, and Everyday Life.* Oxford: Berg, 2002.

———. "National Identity and the Politics of Memory: Remembering Bruce and Wallace in Symbolic Space." *Environment and Planning D: Society and Space* 15, no. 2 (1997): 175–94.

Fentress, James, and Chris Wickham. *Social Memory.* Oxford: Blackwell, 1992.

Fiske, Turbese Lummis, and Keith Lummis. *Charles F. Lummis: The Man and His West.* Norman: University of Oklahoma Press, 1975.

Foote, Kenneth E. *Shadowed Ground: America's Landscapes of Violence and Tragedy.* Austin: University of Texas Press, 1997.

Foote, Stephanie. *Regional Fictions: Culture and Identity in Nineteenth-Century Literature.* Madison: University of Wisconsin Press, 2001.

Glassberg, David. *American Historical Pageantry: The Uses of Tradition in the Early Twentieth Century.* Chapel Hill: University of North Carolina Press, 1990.

Gordon, Dudley. *Charles F. Lummis: Crusader in Corduroy.* Los Angeles: Cultural Assets Press, 1972.

Goss, Jon. "Once-Upon-a-Time in the Commodity World: An Unofficial Guide to Mall of America." *Annals of the Association of American Geographers* 89, no. 1 (1999): 45–75.

Gottlieb, Robert, and Irene Wolt. *Thinking Big: The Story of the Los Angeles Times, Its Publishers and Their Influence on Southern California.* New York: Putnam's Sons, 1977.

Gutiérrez, Ramón. *When Jesus Came, the Corn Mothers Went Away. Marriage, Sexuality, and Power in New Mexico, 1500–1846.* Stanford, Calif.: Stanford University Press, 1991.

Haas, Lisbeth. *Conquests and Historical Identities in California, 1769–1936.* Berkeley: University of California Press, 1995.

Halbwachs, Maurice. *The Collective Memory.* 1950; New York: Harper and Row, 1980.

Hall, Sharlott M. "A 'Ramona' Luncheon." *The Delineator. A Journal of Fashion, Culture and Fine Arts* 48 (1896): 506–7.

Hanna, Stephen. "Is It Roslyn or Is It Cicely? Representation and the Ambiguity of Place." *Urban Geography* 17 (1996): 633–49.

Hannaford, Katherine W. "Culture Versus Commerce: The Libby Prison Museum and the Image of Chicago, 1889–1899." *Ecumene* 8, no. 3 (2002): 284–316.

Herbert, David. "Literary Places, Tourism, and the Heritage Experience." *Annals of Tourism Research* 28, no. 2 (2001): 312–33.

Hobsbawm, Eric, and Terrence Ranger. *The Invention of Tradition.* Cambridge: Cambridge University Press, 1983.

Houston, John M. *San Pedro City Dream,* vol. 1, *A City Is Born.* San Pedro, Calif.: San Pedro Historic Publications, 1983.

Irwin-Zarecjka, Iwona. *Frames of Remembrance: The Dynamics of Collective Memory.* London: Transaction Publishers, 1994.

Israels, Josef, II. "Twelve Million Dollars a Year for Memories." *Coronet* (August 1948): 91–95.

Jakle, John. *The Tourist: Travel in Twentieth-Century North America.* Lincoln: University of Nebraska Press, 1985.

Kropp, Phoebe Schroeder. "'All Our Yesterdays': The Spanish Fantasy Past and the Politics of Public Memory in Southern California, 1884–1939." Ph.D. diss., University of California, San Diego, 1999.

Lears, T. J. Jackson. *No Place of Grace: Antimodernism and the Transformation of American Culture, 1880–1920.* New York: Pantheon Books, 1981.

Levitt, Shelley, with Lois Armstrong, Lynda Wright, Margaret Nelson, David Cobb Craig, and Maria Speidel. "Meryl's Passion." *People,* 26 June 1995, 70–76.

Lewis, Peirce. "Axioms for Reading the Landscape, Some Guides to the American Scene." In *The Interpretation of Ordinary Landscape,* ed. D. W. Meinig, 11–32. Oxford: Oxford University Press, 1979.

Lipsitz, George. *Time Passages: Collective Memory and American Popular Culture.* Minneapolis: University of Minnesota Press, 1990.

Lowenthal, David. *The Past Is a Foreign Country.* Cambridge: Cambridge University Press, 1985.

———. "Past Time, Present Place: Landscape and Memory," *Geographical Review* 65, no. 1 (January 1975): 1–36.

Luftig, Victor. "Literary Tourism and Dublin's Joyce." In *Joyce and the Subject of History,* ed. Mark A. Wollager, Victor Luftig, and Robert Spoo, 141–54. Ann Arbor: University of Michigan Press, 1996.

MacCannell, Dean. *The Tourist: A New Theory of the Leisure Class.* London: Macmillan, 1976.

Mandel, Brett H. 2002. *Is This Heaven? The Magic of the Field of Dreams.* Lanham, Md.: Diamond Communications.

Marling, Karal Ann. *George Washington Slept Here: Colonial Revivals and American Culture, 1876–1986*. Cambridge: Harvard University Press, 1988.

McCabe, Shauna. "Contesting Home: Tourism, Memory, and Identity in Sackville, New Brunswick." *Canadian Geographer* 42, no 3 (1998): 231–45.

McWilliams, Carey. *North from Mexico: The Spanish Speaking People of the United States*. Philadelphia: J. B. Lippincott, 1949.

Meinig, Don W. *The Shaping of America. A Geographical Perspective on 500 Years of History*, vol. 3, *Transcontinental America, 1850–1915*. New Haven: Yale University Press, 1998.

———. "Symbolic Landscapes: Models of American Community." In *The Interpretation of Ordinary Landscape*, ed. D. W. Meinig, 164–92. Oxford: Oxford University Press, 1979.

Middleton, David, and Derek Edwards. *Collective Remembering*. London: Sage, 1990.

Mitchell, Don. *The Lie of the Land: Migrant Workers and the California Landscape*. Minneapolis: University of Minnesota Press, 1996.

———. "The Lure of the Local: Landscape Studies at the End of a Troubled Century." *Progress in Human Geography* 25, no. 2 (2001): 269–81.

Monroy, Douglas. *Thrown Among Strangers: The Making of Mexican Culture in Frontier California*. Berleley: University of California Press, 1990.

Neumann, Mark. *On the Rim: Looking for the Grand Canyon*. Minneapolis: University of Minnesota Press, 1999.

Nochlin, Linda. *The Politics of Vision: Essays on Nineteenth-Century Art and Society*. New York: Harper and Row, 1989.

Nordhoff, Charles. *California for Health, Pleasure and Residence*. 1874; New York: Harper and Brothers, 1882.

Pemberton, T. Edgar. *Dickens's London; or, London in the Works of Charles Dickens*. 1876; New York: Haskell House Publishers, Ltd., 1976.

Phillips, George Harwood. *Chiefs and Challengers: Indian Resistance and Cooperation in Southern California*. Berkeley: University of California Press, 1975.

Pitt, Leonard. *The Decline of the Californios: A Social History of the Spanish-Speaking Californians, 1846–1890*. Berkeley: University of California Press, 1966.

Pocock, Douglas. "Haworth: The Experience of a Literary Place." In *Geography and Literature*, ed. W. E. Mallory and P. Simpson Housley, 135–42. Syracuse, N.Y.: Syracuse University Press, 1987.

Pomeroy, Earl. *In Search of the Golden West: The Tourist in Western America*. 1957; Lincoln: University of Nebraska Press, 1990.

Reimer, Mavis. Introduction to *Such a Simple Little Tale: Critical Responses to L.M. Montgomery's Anne of Green Gables*, ed. Reimer, 1–10. Metuchen, N.J.: The Children's Literature Association and Scarecrow Press, 1992.

Riley, Roger, Dwayne Baker, and Carlton S. Van Doren. "Movie Induced Tourism," *Annals of Tourism Research* 25, no. 4 (1998): 919–35.

Robinson, W. W. *Land in California*. Berkeley: University of California Press, 1948.

————. *Ranchos Become Cities*. Pasadena: San Pasqual Press, 1939.

Rojek, Chris. "Indexing, Dragging and the Social Construction of Tourist Sights." Pp. 52–74 in *Touring Cultures: Transformations of Travel and Theory*, ed. Chris Rojek and John Urry. London: Routledge, 1997.

Rothman, Sheila M. *Living in the Shadow of Death: Tuberculosis and the Social Experience of Illness in American History*. New York: BasicBooks, 1994.

Rydell, Robert W. *All the World's a Fair*. Chicago: University of Chicago Press, 1984.

Sánchez, Rosaura. *Telling Identities: The Californio Testimonios*. Minneapolis: University of Minnesota Press, 1995.

Sauer, Carl Ortwin. "Historical Geography of the Western Frontier." In *Land and Life: A Selection from the Writings of Carl Ortwin Sauer*, ed. John Leighly. 1929; Berkeley: University of California Press, 1969.

Schein, Richard. "The Place of Landscape: A Conceptual Framework for Interpreting the American Scene." *Annals of the Association of American Geographers* 87 (1997): 660–80.

Sears, John F. *Sacred Places: American Tourist Attractions in the Nineteenth Century*. New York: Oxford University Press, 1989.

Shaffer, Marguerite S. *See America First: Tourism and National Identity, 1880–1940*. Washington, D.C.: Smithsonian Institution Press, 2001.

Shipek, Florence Connolly. *Pushed Into the Rocks: Southern California Indian Land Tenure, 1769–1986*. Lincoln: University of Nebraska Press, 1987.

Squire, Shelagh J. "Valuing Contryside: Reflections on Beatrix Potter Tourism." *Area* 25, no. 1 (1993): 5–10.

Stewart, Susan. *On Longing. Narratives of the Miniature, the Gigantic, the Souvenir, the Collection*. Baltimore: John Hopkins University Press, 1984.

Sturken, Marita. *Tangled Memories: The Vietnam War, the AIDS Epidemic, and the Politics of Remembering*. Berkeley: University of California Press, 1997.

Taft, Robert. *Photography and the American Scene: A Social History, 1839–1889*. New York: Macmillan, 1942.

Urry, John. *The Tourist Gaze*. Thousand Oaks, Calif.: Sage Publications, 1990.

Ward, Stephen V. "Time and Place: Key Themes in Place Promotion in the USA, Canada and Britain Since 1870." In *Place Promotion: The Use of Publicity and Marketing to Sell Towns and Regions*, ed. John R. Gold and Stephen V. Ward, 53–74. New York: John Wiley and Sons, 1994.

Weems, M. L. *The Life of George Washington; with Curious Anecdotes Equally Honorable to Himself, and Exemplary to His Young Countrymen*. 1809; Philadelphia: Lippincott, Grambo, 1918.

Yeoh, Brenda S. A. "Street Names in Colonial Singapore." *Geographical Review* 82 (1992): 313–22.

Young, James E. *The Texture of Memory: Holocaust Memorials and Meaning.* New Haven: Yale University Press, 1993.

Zelizer, Barbie. "Reading the Past Against the Grain: The Shape of Memory Studies." *Critical Studies in Mass Communication* 12 (1995): 204–39.

Zimmerman, Tom. "Paradise Promoted: Boosterism and the Los Angeles Chamber of Commerce." *California History* 64 (1985): 22–33.

INDEX

A native of southern California, **Dydia DeLyser** is a member of the faculty of the Department of Geography and Anthropology at Louisiana State University. She has published articles on ghost towns, on Ramona, and on qualitative research in the journals *Annals of the Association of American Geographers, Geographical Review, Journal of Historical Geography,* and *Journal of Social and Cultural Geography.*